Design for Services

Design for Social Responsibility Series

Series Editor: Rachel Cooper

Social responsibility, in various disguises, has been a recurring theme in design for many years. Since the 1960s several more or less commercial approaches have evolved. In the 1970s designers were encouraged to abandon 'design for profit' in favour of a more compassionate approach inspired by Papanek.

In the 1980s and 1990s profit and ethical issues were no longer considered mutually exclusive and more market-oriented concepts emerged, such as the 'green consumer' and ethical investment. The purchase of socially responsible, 'ethical' products and services has been stimulated by the dissemination of research into sustainability issues in consumer publications. Accessibility and inclusivity have also attracted a great deal of design interest and recently designers have turned to solving social and crime-related problems.

Organisations supporting and funding such projects have recently included the NHS (research into design for patient safety); the Home Office has (design against crime); Engineering and Physical Sciences Research Council (design decision-making for urban sustainability). Businesses are encouraged (and increasingly forced by legislation) to set their own socially responsible agendas that depend on design to be realised.

Design decisions all have environmental, social and ethical impacts, so there is a pressing need to provide guidelines for designers and design students within an overarching framework that takes a holistic approach to socially responsible design.

This edited series of guides is aimed at students of design, product development, architecture and marketing, and design and management professionals working in the sectors covered by each title. Each volume includes:

- The background and history of the topic, its significance in social and commercial contexts and trends in the field.
- Exemplar design case studies.
- Guidelines for the designer and advice on tools, techniques and resources available.

Design for Services

Dr Anna Meroni
Politecnico di Milano, Italy

&

Dr Daniela Sangiorgi
Lancaster University, UK

GOWER

Published by
Gower Publishing Limited
Wey Court East
Union Road
Farnham
Surrey, GU9 7PT
England

Ashgate Publishing Company
Suite 420
101 Cherry Street
Burlington,
VT 05401-4405
USA

www.gowerpublishing.com

British Library Cataloguing in Publication Data
Design for services. -- (Design for social responsibility series)
1. Service industries--Management. 2. Customer services--Management. 3. Social responsibility of business.
4. Service industries--Management--Case studies.
5. Customer services--Management--Case studies. 6. Social responsibility of business--Case studies.
I. Series II. Meroni, Anna. III. Sangiorgi, Daniela.
658-dc22

ISBN: 978-0-566-08920-6 (hbk)
ISBN: 978-0-566-08921-3 (ebk)

Library of Congress Cataloging-in-Publication Data
Meroni, Anna.
Design for services / Anna Meroni and Daniela Sangiorgi.
p. cm. -- (Design for social responsibility)
Includes index.
ISBN 978-0-566-08920-6 (hardback) -- ISBN 978-0-566-08921-3 (ebook) 1. Service industries. 2. Design--Social aspects. I. Sangiorgi, Daniela. II. Title.
HD9980.5.M46 2011
658.5'03--dc22

2010048156

MIX
Paper from responsible sources
FSC® C018575
FSC
www.fsc.org

Printed and bound in Great Britain by the MPG Books Group, UK

CONTENTS

LIST OF FIGURES

RACHEL COOPER

PREFACE

This book is one in a series, looking at the role of design and the designer in a socially responsible context. Being concerned for society is not a new phenomena amongst designers. Indeed Ruskin and Morris at the turn of the 20th century actively pursued design and production in the material world in a manner consistent with moral and ethical values for the benefit of the wider society. However during the 20th century we saw not only a growth in the design professions but also a period in which the economies of the west, consumption and the use of the world's resources continued to grow at an alarming rate, contributing to the ongoing fragility of society and planet earth.

By the 1960s, designers began to actively consider the wider implications of design for society. Several approaches emerged, including green design and consumerism, responsible design and ethical consuming, ecodesign and sustainability, and feminist design. In the 1970s Papanek (1972), amongst others, encouraged designers to abandon 'design for profit' in favour of a more compassionate approach. In the 1980s and 1990s, profit and ethical issues were no longer considered mutually exclusive, more market-oriented approaches emerged, such as the 'green consumer' and ethical investment. The purchase of socially responsible, 'ethical' products and services was facilitated by the dissemination of research into sustainability in consumer publications. Accessibility and inclusivity also saw a great deal of design interest and activity and more recently designers have turned to resolving issues related to crime, health and education.

At the same time governments, businesses and individuals have become increasingly aware of what we are doing, not only to the world, but also to each other. Human rights, sustainability and ethics are all issues of concern, whilst the relationship between national economies and poverty struggles to be resolved. Global businesses have recognised the changing environment and are setting their own corporate social responsibility agendas. However if businesses and organisations are to turn these ideas into reality 'design' is an essential ingredient.

Designers make daily decisions with regard to the use of resources, to the lifestyle and use of products, places and communications. In order to achieve both the needs of businesses, the desires of the consumer and improvement of the world, the designer in making decisions must embrace dimensions of social responsibility. However, there is now a need to shift from focusing on a single issue towards taking a more holistic approach to socially responsible design. This book is part of a series that brings together the leading authors and researchers to provide texts on each of the major socially responsible dimensions.

Services, as a sector and as an important activity, have risen in our economic and social horizon over the past 40 years. So whilst we may have been concerned with the eco-aspects of products, and the inclusive nature of place and product use, designers have only relatively recently turned their attention to the whole system experience and whilst doing so, they have taken on more broader concerns in relation to environmental, social and local innovation.

As part of this series, *Design for Services* illustrates this holistic attitude in a broad and all-encompassing manner.

Services seem to be opening up a room for more promising innovation with regards to sustainability and the human-centred approach, given their focus on interactions, relations and activities rather than on objects. Thinking in terms of services helps designers to deconstruct preconceived ideas about how things should be done, and generate new solutions that have the potential to reshape behaviours, rethink products and places, and eventually transform society.

As Meroni and Sangiorgi point out, the book is not about Service Design or the Design of Services, but about Design *for* Services. It therefore focuses on what design is doing and can do for services. They illustrate how Design for Services pervades and supports many aspects of a civilised society, and how it will be a dominant activity in a future where the digital, the sustainable and the general wellbeing of our world is paramount in everyday life.

ACKNOWLEDGMENTS

Design for Services is one of the first publications in the emerging field of Service Design. Given the huge necessity for foundation books, in particular for education and research aims, we would like to thank Rachel Cooper and Gower Publishing for the opportunity given to us to compile this book.

Given the limited body of knowledge in this area, we chose to use case studies as a main source of data to map the discipline. It has been a significant challenge to identify, collect and edit project work coming from a still disperse and extremely varied scientific and professional community. We therefore would like to thank the 33 contributors (see Notes on Contributors) in this publication that helped us in shaping 17 inspiring case studies that represent the core of the book. Also we would like to thank 17 professionals and researchers (see Annex I) we engaged in an open conversation with about the future of the discipline. Finally Ezio Manzini, who we thank wholeheartedly for the constant support, wrote a significant introduction to this book, already challenging existing preconceptions and projecting the discipline in the near future. This high number of participants makes this book a precious collective piece of work that we are extremely happy to present.

A further thank you goes to the colleagues whom we have been teaching Service Design courses with and who helped us shaping and articulating our thoughts: Tommaso Buganza, Giordana Ferri, François Jégou, Stefan Holmlid, Sabine Junginger, Stefano Maffei, Alessio Marchesi, Nicola Morelli, Elena Pacenti, Lara Penin, Annmarie Ryan, Giulia Simeone, Eduardo Staszowski, Roberto Verganti, Beatrice Villari and Francesco Zurlo. They have all been precious with their critical reflections and support.

Finally we would like to thank Massimo Bianchini for the great graphic design work done in helping us visualising our ideas in the book and its cover.

ABOUT THE AUTHORS

Anna Meroni

Dr Anna Meroni is assistant professor at the INDACO (Industrial Design, Arts, Communication and Fashion) Department of Politecnico di Milano, Italy, an Education and Research Centre in Design. She investigates services from the perspective of strategic social innovation, with a specific emphasis on community centred design. Her main research areas are food systems and innovative housing for sustainable lifestyles. Dr Meroni is co-director of the international Master in Strategic Design and a visiting professor and scholar in schools and universities around the world. She is active in the launch and promotion of the international network DESIS, Design for Social Innovation and Sustainability.

Daniela Sangiorgi

Dr Daniela Sangiorgi is a lecturer at ImaginationLancaster, the creative research laboratory at the Lancaster Institute for Contemporary Arts (Lancaster University, UK). As one of the early scholars looking into Service Design, she has gained international recognition. Her work has been mapping and supporting this emerging field of study and research since its outset. Her doctorate has investigated services as complex social systems, proposing holistic and participatory approaches to Service Design. Recent work has been exploring the role of Design and participation within public services reform, with a focus on commissioning for healthcare. She has been one of the founders of the Service Design Network and Service Design Research initiatives.

NOTES ON CONTRIBUTORS

Sara Bury
Sara Bury is a third year Ph.D. candidate in the Computing Department at Lancaster University. Her area of research is collaborative network operation and management, and methods to enable ordinary users to regulate their usage within community run networks.

Keith Cheverst
Keith Cheverst is a Senior Lecturer with Lancaster University's Computing Department. His research over the last decade has focused on exploring the obdurate problems associated with the user-centred design of interactive systems (typically these systems utilise mobile and/or ubicomp technologies) in complex or semi-wild settings and the deployment and longitudinal study of these systems in order to gain insights into issues of adoption and appropriation by users. He has published over 100 research articles, served on numerous programme committees and co-founded a series of workshops on HCI in mobile guides and locative media.

Carla Cipolla
Carla Cipolla is professor of Design at Federal University of Rio de Janeiro – Coppe, Production Engineering Programme. Her research interests cover service design and design for social innovation and sustainability, which began with a Ph.D. in Design at Politecnico di Milano (Italy) where she was also visiting professor. She devotes particular attention to a design approach based on social innovation to foster innovative service models.

Rachel Cooper
Rachel Cooper is Professor of Design Management at the University of Lancaster, where she is Chair of the Lancaster Institute for the Contemporary Arts and Co-director of ImaginationLancaster. Her research interests cover design management; design policy; new product development; design in the built environment; design against crime and socially responsible design. From 2003–2008 she led 'Vivacity 2020' Sustainable Urban Design for the 24-Hour City and she is currently co-investigator of the research project Urban Futures. She has authored several books in the field, including *The Design Agenda* (1995) and *The Design Experience* (2003) and is currently commissioning editor for a Gower series on socially responsible design. She is President of the European Academy of Design and editor of *The Design Journal.*

Shelley Evenson
Shelley Evenson recently joined FUSE|East Labs as a principal in user experience design. Previously, she was teaching interaction design at Carnegie Mellon University, with courses in designing conceptual models, interaction, and service design, and

collaborated with colleagues from the Tepper School of Business and the Human Computer Interaction Institute. She jumpstarted service design in the US, designing courses and hosting the first international conference – Emergence. She is a founding member of the Service Design Network. She is now focusing on the future of social experience, adding to her interests in design for service, design languages and strategy, and organisational interfaces.

Luca Maria Francesco Fabris
Luca Maria Francesco Fabris is assistant professor in Environmental Design at the Department BEST of the Politecnico di Milano, where he has been teaching since 1997. He is the coordinator of the 'Project' area of the monthly review COSTRUIRE (RCS Media Group – www.costruire.it) and technical editor of the Environscapes series published by Maggioli Editore (www.maggioli.it). A visiting professor at European, American and Asian Universities, Luca focuses on research related to the contemporary built environment and landscape. Since 2007 he has coordinated the C.Scape Design Studio through the PoliDaido interactive digital platform.

Giordana Ferri
Giordana Ferri graduated in architecture from Politecnico di Milano and is the Head of Research and Planning for the Social Housing Foundation, which develops the master plans for new residential dwellings. Since 2006 she has been visiting Professor in Service Design at the School of Design of Politecnico di Milano. In recent years Giordana has been involved in service design for residential dwellings, focussing on building co-housing projects and experimental programmes where residents actively participate in building the settlement. She writes articles for various magazines and is a member of the Service Design Commission for the Compasso D'Oro prize in Italy.

Julia Gillen
Julia Gillen is senior lecturer in Digital Literacies at the Literacy Research Centre, Lancaster University and a member of the Centre for Mobilities Research there. She researches connections between language, literacy, technology, learning and identity in schools, homes and virtual environments. Current publications include *An International Perspective on Early Childhood Research: A Day in the Life* (Palgrave Macmillan; co-edited with C.A. Cameron, 2010) and *Researching Learning in Virtual Worlds* (Springer; co-edited with A. Peachey, D. Livingstone and S. Robbins, 2010).

Valerie Hickey
Valerie Hickey applies design thinking to learning and change strategy solutions for corporate and government organisations. Valerie's tool set enhances the human value added to the product or service that makes an organisation successful, innovative and competitive. She has worked with IBM to deliver enterprise learning and change for 200 to 20,000 employees, in not for profit organizations, and internationally. Valerie has a BA and M.Ed from the University of Toronto.

Stefan Holmlid
Stefan Holmlid is associate professor in Interaction and Service Design at Linköping University. He pioneered the teaching of interaction design and service design in Sweden, and continues to teach user-driven innovation, interaction design and service design. His current research interests are the expressive powers and involvement of stakeholders through design methods and techniques in service innovation. The idea of design objects and materials as dynamic and active, and of design as co-created

'in use' drives his research. He is co-founder of the Nordic Service Design and Service Innovation conference, and of the Service Design Network.

Johnathan Ishmael
Johnathan Ishmael is a researcher at Lancaster University and works in the area of computer communication and distributed systems. His current research activities are focused around the EU FP7 project P2P-Next, looking at future multimedia distribution technologies and their impact on heterogeneous networks. Prior to this he also worked on the EU FP6 ENTHRONE project, providing end-to-end QoS guarantees to the core of the Internet. During his Ph.D. studies Johnathan investigated the deployment of community wireless mesh networks and the emerging requirements for autonomic management and control.

François Jégou
François Jégou, director of the Brussels-based design research company Strategic Design Scenarios, has 20 years of experience in strategic design, participative scenario building and new product-services system definition. He is active in various fields and research projects from investigating creative communities for sustainable living in China, India, Brazil and Africa with UNEP to a European research project building a deliberative platform on food and nanotechnology. François is scientific director of the public innovation lab La 27e Règion in France and teaches strategic design at Politecnico di Milano (Italy) and La Cambre, Brussels (Belgium). His latest book is *Collaborative Services, Social Innovations and Design for Sustainability.*

Sabine Junginger
Sabine Junginger is a faculty member of ImaginationLancaster at Lancaster University and a guest scholar at the Hertie School of Governance in Berlin. She investigates the nature, principles and methods of human-centred design to find out when, how and why its inquiries become vehicles for generating and implementing directed organisational changes. Her work draws on theories and methods from emerging design disciplines, product development, human-centred interaction design, organisational change, management and public policy. She has articulated the relationships that exist between designing, changing, organising and managing in various seminars, workshops, speeches and publications.

Lucy Kimbell
Lucy Kimbell is associate fellow in Design Leadership at Saïd Business School, University of Oxford, where she researches designing for service and teaches design management on the MBA course. She led a multidisciplinary research project bringing together management and design researchers with an interest in designing for services. Previously she taught interaction design at the Royal College of Art, London, and has worked for over 15 years as a designer of mobile and Web services.

Ezio Manzini
For more than two decades Ezio Manzini has been working in the field of design for sustainability. Most recently, his interests have focussed on social innovation and he started and currently coordinates, DESIS: an international network on design for social innovation and sustainability (http://www.desis-network.org).

Throughout his professional life he has explored the design potentialities in different fields, such as: Design of Materials, in the 80s; Strategic Design, in the 90s; Service Design, in the last ten years,

He taught and directed design researches in several design schools. At the Politecnico di Milano he coordinated the Unit of Research DIS, the Doctorate in Design and, recently, DES: the Centre for Service Design in the Indaco Department.

Keith Mitchell
Keith Mitchell is a Research Fellow in the School of Computing and Communications at Lancaster University (UK) and co-founder and technical director of 21media innovations ltd, a media and technology based spin-out company located in InfoLab21, Lancaster University. He focuses both his research and commercial interests within the area of distributed and multimedia computing with an emphasis on context-awareness and personalisation of applications and services. The goal of his research is to develop, deploy and evaluate intelligent and interactive systems through the living lab methodology within real-world environments.

Dianne Moy
Dianne Moy, former project coordinator and design manager of the Victorian Eco-Innovation Laboratory at University of Melbourne, Australia, specialises in service and systems design focusing on sustainable and social innovations. Previous to this she worked in social trends coordinating research projects and workshop materials. In her current role she supports design studios across four Melbourne universities (architecture, industrial design, urban design, visual communications, systems and services) and has designed tools and methods for workshops with large commercial organisations, government, local council and community stakeholders.

Elena Pacenti
Elena Pacenti has been the director of the Domus Academy Research Center (DARC) since 2003, and she is the Director of the Service Design Department at Domus Academy. She develops research for the European Commission and design advice for governmental and private agencies in Italy. She also deals with design of services, design of service interfaces and of new media for everyday use. Since her graduation at Politecnico di Milano, she has investigated service design theory and tools to be applied in traditional sectors, with respect to telecom and Web-related services. She has been Visiting Professor of Interaction and Service Design at Politecnico di Milano.

Margherita Pillan
Margherita Pillan is Professor of Interaction Design at Politecnico di Milano, with a background in physics and a Ph.D. in electronic engineering and communications. Her research interests range from user-centred design methodologies to technology-assisted systems and services design, with a specific focus on the field of communication. She has developed research in the fields of integrated circuits design, CAD tool development and circuit theory.

Nicholas J. P. Race
Nick Taylor is a research associate in Culture Lab at Newcastle University. His research interests involve the use of simple and intuitive technologies to support communities, and the use of participatory methods to engage communities in the design process. This has involved deploying several prototype systems in the wild over prolonged periods. He has recently submitted his Ph.D. thesis at Lancaster University, funded by a Microsoft Research scholarship.

Bas Raijmakers
Bas Raijmakers currently runs his own design research company STBY (Standby) in London and Amsterdam with Dr Geke van Dijk. STBY focuses on design research for service innovation. Bas graduated in 2007 at the Royal College of Art in London, has a background in cultural studies and in the Internet industry. His main passion is to bring the people we design for into design and innovation processes using visual storytelling. Bas is also Associate Professor at Design Academy Eindhoven.

Mark Rouncefield
Mark Rouncefield is a senior research fellow in the Department of Computing, Lancaster University. His research interests involve the study of various aspects of the empirical study of work, organisation, human factors and interactive computer systems design. He was awarded a Microsoft European Research Fellowship for his work on social interaction and mundane technologies. His research is strongly interdisciplinary in nature and his empirical studies of work and technology have contributed to critical debates concerning the relationship between social and technical aspects of IT systems design and use.

Chris Ryan
Chris Ryan is Professor of Eco-innovation and Director of the Victorian Eco-Innovation Lab at the University of Melbourne in Australia. He was Foundation Professor of Design and Sustainability at RMIT University, in Melbourne, initiating the Australian EcoReDesign programme (1993–7). From 1998–2003 he was professor and director of the International Institute for Industrial Environmental Economics at Lund University Sweden. He was coordinator and author of the UN Global Status Report on Sustainable Consumption for the Johannesburg Summit of Sustainable Development 2002. His most recent books are *Imaging Sustainability* (RMIT University Press 2007) and *Design for Sustainability – a Step by Step Guide*, published by the UN Environment Program, Paris 2009.

Susanna Sancassani
Susanna Sancassani is the managing director of METID, the centre of Politecnico di Milano for e-learning and e-collaboration, honoured in 2009 with the Efquel Award (the major European award for e-learning quality). Since 2004 she has coordinated the activities of Side_lab, the laboratory of METID for the creative design of e-learning and digital communications, and is the coordinator of a series of Web 2.0 Workshops – a dissemination initiative about Web 2.0 applications in learning and teaching. Since 1999 she has been Professor of Multimedia Design in the School of Design, of Digital Services Design and Design of e-learning courses for the online degree in Computer Engineering of Politecnico of Milano.

Giulia Simeone
Giulia Simeone is a researcher at DIS (Design and Innovation for Sustainability research unit) in the Department INDACO (Industrial Design, Arts, Communication and Fashion) of Politecnico di Milano. Her research interest is in Service Design for local sustainable development, with a peculiar investigation of the virtuous relationships between the city and the peri-urban area. Her doctoral thesis and her current work is focused on Strategic and Service Design methods and tools, with a centre on collaborative services in peri-urban areas with agricultural purpose.

Paul Smith
Paul Smith is a research associate at Lancaster University's Computing Department. With a background in computer science, he developed a Ph.D. in the area of programmable networking resource discovery. He is interested in the various ways that networked (sociotechnical) systems fail to provide a desired service when under duress from various challenges, such as attacks and mis-configurations, and developing approaches to improving their resilience. In particular, his work has focused on the rich set of challenges that face community-driven wireless mesh networks and how they can be tackled.

Susan L. Spraragen
Susan Spraragen is a service experience researcher at the IBM Research Centre in New York. Her work focuses on the dynamics between technology developers and technology users with the goal of linking these two communities in order to bring joy, understanding, efficiency and efficacy to both of their workplaces. Currently Susan is developing visual and expressive service design techniques to address the emotive qualities in provider–consumer relationships. Susan is a senior editor for *Ergonomics in Design*, a publication of the Human Factors and Ergonomics Society. She earned her BA at the University of Rochester, and her MA at Teachers College, Columbia University

Deborah Szebeko
Deborah Szebeko is the founder of *thinkpublic*, a social innovation and design agency that works with the public and third sector in the UK. She has developed a range of collaborative methods and tools to enable social innovation and service improvement in the public and third sector, which was also part of her Ph.D. topic. Over the past seven years, she has successfully used her co-design approach to grow *thinkpublic*, whilst developing communication products and services that have been rolled out nationally in the UK. In recognition of Deborah's pioneering work she was awarded the British Council's UK Young Design Entrepreneur in 2008/9.

Nick Taylor
Nick Taylor is a research student at the Computing Department at Lancaster University, funded by a Microsoft Research European Ph.D. scholarship. He is studying the use of publicly situated displays to support rural communities, the issues and challenges related to this setting, and the various design and interaction techniques which can be used in developing such displays. He has published several papers in this area.

Paola Trapani
Paola Trapani carries out both research and professional activities in the field of the communication in outdoor, with a specific focus on services for sustainability, social innovation and creative communities.

Mark Vanderbeeken
Mark Vanderbeeken is a founding partner of Experientia, the international user experience design consultancy, with responsibilities for management, project supervision, editorial contributions, design policy and strategic communications. Prior to starting Experientia, he was communications manager of Interaction Design Institute Ivrea (Ivrea, Italy), European communications coordinator for the World Wide Fund for Nature (Copenhagen, Denmark), marketing director of Gwathmey Siegel and Associates Architects (New York, USA) and chief press officer of Antwerp

93, Cultural Capital of Europe (Antwerp, Belgium). He is the author of Experientia's successful blog Putting People First, writes for Core77 and is a contributing editor to *Interactions* magazine.

Jennie Winhall

Jennie Winhall is a designer and social innovator. For Participle she leads a multidisciplinary innovation process that applies design thinking to social problems, starting with the everyday experiences of people and blending policy, enterprise and service design to make radical change in the public sector a tangible and financially sustainable reality. Participle has launched a range of new social enterprises, delivering services to reduce loneliness, for older people to live a rich third age, for 'problem families' to build new lives and young people to thrive. Previously Jennie was Senior Design Strategist for the UK Design Council, and project lead for live|work.

Roger Whitham

Roger Whitham is a visualiser and researcher within ImaginationLancaster at Lancaster University with experience in both academic and commercial settings. His specialisations include information design, user experience design, interaction design and group facilitation. He is currently undertaking a Ph.D. in human–computer interaction and design with research interests around information visualisation and personal information management to investigate individual work practices and their support through digital information technologies.

EZIO MANZINI

INTRODUCTION

Services are complex, hybrid artefacts. They are made up of things – places and systems of communication and interaction – but also of human beings and their organisations. They therefore belong to the physics of natural and technical systems and to biology, but also to sociology and the culture of human beings. Permeated with human activity as they are, with a network of relationships between people, and people and things at their centre, they can never be reduced to the simplicity of mechanical entities. Like all complex entities they are largely un-designable. On the other hand, for this very reason, precisely because they appear to be un-designable, it is both useful and necessary today to develop a new, service-oriented design culture and practice.

To justify such a statement, which may appear paradoxical, we must trace a pathway that leads us from twentieth-century design to that of the twenty-first and which can be summed up as the *loss of the illusion of control,* or *the discovery of complexity*. A loss and a discovery that have, in my opinion, influenced the culture and practice of design in general, but which we will discuss here with particular reference to service design.

This change in design culture obviously reflects a wider change: the ongoing transition towards an economy based on services, networks and sustainability; a new economy that is not as yet the present (as the mainstream is still dominated by the economy of the twentieth century). However, it is no longer only one of many possibilities for the future. What is emerging is the economy of the twenty-first century or, for us today, the *next economy*.

The Next Economy

Let's try to list what are considered to be the expanding activities for the near future: environmental reorientation of production and consumption systems (aiming to dramatically increase their eco-efficiency); the social production of services (to meet new demands and promote social cohesion); and promotion of a new territorial ecology (encouraging variety in biological and sociocultural systems). Operating in these fields, the next economy presents characteristics that are very different from those that until now have been considered 'normal' and which were typical of the economy of the twentieth century (Green 2007, Ogle 2007, Tapscott and Williams 2007, Kling and Schulz 2009).

The first distinctive characteristic of interest to us here is that the next economy is a *social economy*. The nature of the problems to be dealt with calls a variety of actors into play: private enterprise, public institutions, local bodies, endowed institutions, social enterprises, not-for-profit associations, civic society organisations, groups of active citizens. Each of these is driven by a different mix of motivations within the framework of a complex economy where the market, public funding, support from not-for-profit entities and endowed institutions, exchange economies and donations (both in terms of things and, above all, personal capabilities and time) combine in different ways in each case (Murray 2009).

The second distinctive characteristic of the next economy is the way it ties in with the ongoing dynamics of social innovation: changes in ways of living and producing which emerge from the grassroots rather than from above (that is, in social networks rather than in laboratories and in the great centres of decision making) and at the margins more than the centre (in situations seen as peripheral, rather than those until now thought of as central). There are many solid reasons for affirming that over the next few years, driven by increasing problems and supported by the new telecommunications networks, this wave of social innovation will grow, anticipating features of the new economy – the next economy which we are talking about here (Mulgan 2006).

The third distinctive characteristic of the next economy, more directly linked to our reflections on the present and the future of service design, concerns the nature of its products. What is produced in the next economy are not consumer goods (as in the twentieth century), but systems targeted to a particular purpose (Mont 2002, Stahel 2006): distributed energy systems, integrated in the local community; food networks that create new bridges between city and countryside; social services based on active user participation; intelligent systems of multimodal transport; place development and urban regeneration programmes (Thackara 2005, Manzini 2010). It is easy to see that these products of the next economy are mainly systems based on interlinking services: technical and social networks where people, products and places interact to obtain a common result (that is, a value that can be recognised as such by all the actors involved). Therefore, ultimately, the next economy is to a large degree an economy geared towards services.

On the other hand, if we look around us, we can observe countless activities that have been moving in this direction for some time in the complexity of contemporary society. They are widely differing cases, but they possess certain traits in common: they use existing physical and social resources to the best advantage, they make systems more efficient in environmental terms and more cohesive socially, they direct attention towards 'common goods' (both social and environmental) and towards an idea of 'active welfare' (meaning the result of an action to accomplish). Such promising cases are not always easy to recognise because they tend not to appear where, out of habit, we usually tend to look. However, when we learn to recognise them, we can see that together they constitute a phenomenon of extraordinary importance: a great and growing wave of social innovation (Meroni 2007).

DISCOVERING COMPLEXITY

Let's now consider the world of design (designers, their ethos and the way they operate). Twentieth-century designers saw their task as the conception, development and production of simple objects, or rather of objects that grew out of the simplicity of the mechanical ways of thinking then dominant. All the properties of such objects could be defined through a design process in which a team of professionals (or even one single designer) was able to collect the information necessary to identify all the characteristics of the finished artefact in advance and then create it, just as anticipated.

Twenty-first century design has set out on a very different course. The change came when it became apparent that during the process of designing and bringing about results a growing number of unpredictable factors and un-designable actors (that is, whose behaviour was impossible to plan) were increasingly coming into play. In other words, it is the complexity of our world, and what we have seen characterises the new economy, that impacts on the territory of design. As we have already said, this leads us to drop any idea of control and find ways of navigating in unpredictability, which is to say, in complexity.

In this new context, the 'object' of design itself tends to turn into a 'process': something that occurs over time, an activity that aims to achieve results. In this perspective, design no longer 'designs something' but rather 'designs for something (or to get something to happen)': it designs entities in the making, whose final characteristics will emerge only in the complex dynamics of the real world. Consequently, they are unpredictable because they lie outside the control of the design team.

Action Platforms

The book I am introducing is entitled *Design for Services*. The 'for' is very important because it encapsulates the idea of transformation in progress (a transformation that effects the entire design world, but the impact of which is most evident in service design). What exactly does 'designing *for* something' (rather than 'designing something') mean? In the case of service design, the answer is already clear enough: what is in effect being designed is not the end result (the interaction between people), but an *action platform*. This means a system that makes a multiplicity of interactions possible. It does so by fixing use modes, making certain kinds of behaviour more difficult and others more probable while leaving opportunities for action and interpretation open. It should be said that this basic element, the need to find a balance between what we try to fix and what is to be left free, may be seen and evaluated completely differently according to the specifics of each service and the design culture of its proponents. It may consequently lead to different strategies for the reduction or enhancement of the components that cannot be planned in advance.

In the range of possibilities, one extreme is that the interactions that cannot be planned (which ultimately means the human interactions) are seen as a problem to be minimised. The declared objective is to guarantee efficient service performance by carefully planning acceptable behaviour. We can call this the *McDonald's model* (where there is a precise protocol for every interaction).

At the other extreme, the human component of the service is seen as a value to cultivate. Here the aim is to leave people free to behave as best suits the circumstances, experimenting an idea of efficiency based on the distributed intelligence of the various operators and on high relational quality. We can call this the *Radio taxi* model (where the taxi drivers are intelligent knots in a traffic and client distribution information network).

The search for the right balance in each case, or for the correct combination of the two approaches, is an open problem under discussion: a discussion that can be found in the background of many pages in this book.

THE USER AS A RESOURCE

Most of the contents of *Design for Services* refers to the role of the designer as an actor able to listen to users and facilitate the discussion about what to do. They show very clearly how a multiplicity of dedicated tools have been made available to support the designer in this role: tools that can be used in all design practices, but which have found their most advanced field of action in *Design for Services*. Indeed, while ethnographic research and notions of user-centred design are still optional when speaking of products, they are no longer so where services are concerned. No one today can consider proposing a service without listening to users and without discussing and testing out the proposal with them.

The moment the value of users as a resource is discovered, a discussion opens as to how and when to use it. Here too design culture and behaviour may vary. Users may be valued as a resource in the design process or also in its application. They may be seen as individuals or as a community. Let's look at this more closely.

The most common approach is to see the user as an individual, bringing needs, desires and knowledge to be listened to and integrated into the design stage and the assessment of proposals and end results. The profile that emerges is one of an aware and informed user looking for efficiency and pleasantness; a user active in proposing but passive in action. Alongside the initial approach (the user bringing needs), a second appears where the user is also seen to bring ability and skills (Nussbaum and Senn 1993); a user who participates actively in the designing of a service in which they will themself be an active component, with their own capabilities. The profile that emerges here is one of a user who plays an active part both in the service proposal and its performance (Bruns et al. 2006, Leadbeater 2008).

The second approach (user as a bringer of capability) also presents an interesting variation where the subject is not an individual but a community: a collective subject who asks questions and possesses the skills and abilities to conceive, perform and manage new kinds of services. This is giving rise to an evolution in traditional user-centred design, extending it towards the community: towards community-centred design (Meroni 2007).

It is clear that the first profile corresponds to the conventional idea of service relationship: the kind which a client experiences in a taxi, in a bar or in a hotel or that a patient receives in a hospital.

All of these are situations where the difference between provider and receiver is clear-cut. The second profile on the other hand brings us to a situation where this difference is not so clear because the roles of the service provider and receiver are blurred. Here we are looking at a service where users are also co-producers of the result they intend to achieve (think of an automatic banking service, a self-service petrol station, a transport service based on bicycles and cycling paths). Finally the third profile, the collective subject, corresponds to services where the efficiency and relational quality arise from the fact that users collaborate to achieve a result. This innovative type of service, *collaborative services*, is expanding: from services for the elderly based on mutual help, to services for public green spaces managed by neighbourhood communities, or the new range of collaborative services made possible by digital platforms, which are spreading thanks to the Internet and mobile phones (Jégou and Manzini 2008).

THE DESIGNER AS FACILITATOR/PROVOKER

The discussion on design for services has so far focused on the tools: what a professional must be able to do to operate as facilitator in a user-centred design process. However, in my view what is still missing (but which *Design for Services* starts to bring to light) is a discussion that shifts from tools to content. What do we want to do with these tools? Does basing one's own action on listening and collaboration with users absolve the designer from any responsibility concerning what we want to or must do?

Personally I believe that the answer to this question should be negative. Design, and therefore also design for services, is or should be a culture. Consequently the designer has, or should have, their own view about the world. If this is the case, the new question to pose is: how do we conciliate the role of designer as facilitator (of a conversation about what to do), with that of a proponent (that is, bringer of visions and proposals)?

I think the answer to this new question is the following: the designer is certainly an actor in the design process whose task is to listen and facilitate discussion between actors, however it is also to bring proposals to the discussion table that are capable of going beyond what the user community could have imagined; proposals that are provocative (that is, are able to provoke discussion) and that motivate in such a way as to be open to discussion. In this way designers can be both facilitator and provoker: the tools they use do not serve only to make ideas co-created by the group more visible and assessable (*visualising*) but also stimulate the group by feeding the discussion with original visions and proposals (*visioning*).

A NEW GENERATION OF SERVICES

The designer therefore takes the role of a 'design specialist', able to listen, but whose proposals are also able to generate new discussions. Consistent with this position, I would like to conclude these introductory notes with a final reflection on design for services, which will hopefully be both provocative and debateable in this way. To do so however I must go back to the issues mentioned at the start, inherent as they are to the context in which design for services is operating (and will presumably be operating in the near future).

In order to act within the next economy as agent of change, design must rethink itself and the nature of the services it is working on. It must therefore also rethink what design for services is and could be.

We said at the outset what *rethinking* design means: shifting from a (mainly) product-oriented design culture and practice towards a (predominantly) service orientation. That is, from a way of thinking and doing where products are at the centre of the scene and services are considered as product extensions and/or additional features, towards a service approach to design where the interactions between people, things and places lie at the centre, and where (physical) products are the 'evidence' that testify to the service's existence.

However, I believe that this necessary evolution towards a service-oriented design culture and practice is not sufficient. What is required at the same time is a rethinking of the nature and operating modes of design for services itself (Manzini 2009) – a rethinking that includes both standard service (taxis, hotels, hospitals etc.) and the innovative services emerging on the Internet and in processes of diffuse social innovation, meaning the innovative kind of services that we referred to in the previous paragraph as *collaborative services*. In the sustainable network society we should promote, there will undoubtedly still be taxis, hotels and hospitals (which will certainly have to be carefully designed), but it is not here that the real challenge lies. The issues of the future (environmental re-conversion and the promotion of a new sustainable social economy) highlight the need to develop and popularise new types of services able to promote, systemise and enhance diffuse social resources. In a small, densely populated planet like ours, it is the sensitivity, intelligence and capability of people to set to and resolve problems that is potentially the most widespread resource. It is a question of knowing how design for services needs to evolve into something far larger than it is today, to become an agent for change capable of operating in the new social networks, able to catalyse available social resources and feed the strategic conversation with visions and proposals, at all levels from the problems of everyday to the future of the planet.

References

Bruns, C., Cottam, H., Vanstone, C. and Winhall, J. 2006. *Transformation Design. RED Paper 02*, London: Design Council.

Green, J. 2007. *Democratizing the future. Towards a new era of creativity and growth.* Eindhoven: Philips Design. Available at: http://www.newscenter.philips.com/shared/assets/Downloadablefile/democratizing-the-future-16071.pdf, accessed 31 January 2010.

Jégou, F. and Manzini, E. 2008. *Collaborative Services Social Innovation and Design for Sustainability*. Milan: Polidesign.

Kling, A. and Schulz, N. 2009. *From Poverty to Prosperity*. New York: Encounter Books

Leadbeater, C. 2008. *We Think: The Power of Mass Creativity*. London: Profile Books LTD.

Manzini, E. 2009. Service design in the age of networks and sustainability, in *Designing Services with Innovative Methods*, edited by S. Miettinen, and M. Koivisto. Helsinki: University of Arts and Design.

Manzini, E. 2010. Small, local, open and connected: design research topics in the age of networks and sustainability. *Journal of Design Strategies*, 4(1).

Meroni A. 2007. *Creative Communities. People Inventing Sustainable Ways of Living.* Milan: Polidesign.

Mont, O. 2002. *Functional Thinking. The Role of Functional Sales and Product Service Systems for a Functional Based Society*. Research report for the Swedish EPA, IIIEE. Lund: Lund University.

Mulgan, J. 2006. *Social Innovation. What it is, Why it Matters, How it can be Accelerated.* London: Basingstoke Press.

Murray, R. 2009. *Danger and Opportunity. Crisis and the New Social Economy. Provocation 09*. London: NESTA.

Nussbaum, M. and Sen, A. 1993. *The Quality of Life*. New York: Oxford University Press.

Ogle, R. 2007. *Smart World*. Boston, MA: Harvard Business School Publishing.

Stahel, W. 2006. *The Performance Economy*. London: Basingstoke Press.

Tapscott, D. and Williams, A.D. 2007. *Wikinomics. How Mass Collaborations Changes Everything*. New York: Portfolio.

Thackara, J. 2005. *In the Bubble, Designing in a Complex World*. London: The MIT Press.

Section 1

Introduction to Design for Services

1.1
A New Discipline

Service design, as a new discipline, emerged as a contribution to a changing context and to what a certain group of design thinkers (notably Morello 1991,[1] Hollins and Hollins 1991, Manzini 1993, Erlhoff et al. 1997, Pacenti 1998) started to perceive and describe as a new design agenda. In the 1990s the growing economic role of the service sector in most of the developed economies was in clear contrast to the then dominant practices and cultures of design, which still focused on the physical and tangible output of the traditional industrial sectors.

As Richard Buchanan has asserted 'design problems are "indeterminate" and "wicked" because design has no special subject matter of its own apart from what a designer conceives it to be' (Buchanan 1992: 16). This means that the objects and practices of design depend more on what designers perceive design to be and not so much on an agreed on or stable definition elaborated by a scientific community.

> *The subject matter of design is potentially universal in scope, because design thinking may be applied to any area of human experience (Buchanan 1992: 16).*

The growing relevance of the service sector has affected not only design but several disciplines, starting from marketing and management moving to engineering, computing, behavioural science, etc.; recently a call for a convergence of all these disciplines has claimed the need for a new science, a 'Service Science' (Spohrer et al. 2007, 2008, Pinhanez and Kontogiorgis 2008, Lush et al. 2008), defined as 'the study of service systems, aiming to create a basis for systematic service innovation' (Maglio and Spohrer 2008: 18).

This book explores what design brings to this table and reflects on the reasons why the ideas and practices of service design are resonating with today's design community. It offers a broad range of concrete examples in an effort to clarify the issues, practices, knowledge and theories that are beginning to define this emerging field. It then proposes a conceptual framework (in the form of a map) that provides an interpretation of the contemporary service design practices, while deliberately breaking up some of the disciplinary boundaries framing designing for services today.

Given the richness of this field, we followed some key principles to build and shape the contents of this publication:

1. We decided to select service projects that have a direct and clear relationship with consolidated design specialisations (such as interaction design, experience design, system design, participatory design or strategic design)

1 Morello, A. 1991. Design e mercato dei prodotti e dei Servizi. Document for the Doctorate programme in Industrial Design, Milano: Politecnico di Milano.

or manifesting a *designerly* way of thinking and doing (Cross 2006), despite the diverse disciplinary backgrounds;

2. We aimed at organising the different contributions into a systemic framework delineating a field of practice characterised by some clear core competences, but having blurred and open boundaries. This framework in particular illustrates the multidimensional nature of contemporary design practice and knowledge, apparently fragmented in its description, but actually able to identify, apply and assimilate multiple relevant contributions coming from other disciplines;

3. We recognised how services, like most contemporary artefacts (Morin 1993), are impossible to control in all their aspects, because of their heterogeneity and high degree of human intensity. In this book we therefore applied the principles of '*weak thinking*' (Vattimo and Rovatti 1998), meaning accepting the fundamental inability of design to completely plan and regulate services, while instead considering its capacity to potentially create the right conditions for certain forms of interactions and relationships to happen.

For these reasons the title of this publication is *Design for Services* instead of Service Design (or Design *of* Services). While acknowledging service design as the disciplinary term, we will focus more on articulating what design is doing and can do *for* services and how this connects to existing fields of knowledge and practice.

This reflection is timely and extremely relevant as more and more universities, design consultancies and research centres are willing to enter the field of design for services; we hope that by proposing an orienting framework and a sort of service designers' 'identikit', we will provide a foundation for these growing initiatives while stimulating further conversations and research.

The book introduces a map (described in Chapter 2.5) that illustrates how designers and design research are currently contributing to the design for services. We generated this map by collecting and reflecting on 17 case studies of design and research projects that have been reported and described in Section 2 of this publication.

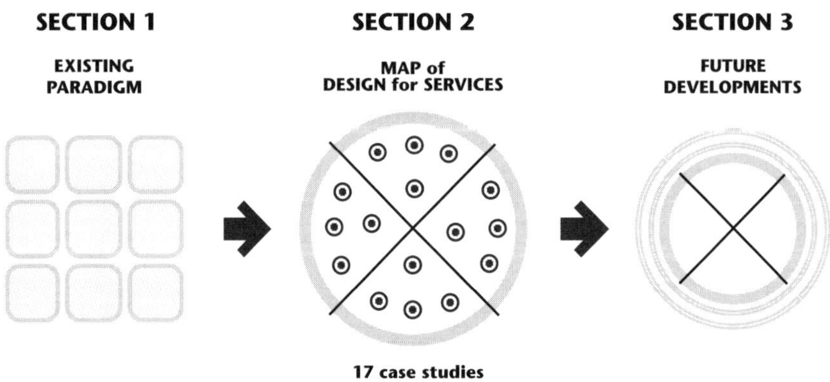

Figure 1.1 The structure of this book

As a support and complementation to the case studies, Section 1 links design for services to existing models and studies on service innovation and service characteristics; while Section 3 projects design for services into the emerging paradigms of a new economy to help us reflecting on its possible future development.

As Kimbell pointed out (Kimbell and Seidel 2008, Kimbell 2009) design for services is still an emerging discipline based on mainly informal and tacit knowledge, but it may develop into a more structured discipline if it develops a closer dialogue with existing disciplines such as service management, service marketing, or service operations. We have opened up and engaged in this closer dialogue throughout this book, in particular considering 'service marketing' as historically encompassing all research study in services (Pinhanez and Kontogiorgis 2008). This book represents a first attempt in that direction that will require further efforts and collaboration across disciplines. Appendix 1 actually opens up reflection on future research on design for services by starting a conversation with a selection of key researchers and professionals of the field of services. Finally, Appendix 2 presents a selection of tools as introduced in the case studies.

Before introducing the case studies that will feed into the map of design for services, we are going to address two key questions that will help us position and motivate this new field of studies: *Why is it necessary to introduce a new subdiscipline in design?* and *How has design approached the realm of services so far?*

As a response to these questions in the next chapters we will briefly consider the role and recognition of services and of design in the current economy and, following a similar path to service marketing in its original development, we will refer design to the IHIP (Intangibility, Heterogeneity, Inseparability and Perishability) framework,[2] looking at how design developed alternative strategies in dealing with service characteristics to traditional design fields and service related disciplines.

Why Design for Services?

It is widely acknowledged that in recent decades the developed economies have moved to what is called a 'service economy', an economy highly dependent on the service industry. In 2007, services represented 69.2 per cent of total employment and 71.6 per cent of the gross value added generated by EU27[3] (Eurostat 2009).[4] This means that services in their different forms and characteristics have developed a fundamental role for the growth and sustainability of innovation and competitiveness. This role has been fully recognised of late with a flourishing of innovation studies and policy debates and programmes specifically aimed at deepening the understanding and at supporting the development of the service sector at different levels. As a consequence the European Council called for the launch of a European plan for innovation (PRO INNO Europe) that could include and generate new understandings of innovation in general and of service innovation in particular.

2 IHIP is a 'core paradigm of services marketing, namely, the assertion that four specific characteristics – intangibility, heterogeneity, inseparability, and perishability – make services uniquely different from goods' (Lovelock and Gummesson 2004: 21).

3 EU27 is the European Union in its latest composition of 27 member states.

4 By services we mean the following sectors: financial, real estate, renting and business activities (NACE Sections J and K); distribution, hotels, restaurants and catering (HORECA), communications and transport services (NACE Sections G to I); public administration, health, education, other services and households (NACE Sections L to P).

Some of the key changes in these late policies have been a growing attention for the role of design and creativity as well as for user-centred approaches to innovation. PRO INNO Europe, the focal point of innovation policy analysis and development throughout Europe, dedicated a series of studies within this platform specifically to 'design and user-centred innovation' and to 'design as a tool for innovation'.[5] Initial studies at EU levels are suggesting the need for a more integrated and coherent measurement of design impact and design policies; recognition is growing on the role of design for innovation and on the importance to integrate design strategies at higher executive levels as well as to engage users on an early basis as co-designers (Bitard and Basset 2008).

The Community Innovation Survey (CIS), the most comprehensive European-wide approach to measure innovation based on surveys, has been gradually improved to better capture and report service innovation processes. The Oslo Manual (OECD/Eurostat 2005), on which the CIS surveys are based, has been updated since 2005 to include, besides product and process innovations, marketing and organisational innovation, and now considers non-R&D (research and development) sources of innovation as strategic for the development of service industries. A first attempt to produce a common measurement for service industry performance at a national level has resulted in the Service Sector Innovation Index (SSII). Different initiatives on the national level emerged out of this framework. For example, in the UK, the National Endowment for Science, Technology and the Arts (NESTA) has coordinated the development of a new Innovation Index (http://www.innovationindex.org.uk) in response to the Innovation Nation White Paper by the Department of Industries and Universities (DIUS 2008), which called for a more accurate measure of innovation in the UK's increasingly important services sectors, creative industries and in the delivery of public services.

The need for a new Innovation Index emerged based on investigations into UK innovation practices, that revealed a gap between what 'traditional innovation' performance metrics – focused on scientific and technological innovation – were measuring and how 'hidden innovation' (NESTA 2006, 2007) was not being captured through them. At the same time it was being recognised that hidden innovation was one of the keys to success for the UK economy. Studies suggested the level of complexity involved in innovation, ill represented by linear models of innovation, the importance of incremental changes, and the role of diffusion. Moreover, further attention was to be given to the adoption and exploitation of technologies, organisational innovation and innovation in services (including public services and non-commercial settings). This example from the UK shows how our understanding of innovation needs to go beyond the traditional 'hard' dimensions of technologies and physical matter. Instead, we need to include the 'soft' dimensions that are directly related to people, people skills and organisations (Tether and Howells 2007).

In synthesis, service innovation is 'more likely to be linked to disembodied, non-technological innovative processes, organisational arrangements and markets' (Howells 2007: 11). The main sources of innovation in service industries are employees and customers (Miles 2001) and new ideas are often generated through the interaction with users (user-driven innovation) and through the application of tacit knowledge or training rather than through explicit R&D activities (ALMEGA 2008). A dedicated study on service innovation by Tekes (2007), the Finnish Funding Agency for Technology

5 For more information see the INNO-Grips web-pages: http://grips.proinno-europe.eu/key_topics/2/design-user-centred-innovation, accessed 31 July 2010.

and Innovation,[6] confirmed how customers have replaced the role of competitors as main source for innovation and how 'customer services' is the main area of service improvement (instead of 'product–service performance' in the manufacturing sector). Given the interactive nature of services, customer services and in general 'delivery (or relationship) innovation' (Gallouj 2002) have been looked at as the most characteristic form of innovation of services; however this practice is still poorly captured and understood. Other successful transformations into service companies often concern their organisational and financial models, moving from improving processes to the reformulation of their value networks and business models (Tekes 2007).

Service innovation is a complex interdisciplinary effort (Figure 1.2). Even if the role of design within this process is still not clear, it is starting to gain some visibility. Tekes for example suggests how design for services can apply design methods to develop a new offering or improved experiences by bringing 'many intangible elements together into a cohesive customer experience' (2007: 18).

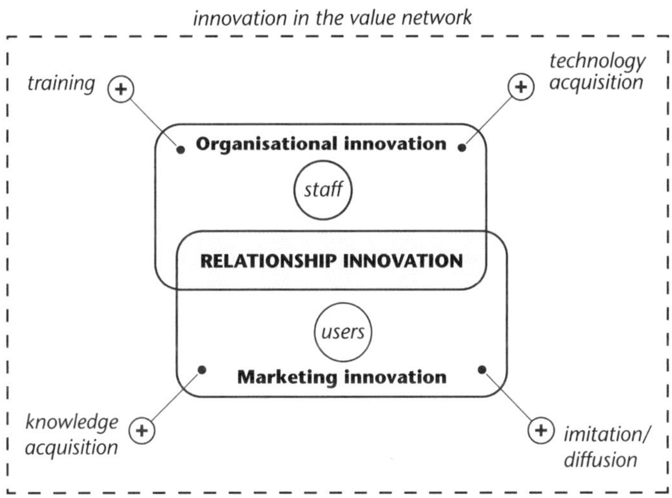

Figure 1.2 A representation of the main areas of and sources for service innovation

THE TRANSFORMATIONAL POTENTIAL OF SERVICES

Among service innovation studies, special attention is being paid to the role services have in supporting the development of a knowledge-based economy; moreover services are often associated with the desired shift from a traditional resource-exploiting manufacturing-based society to a more sustainable one.

Knowledge-intensive Services (KIS)[7] have been identified as an indicator for the overall 'knowledge intensity' of an economy representing a significant source for

6 Applying the Ten Types of Innovation framework as developed by Larry Keeley at Doblin, Tekes compared the analysis of 12 successful service companies in the USA with a previous investigation into 100 service projects by Peerinsights.

7 KIS can be defined 'as economic activities conducted by private sector organisations that combine technology, knowledge (such as R&D) and highly skilled employees to provide a service to the market' (European Commission 2009: 95). Following the NACE classifications KIS are services such as water and

the development and exchange of new knowledge. These special kinds of services are now considered as connected to the overall wealth and innovation capability of a nation. As a subset of KIS, Knowledge-intensive Business Services (KIBS) have attracted significant attention. KIBS are services[8] that 'provide knowledge-intensive inputs to the business processes of other organisations' (Miles 2005: 39) to help solving problems that go beyond their core business. Their growth is associated mainly with the increase in outsourcing and the need for acquisition of specialised knowledge, related to, among others, technology advancement, environmental regulations, social concerns, markets and cultures.

Services have been traditionally looked at as a possible alternative to the manufacturing driven model of consumption based on ownership and disposal. The concept of the Product Service System (PSS) developed out of the engineering and environmental management literature as an area of investigation to balance the need for competitiveness and environmental concerns. A PSS 'consists of a mix of tangible products and intangible services designed and combined so that they jointly are capable of fulfilling final customer needs' (Tukker and Tischner 2006: 1552). Research has not yet produced evidence that PSS is a win–win strategy in terms of sustainability. That is, companies employing PSS have not been able to achieve significant or radical reductions in their environmental impact (Tukker 2004). Despite this, PSS has helped to show that service-oriented solutions are potentially better in addressing environmental concerns than approaches that focus on the product when combined with dimensions of localisation (Walker 2009), shared strategies and changes in consumption behaviours (Tukker and Tischner 2006, Marchand and Walker 2008), community engagement (Meroni 2007) or lightness (Thackara 2005).

In addition to the impact on the economy and employment, service innovation is increasingly viewed as an enabler of a 'society-driven innovation' with policies at national and regional level that are 'using service innovation to address societal challenges and as a catalyst of societal and economic change' (European Commission 2009: 70). Tekes positions service innovation as a core lever for transformative changes in areas such as health and well-being, clean energy, built environment and the knowledge society (Tekes 2008).

This transformative potential of services is due to different characteristics: service innovation brings to the fore new 'soft' dimensions that help in reframing artefact and technologically focused innovation paradigms (Miles 2005); services don't imply ownership and therefore can potentially overcome traditional consumption patterns (Lovelock and Gummesson 2004); services depend on users' behaviour and direct participation in the delivery system that can require changes in lifestyles and consumption modes (Meroni 2007); and their focus on providing solutions (instead of necessarily products) means that there is an inherent potential for systemic changes, resource optimisation and value-driven offerings (Manzini and Vezzoli 2003, Manzini et al. 2004).

FINAL CONSIDERATIONS

We can see that the perception of services as a means to tackle society and economic challenges is gaining increased attention. In taking this perspective forward certain

---

air transport; post and telecommunications; financial intermediation; real estate, renting and business activities; education; health and social work; and recreational, cultural and sporting activities.

8 KIBS services include computer services, R&D services, legal, accountancy and management services, architecture, engineering and technical services, advertising and market research (Miles, 2005). In the NACE classifications are identified with the Business Services (NACE 70–74).

important factors come into focus. For example, we need to understand more clearly how services are and can be innovative, how they complement traditional science and technology based models of innovation, how they can address societal and environmental challenges and finally the role of design and creativity as significant contributors to such innovation and growth. If the relevance of design for services as a field of action and expertise for designers is accepted, then we need to be clear on what it is that design contributes, can contribute or cannot contribute to this context. Considering the multidisciplinary nature of a service project and the current building of a 'service science', it is not easy to identify the role and identity of a 'designer'.

What is evident however, and is documented in this book, is that design and design research are practically and necessarily entering into new 'orders' (Buchanan 2001) of practice and research as a way to answer new project and society demands.

Buchanan (2001), reflecting on the evolution and future development of design, talks about 'places' or 'placements', as areas of discovery and invention that characterise the practice of design; in doing so he suggests a movement from 'signs' (graphic and communication design), to 'objects' (product design), to 'interactions' (interaction design) and 'systems' (environment and system design). These placements, or 'design orders', which are not rigidly fixed and separated from each other, represent perfectly the growing of scale and complexity of design objects and problems in the last two decades. Moreover they represent the interconnectedness of their dimensions, from single products to larger environments of living, working, playing or learning. What Buchanan is suggesting is how the growth of scale and complexity of design interventions is related to the growth of scale and complexity of contemporary challenges. Working on higher scales of interventions allows designers to intervene at an earlier stage and at a more strategic level.

Design for services has been generally identified with the 'interaction' order, where 'interaction' refers to how 'human beings relate to other human beings through the mediating influence of products' (Buchanan 2001: 11) and 'products' can be interpreted as physical artefacts, experiences, activities or services.

If design is entering into new 'orders' of practice, the next question is then how design, being traditionally linked with tangible artefacts, has approached the realm of services. The next section will adopt an existing framework in marketing literature, as a conceptual tool to relate design practice and research to the main characteristics of services, i.e. intangibility, heterogeneity, inseparability and perishability (the IHIP framework); while acknowledging the limitations implicit in this framework in the contemporary debate on services (Lovelock and Gummesson 2004), we suggest how this classification can help to systematise and reflect on the work and knowledge developed in design for services; while doing so we will also aim to bridge and compare its practice with other service-related studies.

Services and Design for Services

As we have demonstrated, the global economy is moving towards models in which a 'service logic' dominates (Vargo and Lush 2004), challenging traditional ways of evaluating productivity, innovation and growth. Along with this change, we can identify shifts in the perception and function of services: for example, service marketing in the 1970s through to the early 1980s conceptualised the nature of services as substantially different from that of products.

These initial studies identified four main characteristics (or shortcomings as compared to products) of services that researchers seemed to agree on. These four characteristics are intangibility, heterogeneity, inseparability of production and consumption, and perishability (Zeithaml et al. 1985, Edgett and Parkinson 1993). *Intangibility* refers to the quality of services that escape our physical human touch. Services are thus described as 'performances, rather than objects, they cannot be seen, felt, tasted or touched in the same manner in which goods can be sensed' (Zeithaml et al. 1985: 33). A further distinction has been made between 'physical intangibility' and 'mental intangibility', this last related to the difficulty of evaluating the service before buying it (Bateson 1979).

The characteristic of *inseparability of consumption and production* alludes to the fact that services require the presence of customers for the service to exist. This means that most services are highly interactive and depend on people-to-people or person-to-person interactions. *Heterogeneity* thus suggests how, in particular for labour-intensive services, the quality of the performance may vary from time to time depending on the situation and service participants.

Finally, a key characteristic identified for services is the fact that services in general cannot be stored and therefore depend on the service provider's ability to balance and synchronise demand with supply capacity. This brings in elements of just-in-time delivery and relates to *perishability* as services come into being but can also fall back into non-existence.

These characteristics, as Lovelock and Gummesson have demonstrated (2004), have not been grounded in empirical research and can be subject to an ambiguous interpretation.[9] Nonetheless, as the IHIP framework has served as a basis for the growth of service marketing and the development of dedicated service management strategies, we chose to use its four widely acknowledged parameters to start our reflection on the peculiar contributions of design for services.

Design has been traditionally associated with shaping tangible artefacts. The IHIP characteristics, in particular intangibility, explain the resistance in the practising design community to accepting and understanding design for services. Moving from tangibles to intangibles questions what design is actually designing. If services are defined as acts or performances how can design contribute to their shaping? What is the aesthetic of a performance? And what is the designed outcome?

Design research and practice have approached services from two main perspectives that have represented two main distinct research streams: the 'interaction paradigm', which has focused mainly on *how* services are performed, and the 'functional paradigm', which has instead considered *what* services represent and can offer. We will introduce both the perspectives and then relate their arguments to the IHIP framework.

The interaction paradigm has considered the *interactive nature of services* as its main focus, applying design methods and skills to improve the user experience. It did so, for example, by better designing the service interface (the visible part of the service through which users can interact and orient their behaviours and choices). By focusing on the interactivity dimension, design for services has identified service experiences as an area of design intervention. Elena Pacenti proposed this perspective

9 Lovelock and Gummesson recognise that the IHIP framework helped to generate the impetus for and legitimacy of studies about the new field of service marketing; also, if taken separately, the IHIP characteristics help explain some of the behaviours of specific services. They suggest devoting attention to another property that seems to fully represent service nature, which is 'non-ownership': 'services involve a form of rental or access in which customers obtain benefits by gaining the right to use a physical object, to hire the labor and expertise of personnel, or to obtain access to facilities and networks' (2004: 34).

for the first time in her Ph.D. research in 1998 where she defined service design as the design of the area and scene where the interactions between the service and the user take place. She made an analogy between the design of advanced interactive devices and the design of services to suggest a shift from the interpretation of services as complex organisations to one that sees services as complex interfaces to the user. The introduction of the interaction perspective has enabled a deeper understanding of the nature of services and of design for services, opening up a liaison with the research and methodology of human-centred interaction design.

This correlation and analogy between interaction design and design for services has been further developed, mainly from a methodological perspective, in a reciprocal way. For example, Holmlid (2007) points out how the service perspective has become a challenge to interaction design, while technology usage has become a challenge to design for services. A set of design tools has been adopted and adapted mainly from interaction design disciplines and practices, including such things as drama, scenarios, service interface analysis (Mager 2004), storyboards, flow charts, storytelling (Evenson 2006), use case (Morelli and Tollestrup 2007), scripts, personas, role play and experience prototypes. These tools and methods support the design practice and, at the same time, contribute to the visualisation and testing of the service experience and interface, from a general description to detailed implementation specifications.

The functional paradigm instead derives from studies about strategies for sustainable consumption and production, conducted by a network of scholars in Europe at the beginning of the Millennium. Among these studies we can mention SusHouse (1998–2000), an EU-funded[10] research project concerned with developing and evaluating scenarios for transitions to sustainable households (Vergragt 2000); a series of research projects funded by the Swedish Environmental Protection Agency and developed at Lund University (Mont 2000, 2002); studies funded by UNEP about Product–Service System sustainability and developed at Politecnico di Milano (Manzini and Vezzoli 2002); the EU-funded[11] Thematic Network of industries and institutes SusProNet (2002–04) developing expertise on design of product–service systems for sustainable competitive growth; HiCS (Highly Customerised Solutions), an EU-funded[12] research project (2001–04) aiming to produce methodologies and tools for designing sustainable solutions (Manzini et al. 2004); and MEPPS (Methodology for Product–Service System; development of a toolkit for industry), a European research project coordinated by PricewaterhouseCoopers N.V. (2001–04) aimed at developing a methodology for product service systems bringing together design with sustainability evaluation methods (van Halen et al. 2005).

These initiatives apply the 'functional thinking' approach (Mont 2000, 2002), which claims that to reduce material throughput in the economy, 'functions' should be provided, not products. The proposed approach is *thinking by functions* instead of by products, using a *solution-oriented* perspective (Manzini et al. 2004). The underlying hypothesis is that it is possible to create offerings that provide consumers with the same level of performance of traditional ones, but using less stuff (dematerialisation) and therefore having a lower environmental impact (Mont 2000: 6). The basis of this approach is the so-called 'revolution of efficiency', that is a change of values, consumption modes and lifestyles related to the selling of services instead of products, which enables an optimisation of logistics and distribution (Mont 2000: 15).

---

10 EU Environment and Climate Research Programme Theme 4, Human Dimensions of Environmental Change.

11 EU Fifth Framework Programme (FP5).

12 EU Growth Programme, Fifth Framework Programme (FP5).

Based on these two original focuses on interaction and functions, design for services dealt with service specificities adopting different tactics. We have used the IHIP characteristics as a trigger and as a framework to reflect on and systematise these tactics. We will outline our considerations in detail below, relating each service quality with current research and practice of design for services as summarised in Table 1.1.

Table 1.1 A summary of design for services approaches in relation to the main IHIP service characteristics

Service characteristics	Description	Design for Services contribution
Intangibility	Services cannot be seen, felt, tasted or touched in the same manner in which goods can be sensed	• 'Evidencing' the service offering and service experience • Making the intangible tangible • 'Empathic' design • 'Dematerialisation' as an innovation lever
Inseparability	Most services require the presence of customers for the production of services	• Users as sources and not as problems • Co-design approaches • Collaborative services
Heterogeneity	The quality of the performance may vary from time to time, depending on the situation and service participants	• Services as 'situated actions' • Design the conditions for possible behaviours and interactions to emerge • System design • Customisation and modular service architecture
Perishability	Most services can't be stored and therefore depend upon the ability to balance and synchronise demand with supply capacity	• Replication strategies • Distributed and interconnected service solutions • Enabling platforms

DESIGN FOR SERVICES AND INTANGIBILITY

> *Intangibility*: services cannot be seen, felt, tasted or touched in the same manner in which goods can be sensed.

From an interaction design perspective design for services has been dealing with the intangible dimension of services by mainly working on its opposite, that is endeavouring to make service more tangible by way of 'evidencing' the service offering and service experience. When dealing with intangible performances and interactions that are hard to communicate and anticipate, designers apply one of their key competencies, i.e. the capacity to make things and ideas visible and tangible. In design for services this capacity has proved significant in the design of service evidences (also known as touch-points) or service interface to better guide the interaction process (usability), anticipate service outputs and rules (transparency) and create a coherent service identity. Adopting a theatre metaphor, service designers are described as 'directors' that 'manage the integrated and coherent project of all elements that determine the quality of interaction' (Pacenti 1998: 123). Live|work (the first service design studio based in London) describes design for services as the 'design for experiences that reach people through many different touch-points, and that happen over time' (www.livework.co.uk).

In order to achieve this design for services starts at the service interface, applying methodologies that augment the capacity to deeply understand (*empathise with*) users and service participants' needs and evaluate existing or imagine future interactions (i.e. storytelling, video-based ethnography, observations, interviews, shadowing, emotional mapping, users' diaries).

At the same time in a design process designers use different kinds of visualisations and prototypes to make ideas tangible and let people explore possible future experiences: this helps experimenting with new service models and behaviours, reducing perceived risk for organisations and communities and enhancing the capacity for multidisciplinary teams to engage in co-design processes.

From a functional perspective 'intangibility' recalls the concept of *dematerialisation*, which means lightening the solution in both a physical and cognitive way. Solutions based on 'access' instead of ownership (Rifkin 2000) can actually reduce the human, social and environmental burden of owning and managing products. Design for services has a crucial role in making this change possible: 'thinking by functions' in a creative way can help to imagine everyday life activities and consumption behaviours in completely different ways. It is about *what* a solution offers and not only *how* it works. In this case 'intangibility' is seen as a strategic quality to stimulate innovation. Design capacities to generate visions via scenarios and to redefine service life cycles are relevant here.

DESIGN FOR SERVICES AND INSEPARABILITY

Inseparability: most services require the presence of customers for the production of services.

Design for services has, since its origins, considered the role and presence of users in the service delivery process as its main focus. Design for services generally conceives users as a resource rather than a burden or a problem. Besides being a source of insights and ideas, users have been engaged in design processes to generate more desirable and usable solutions, and to explore new collaborative service models. The relevance of co-production in design for services has been explored in particular in two interconnected fields of study, one oriented to explore more sustainable ways of living (Meroni 2007, Jégou and Manzini 2008, Thackara 2007) and one specifically concerned with the redesign of public services (Cottam and Leadbeater 2004, Parker and Heapy 2006, Parker and Parker 2007, Bradwell and Marr 2008, Thomas 2008).

Research on sustainability has been looking at existing examples of inventiveness and creativity among 'ordinary people' to solve daily life problems related to housing, food, ageing, transport and work. Such cases represent a way of 'living well while at the same time consuming fewer resources and generating new patterns of social cohabitation' (Manzini 2008: 13). The idea behind this research was to consider these as promising signals for a sustainable society and examples of systemic change at a local level that could be replicated and diffused on a larger scale. All solutions were based on collaborative service and business models giving birth to new forms of community and new ideas of locality. Defined as 'collaborative services' they have the potential to develop into a new kind of enterprise, a 'diffused social enterprise', which needs a supporting environment to grow (Stø and Strandbakken 2008). The designers' role here is to contribute to the development of these promising cases by designing 'enabling solutions' – 'a system of products, services, communication and whatever is necessary, to improve the accessibility, effectiveness and replicability of a collaborative service' (Manzini 2008: 38).

The emphasis on collaborative solutions and co-production – and therefore on a more active citizenship – is strongly linked to the contemporary debate on the redesign of public services. At the centre of this debate is the emphasis on *co-design* as a strategic approach to innovation that brings together the need to identify new sources and modes for innovation (user-driven innovation) with that for radical transformation of service models. A common statement within these studies is the requirement to move beyond simple citizens' consultation toward more participatory design approaches (Bate and Robert 2007), where citizens become co-designers of their services; in this sense design for services has been looking at the longer tradition of Scandinavian studies and practice of participatory design (Greenbaum and King 1991, Schuler and Namioka 1993); what is different from traditional participatory approaches is the addition of the 'co-creation' concept where users are now looked at as the biggest untapped resources in the public service delivery system. The co-creation model, suggested by Cottam and Leadbeater (2004), looking at the open source paradigm as main inspiration, implies the use of distributed resources (know-how, tools, effort and expertise), collaborative modes of delivery and the participation of users in 'the design and delivery of services, working with professionals and front-line staff to devise effective solutions' (Cottam and Leadbeater 2004: 22).

With this perspective the role of designers is moving toward the one of facilitator of multidisciplinary design processes, forging connections among people and organisations, bringing users to the centre of each project and defining the platforms and tools needed to enable and encourage participation (Cottam and Leadbeater 2004).

DESIGN FOR SERVICES AND HETEROGENEITY

> *Heterogeneity*: the quality of the performance may vary from time to time, depending on the situation and service participants.

Design for services has been considering the heterogeneity of service performance looking at service encounters not as abstract processes, but as 'situated actions' (Sangiorgi 2004, Maffei and Sangiorgi 2006); meaning that service performances are affected by the conditions of the service situation, but also shaped by the wider sociocultural and organisational contexts.

Service heterogeneity depends on the interaction among different factors that can't be predicted in advance, but that manifest only during each service encounter; that is people interpret the service situation based on their experience, motivations and personal characteristics, while their actions are shaped by the way the service interface supports or inhibits certain tasks. At the same time the way people behave during the service performance is also influenced by factors that transcend the situation at hand. Klaus (1985) developed an 'interaction framework' representing the service encounter in between two circles, one representing the user's sociocultural context and the other representing the organisational context, both determining behavioural norms, conventions, values, meanings and roles.

Developing models and tools to understand the conditions that influence the quality and heterogeneity of service interactions has become a key issue within design for services: the focus is on not attempting to control or standardise service practice but rather to design better conditions for possible behaviours to emerge.[13] This acknowledges that the analysis and the design of service interactions cannot be separated from the overall service system and organisation; nor can it be separated from the user context. As Morelli describes it, reinterpreting Manzini's definition of service design (1993),[14] designers of services need to enter new domains of knowledge (see Figure 1.4): 'the domain of the organizational and design culture and the domain of the social construction of technology' (Morelli 2002: 5).

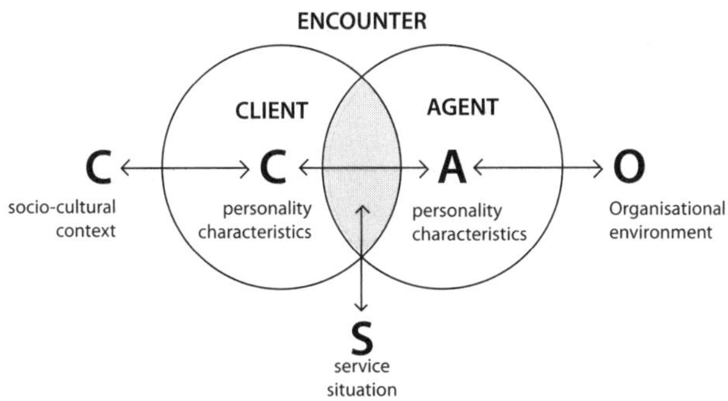

Figure 1.3 The service encounter

Source: Czepiel, J.A., Solomon, M.R. and Surprenant, C.F. (eds) 1985. Lexington, MA: Lexington Books. Reprinted by permission, 1985.

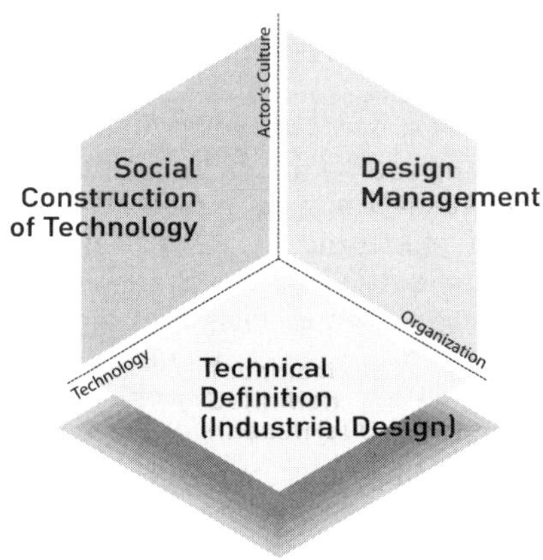

Figure 1.4 Multidimensional values implied in design for services activities

Source: Morelli (2002).

13 This is particularly true for services relying on human interactions where it is fundamental to create the conditions for service participants to empathise with each other (Forlizzi and Battarbee 2004).

14 Manzini (1993) described the design of new services as an activity that should be able to link the techno-productive dimension (what is the realm of the possible?) to the social (what are the explicit areas of demand and what the latent ones?) and cultural dimensions (what behavioural structures should one seek to influence? What values and qualitative criteria should we base our judgments on?).

In the same way interaction design has developed studies and theories to contextualise and locate interactions within wider systems and practices (Bødker and Sundblad 2008), design for services has explored the contextual and systemic dimension of services in different ways and adopted different theories in order to build conceptual models and theoretical frameworks that support designers. These models and frameworks enable the designer to observe, understand and visualise complex social systems of service organisations and to understand their manifestations.

One such research project has explored the application of activity theory[15] to the analysis and design of services (Sangiorgi 2004, Sangiorgi and Clark 2004). In a similar way to interaction design (Kaptelinin and Nardi 2006), activity theory has provided a framework to go beyond one-to-one (user-service interface) and sequential interaction models (service scripts) to include wider systems of action and interactions. The benefit of this approach is that the encounters and potential conflicts among service participants can be better understood when their behaviour is situated within their wider context of action. The success of designing good services can therefore be increased by synchronising the perspectives, goals and existing practices of service participants.

With the similar intent to understand the wider context influencing service interactions, designers have adopted and adapted the concept of 'information ecology' by Nardi and O'Day (1999) to services, introducing the idea of 'service ecology'. An 'information ecology' is defined by Nardi as 'a system of people, practices, values and technologies in a particular local environment' (Nardi and O'Day 1999: 49); Live|work defines a 'service ecology' as a 'system of actors and the relationships between them that form a service' (www.livework.co.uk) considering both direct service participants and people indirectly affected by the service. Understanding and mapping out service ecologies, including artefacts and practices that form them, becomes a way to identify unnoticed opportunities and/or resources to be able to reframe service configurations and interactions; at the same time, as Morelli suggests, adopting interpretations coming from social constructivist accounts of technology (Pinch and Bijker 1984, Bijker 1995), services are the convergence between 'the social, technological and cultural frames of the actors participating in the development system' and the 'technological knowledge embedded in the artefacts used for the service' (Morelli 2002: 6). Understanding these factors helps 'to determine the paradigmatic context in which new technologies, products and services can be accepted or refused' (Morelli 2002: 6).

When designers aim to reframe service systems or ecologies to generate new ideas and improve service interactions and behaviours, they necessarily touch wider issues of organisational change and community development. Studies have explored the role of design inquiries into service organisations as a way to facilitate radical change (Junginger and Sangiorgi 2009, 2011); while a further research strand is applying transformational approaches for socially progressive ends (Burns et al. 2006, Thackara 2007) looking at communities and their resources as part of the design team and as part of the solution as well.

Finally, service heterogeneity can be interpreted as a resource for customisation; the aim is not to reduce heterogeneity, but to valorise and develop service differences to personalise solutions. Services have an intrinsic flexibility that products lack due to the localisation of provision and the variety of contexts and people engaged. This flexibility potentially allows to fit different users' preferences and needs according

15 Activity theory refers to an interdisciplinary approach to human sciences and to a set of concepts and perspectives for the study of human activity that has its roots in Russian psychology of the 1920s.

to the service situation. Customising the solution requires a change to the actors system and their reciprocal relations; this can be achieved by designing modularity into services, thus supporting economies of scope and scale for the producers, while enabling personalisation for users (Manzini et al. 2004).

SERVICE DESIGN AND PERISHABILITY

> *Perishability*: most services can't be stored and therefore depend on the ability to balance and synchronise demand with supply capacity.

Designers have considered the balance between demand and supply capacity, starting from different perspectives, without necessarily focusing directly on efficiency and productivity issues. Rather reflections are related to the need to replicate, scale up or transfer services and service ideas, maintaining the qualities that characterise the original service model, or to generate new solutions that provide a response to an increased or varied service demand in radically new ways.

The scaleability and diffusion of new solutions as well as the need for radical innovation are key issues in innovation studies, with a particular focus on the redesign of public services (Harris and Albury 2009). Here an increase in productivity is a pressing requirement, but there is an increasing awareness that drivers to increase efficiency are not enough any more (Mulgan and Tucker 2007).

To replicate and successfully diffuse new or good solutions is a challenge. Scaled up or replicate service solutions need to consider the interactive nature of services and their local dimensions.

As an example, cultural diversity is a crucial factor when replicating services: in an investigation on case studies of internationalisation of trade services,[16] Morelli and Sangiorgi (2006) report how the immaterial and interactive nature of services requires a transfer process that is flexible enough to adapt the service solution to the specificity of the new context. To transfer services to new contexts both knowledge sharing and codification strategies are required (Rullani 2004a, 2004b). Designers can act as observers, interpreters and mediators (in collaboration with anthropologists) of local and foreign cultures; they work to codify knowledge into the design of signs, kits, manuals, web platforms and space layouts. They can also facilitate the transfer of tacit knowledge (such as skills, competences, values) via sharing strategies mainly thanks to the activity of trained trainers and to the organisation of on-site workshops and pilot activities.

Along with this replication process, interaction qualities can be compromised. Ritzer explains the concept of *nothing* as 'a social form that is generally centrally conceived, controlled and comparatively devoid of distinctive substantive content' (Ritzer 2007: 36). Distinctiveness and authenticity are intentionally or accidentally sacrificed for the benefit of the globalisation of service procedures, and for the convenience of users who can repeat well-known interaction patterns and recognise brand provisions. The relational qualities that belong to people's dialogical capabilities and to the 'intimacy' that a relationship can establish because of a certain degree of

16 Morelli and Sangiorgi investigated how an Italian design studio (Logotel) supported the introduction of the Italian phone company TIM within the Brazilian market acting as observer and interpreter of a foreign culture, and the introduction of the French car accessories retail network, Eurorepar in Italy acting as mediator of its own Italian culture and market.

spontaneity (Cipolla 2006), are impossible to replicate or plan in advance. After the initial enthusiasm, or because of different circumstances, these qualities can perish, just like the service. Engagement and enthusiasm can hardly be replicated. Design for services cannot avoid this limitation, but can work to support responsive and trustful interactions, recognising the person behind each individual (Cipolla 2006).

From a similar perspective Manzini (2008) describes a possible way to diffuse promising solutions[17] trying not to compromise their relational qualities. In his opinion this kind of diffusion can be obtained, rather than scaling up single organisations, by connecting small and diverse initiatives via networks and platforms. This strategy is possible thanks to the convergence of emerging trends, such as distributed systems, social networks and collaborative services. The combination of these three phenomena has the potential to provide small enterprises and local initiatives with the support they need to develop their ideas, gain visibility, acquire tools, knowledge and skills and have a stronger presence in the market.

A radically new model of welfare, defined as *open welfare* by Cottam and Leadbeater (2004), follows a similar direction. Cottam and Leadbeater suggest that the problem of an inbalance between demand and supply capacity, particularly true for the public sector, cannot be solved by improving the efficiency of existing services. Instead of stretching the productivity of existing organisations, open welfare relies on mass participation in the design and delivery of services, while reconfiguring the existing service system by introducing new innovation actors (Harris and Albury 2009).

Designers contribute to these innovation and replication strategies, bringing their capacity to interpret local contexts, design enabling tools and platforms and generate scenarios that provide a vision for different stakeholders to converge and work together.

TOWARD A NEW PARADIGM

This overview has summarised some of the approaches and focuses design has been considering when approaching the service realm: making the intangible tangible and exploring the concept of dematerialisation when dealing with service *intangibility*; engaging users in co-creating services when valuing the *inseparability* of service production and consumption; understanding and designing the factors influencing the quality of service interactions and facilitating service customisation when considering service *heterogeneity*; and defining replication strategy or radically new collaborative service models when dealing with service *perishability*.

This categorisation of design contributions is still valid today and we suggest that it could be used to facilitate a conversation between design research and the different disciplines that are now to converge into a wider 'service science'. What is changing is that the distinction between products and services, as suggested by the IHIP model, is blurring together with the traditional supplier and user distinction. Information technology has multiplied possibilities for service delivery via the Web and ubiquitous computing is reducing the inseparability of production and consumption, and, in some ways, service heterogeneity and perishability. Social technologies and emerging collaborative solutions have generated the conditions for people to interact and collaborate in new ways that can hardly be described as services. Products themselves are increasingly entangled with services as an additional offering, or integrated with service functionalities by becoming smarter and interconnected (see for example digital appliances or GPS).

17 We consider solutions promising when they are potentially more sustainable and when they are capable of generating social capital.

This has caused design for services to start changing and questioning itself and its main focus of practice. By looking at the emergence of a new kind of underground communities enabled by networking technologies, Singleton (2009) questions traditional definitions of services derived from management science that tries to 'define services purely negatively – in terms of what they lack, that material products do' (Singleton 2009: 3), not contributing much to a real understanding of what a service is. He suggests looking at services as 'regulated forms of exchange' to explore the range of motivations and apparatuses of obligations that bring people to do something for someone else. In a similar way Penin and Tonkinwise (2009) recalls the political dimension of design for services being related to the design of 'relations of servility' and therefore in need of methods able to explore the 'plausibility' and 'ethicality' of service interactions. Manzini considers the growth of community-based services that rely on reciprocal exchanges of benefits as a reason to rethink services. He suggests how the products of what he calls the Next Economy are 'mainly systems based on interlinking services: technical and social networks where people, products and places interact to obtain a common result (i.e. a value that can be recognised as such by all the actors involved)' (see Introduction).

Focusing similarly on the dimensions of exchange and interactions, but adopting a different rhetoric, marketing scholars (e.g. Vargo and Lush 2004) have suggested that a service logic (instead of services) offers a new way to approach marketing and indeed the economy more generally, thus arguing for a paradigm shift in the discipline. At the core of this is a renewed interpretation of value (Normann and Ramirez 1993, 1994). This is achieved by developing two distinct models: the good dominant logic and the service dominant logic. The former is characterised by tangible resources, embedded value and transactions. The latter involves a shift from the exchange of 'goods' (interpreted as *operand resources*) to the exchange of 'benefits' obtained through the application of 'knowledge and skills' (interpreted as *operant resources*). In this framework a service is generally conceived as 'the application of competences for the benefit of others' (Spohrer et al. 2008, Vargo and Lush 2004) and goods 'serve as appliances for service provision rather than ends in themselves' (Vargo and Lush 2004: 13). In this approach there is no more separation between products and services because products are also interpreted as 'embodied knowledge or activities' (Normann and Ramirez 1993). The focus on benefits, knowledge and skills and value co-creation in interaction with users helps to reframe the way we look at systems of production and delivery, blurring the distinctions between users and suppliers. Service systems are interpreted here as 'value co-creation configurations of people, technology, value propositions connecting internal and external service systems, and sharing information (e.g. language, laws, measures, and methods)' (Maglio and Spohrer 2005: 40).

These considerations suggest a paradigm shift in the fundamentals of value creation in the contemporary economy that we will explore further in the last section of the book. It is enough here to say that from a design perspective the service dominant logic suggests a shift of focus and scale that is already happening in design, but not in a systematic way. The exponential increase in interactivity, connectivity and co-production of current offerings (being single artefacts or service solutions) requires designers to work in a more integrated, collaborative and systemic way; this doesn't necessarily mean that designers are currently equipped with the required conceptual frameworks and methodologies to do so. Marketing studies suggest a move from a 'marketing to' toward a 'marketing with', that is to adopt a more collaborative approach and philosophy to businesses (Lush et al. 2008). Design is exploring transformations in its identity, reflecting on its own role and practice, when inquiring for example into the emergence of the open source paradigm (Leadbeater 2008) or valuing the innate creativity of people in their daily life and within co-design processes (Meroni 2007). Observing designers' practice in Dott07 public design commission projects,[18] Lauren Tan, for example, identifies seven emerging roles: designers as facilitator, researcher, co-creator, communicator, strategist, capability builder and entrepreneur (Yee et al. 2009). This research is part of a wider debate into the future of design industry (Inns 2007).

We have chosen to explore these emerging roles and 'geographies of design' (Inns 2009) in practice, looking at existing research and design projects related to the service realm. The next chapter will introduce the case studies and their relation to design for services as a bridge to the next section where they will be described and commented on in more detail.

Design for Services in Practice

In the previous paragraphs we have explored the reasons why services and design for services have a significant role in today's economy and society; moreover we have applied the IHIP framework to describe some of the contributions design has brought, in theory and in practice, when dealing with services.

Notwithstanding this existing work design for services is still a young discipline where research and theory appear to be still weak and dispersed; in addition the nature and definitions of services are, as we have anticipated, already changing. We decided then to build this book around a collection of 17 case studies, adopting a phenomenological and grounded theory approach, meaning observing and interpreting these case studies to further reflect and theorise on the role and contributions of design within the emergent 'service science'. As a result a map summarising these observations will follow at the end of Section 2.

In particular we have asked six design companies – *thinkpublic*, UK: STBY, Holland; Participle, UK: Strategic Design Scenarios, Belgium; Experientia, Italy; Domus Academy, Italy – eight academic research centres – Carnegie Mellon University, USA; Linköping University, Sweden; ImaginationLancaster and Computing Department, Lancaster University, UK; Saïd Business School, University of Oxford, UK; Department INDACO, Centro Metid and Dept. BEST, Politecnico di Milano, Italy; Melbourne University, Australia – and one company – IBM Research USA and IBM Corporation, Canada – to write about their project experiences. These case studies were chosen as representing significant areas of research and practice such as social innovation, public services, science and technology-based services, interaction and experience design for services.

Having collected the case studies, we carefully read through the project experiences to mark out and group the emergent roles and contributions of design for services in order to identify the main areas of interventions and core competences of designers; these areas have been used to organise the case studies in four groups as they appear in Section 2.

We will here briefly introduce the four areas of intervention and the related case studies before moving to the next section of the book.

18 Design of the Time (DOTT) is a ten-year programme of public design commissions co-funded by the UK Design Council and local regional development agencies. Dott07 is the 2007 edition conducted in the north-east of England.

DESIGNING INTERACTIONS, RELATIONS AND EXPERIENCES

The projects within this area report on the capacity of designers to understand experiences through empathic conversations and research methodologies. Understanding experiences helps to inform the design of service interactions, relationships and interfaces, to facilitate the engagement of users in the redesign of their experiences (co-design), and to generate service ideas consistent with existing behaviours. The case studies of this area are:

- *Co-designing services in the public sector*: Szebeko (*thinkpublic*) describes the use of an experience-based approach to redesigning health services in a collaborative way;

- *Developing collaborative tools in international projects: the PoliDaido project*: Sancassani and Fabris (Politecnico di Milano) report on the design of an e-learning service platform to enable students from distant universities to co-design;

- *Designing empathic conversations about future user experiences*: Raijmakers (STBY) describes how empathic conversations with citizens can inspire the design of meaningful services for the regeneration of a region;

- *Driving service design by directed storytelling*: Evenson (Carnegie Mellon) describes the use of storytelling as a way to inform the redesign of health services;

- *Exploring mobile needs and behaviours in emerging markets*: Vanderbeeken (Experientia) describes a project on the use of mobile phones to deliver services in emerging markets.

DESIGNING INTERACTIONS TO SHAPE SYSTEMS AND ORGANISATIONS

The projects within this area illustrate how designing and redesigning interactions between users and the service system are the core activities of design for services; at the same time they also demonstrate how, in order to improve user–service interactions, designers often reach into the organisation, participating in deeper transformation processes and suggesting new business configurations and service models. The case studies of this area are:

- *There is more to service than interactions*: Holmlid (Linköping University) investigates into the Swedish Customs' service operations to show how service designers need to deepen their understanding of the service system that is behind user–service interactions;

- *How service design can support innovation in the public sector*: Pacenti (DARC) reflects on how the application of interaction design guidelines at the service operation level can bring to deeper transformation, processes of an organisation service culture;

- *From novelty to routine: services in science and technology-based enterprises:* Kimbell (Oxford University) reports how designers work across boundaries of knowledge domains, therefore helping to reframe business models and service configurations;

- *Enabling excellence in service with expressive service blueprinting*: Spraragen and Hickey (IBM) explore service design methods to understand employee's behaviours and inform internal service processes.

EXPLORING NEW COLLABORATIVE SERVICE MODELS

This area reports on the role of designers to generate new service ideas, interpreting emerging behaviour patterns and technological potential, whilst dealing with societal challenges. Here projects reflect on the role of participation, on the conditions and methodologies to explore and develop collaborative solutions where users become co-producers of their services, and where resources are accessed and managed in a more distributed way. The case studies in this area are:

- *Service design, new media and community development*: Bury et al. (Lancaster University) observe the emergence of community network-based services and initiatives by providing a rural village with access to broadband;

- *Designing the next generation of public service*: Winhall (Participle) describes and reflects on the application of co-creation principles to rethink the welfare state model;

- *A service design inquiry into learning and personalisation*: Sangiorgi, Gillen, Junginger and Whitham (Lancaster University) describe a design inquiry into issues of personalisation and participation within a secondary school in the UK;

- *Mobile and collaborative. Mobile phones, digital services and sociocultural activation*: Pillan et al. (Politecnico di Milano) comment on students' projects exploring more collaborative solutions to issues related to immigration, identity and social inclusion.

IMAGINING FUTURE DIRECTIONS FOR SERVICE SYSTEMS

The projects within this area explore the role of designers in helping communities and organisations to imagine future scenarios for their regions and businesses while exploring how these visions could transform their activities and lifestyles on a daily basis. In this area services are used as tangible manifestations of wider and systemic transformations. The case studies of this area are:

- *Using scenarios to explore system change: VEIL, Local Food Depot*. Moy and Ryan (Melbourne University) describe the design of food service scenarios for Melbourne to guide producers and consumers' expectations of the future;

- *Designing a collaborative projection of the 'Cité du Design'*: Jégou (Strategic Design Scenario) reports on a collaborative design process to imagine, with the local government and the community, possible futures for the Cité du Design in Saint-Etienne.

- *Supporting social innovation in food networks*: Meroni et al. (Politecnico di Milano) describe how service design proposals have been used to build a scenario and activate social and economic resources of a peri-urban area of Milan (Italy) and support its sustainable development.

- *Enabling sustainable behaviours in mobility through service design*: Meroni (Politecnico di Milano) and Sangiorgi (Lancaster University) describe service scenarios as a way to support a company, working in the intelligent transport system sector, to imagine business opportunities for the Italian market.

References

ALMEGA (2008). *Innovation in Service Companies, a Survey of 778 Swedish Service Companies on Innovation and Research*. Available at: http://www.almega.se/Files/ALMEGA/Caradoc_Members/Rapport/Innovativa_tjänsteföretag_2008_B.PDF.

Bate, S.P. and Robert, G. 2007. *Bringing User Experience to Health Care Improvement: The Concepts, Methods and Practices of Experience-based Design*. Oxford: Radcliffe Publishing.

Bateson, J.E.G. 1979. Why we need service marketing. In *Conceptual and Theoretical Developments in Marketing*, edited by O.C. Ferrell, S.W. Brown and C.W. Lamb. Chicago, IL: American Marketing Association, 131–46.

Bijker, W.E. 1995. *Of Bicycles, Bakelites, and Bulbs: Toward a Theory of Sociotechnical Change*. Cambridge, MA: MIT Press.

Bitard, P. and Basset, J. 2008. *Mini Study 05 – Design as a Tool for INNOVATION*. Pro Inno Europe Innogrips. Global Review of Innovation Intelligence and Policy Studies. Available at http://grips.proinno-europe.eu/knowledge_base/view/550/design-as-a-tool-for-innovation-mini-study-05/, accessed 7 January 2010.

Bødker, S. and Sundblad, Y. 2008. Usability and interaction design – new challenges for the Scandinavian tradition. *Behaviour & Information Technology*, 27(4), 293–300.

Bradwell, P. and Marr, S. 2008. *Making the Most of Collaboration: an International Survey of Public Service Co-design*. London: Demos.

Buchanan, R. 1992. Wicked problems in design thinking. *Design Issues*, 8(2), 5–21.

Buchanan, R. 2001. Design research and the new learning. *Design Issues*, 17(4), 3–23.

Burns, C., Cottam, H., Vanstone, C. and Winhall, J. 2006. *Transformation Design*. RED paper 02, London: Design Council.

Cipolla, C. 2006. Sustainable freedoms, dialogical capabilities and design. *Cumulus Working Papers. Nantes*, edited by E. Salmi and L. Anusionwu. Helsinki: University of Art and Design, 59–65.

Cottam, H. and Leadbeater, C. 2004. *Open Welfare: Designs on the Public Good*. London: Design Council.

Cross, N. 2006. *Designerly Ways of Knowing*. London: Springer-Verlag.

Czepiel, J.A., Solomon, M.R. and Surprenant, C.F. (eds) 1985. *The Service Encounter*. Lexington, MA: Lexington Books.

DIUS (Department for Innovation, Universities and Skills) 2008. Innovation Nation. White Paper presented to Parliament March, Cm 7345. Norwich: Tso.

Edgett, S. and Parkinson S. 1993. Marketing for service industries – a review. *The Service Industries Journal*, 13 (July), 19–39.

Erlhoff, M., Mager, B. and Manzini, E. 1997. *Dienstleistung braucht Design, Professioneller Produkt- und Markenauftritt für Serviceanbieter*. Herausgeber: Hermann Luchterhand Verlag GmbH.

European Commission 2009. *Challenges for EU Support to Innovation in Services – Fostering new Markets and Jobs through Innovation*. Commission Staff Working Document, SEC(2009)1195 final. Luxembourg: Publications Office of the European Union.

Eurostat 2009. *European Business. Facts and Figures*. Luxembourg: Eurostat Statistical Books. Available at: http://epp.eurostat.ec.europa.eu/cache/ITY_OFFPUB/KS-BW-09-001/EN/KS-BW-09-001-EN.PDF, accessed 7 January 2010.

Evenson, S. 2006. Directed storytelling: interpreting experience for design. In A. Bennett and S. Heller (eds), *Design Studies: Theory and Research in Graphic Design*. Princeton, NJ: Princeton Architectural Press.

Forlizzi, J. and Battarbee, K. 2004. Understanding experience in interactive systems. Paper to the conference: DIS – Designing Interactive Systems: Processes, Practices, Methods and Techniques 2004, Cambridge, MA, 1–4 August.

Gallouj, F. 2002. Innovation in services and the attendant old and new myths. *Journal of Socio-Economics*, 31, 137–54.

Greenbaum, J. and King, M. (eds) 1991. *Design at Work: Cooperative Design of Computer Systems*, Hillsdale, New Jersey: LEA Publishers.

Harris, M. and Albury, D. 2009. *The Innovation Imperative. Why Radical Innovation is Needed to Reinvent Public Services for the Recession and Beyond*. Discussion paper. London: The Labe, Nesta.

Hollins, G. and Hollins, B. 1991. *Total Design: Managing the Design Process in the Service Sector*. London: Pitman.

Holmlid, S. 2007. *Interaction Design and Service Design: Expanding a Comparison of Design Disciplines*. Nordic Design Research Conference: Design Inquiries, 27–30 May, Stockholm, Sweden.

Howells, J. 2007. *Fostering Innovation in Services*. A Report of the Expert Group on Innovation in Services. Brussels: Commission of the European Union.

Inns, T. (ed.) 2007. *Designing for the 21st Century: Interdisciplinary Questions and Insights*. Aldershot: Gower Publishing Ltd.

Inns, T. 2009. New geographies of design: exploring the strategic use of design thinking. In *Connexity*, 8th European Academy of Design Conference, 1–3 April, Aberdeen, Scotland.

Jégou, F. and Manzini, E. 2008. *Collaborative Services. Social Innovation and Design for Sustainability*. Milan: Edizioni Polidesign.

Junginger, S. and Sangiorgi, D. 2009. Service design and organizational change: bridging the gap between rigour and relevance, *Conference Proceedings of the IASDR09 Conference*, 18–22 October, Seoul.

Junginger, S. and Sangiorgi, D. 2011. Public policy and public management: contextualising service design in the public sector. In *Handbook of Design Management*, edited by R. Cooper, S. Junginger and T. Lockwood. Oxford: Berg Press.

Kaptelinin, V. and Nardi, B.A. 2006. *Acting with Technology: Activity Theory and Interaction Design*. Cambridge, MA: MIT.

Kimbell, L. 2009. The turn to service design. In *Design and Creativity: Policy, Management and Practice*, edited by J. Gulier and L. Moor. Oxford: Berg, 157–73.

Kimbell, L. and Seidel, V.P. (eds) 2008. *Designing for Services in Science and Technology based Enterprises*. Oxford: Saïd Business School.

Klaus, P.G. 1985. Quality epiphenomenon: The conceptual understanding of quality in face-to-face service encounters. In *The Service Encounter*, edited by J.A. Czepiel et al. Lexington, MA: Lexington Books.
Leadbeater, C. 2008. *We Think: The Power of Mass Creativity*. London: Profile Books Ltd.
Lovelock, C. and Gummesson, E. 2004. Whither services marketing? In search of a new paradigm and fresh perspectives. *Journal of Service Research*, 7(1), 20–41.
Lush, R.F., Vargo, S.L. and Wessels, G. 2008. Toward a conceptual foundation for service science: Contributions from service-dominant logic. *IBM Systems Journal*, 47(1), 5–14.
Maffei, S. and Sangiorgi D. 2006. From communication design to activity design. In *Designing Effective Communications: Creating Contexts for Clarity and Meaning*, edited by J. Frascara. New York: Allworth Press, 83–100.
Mager, B. 2004. *Service Design. A Review*. Köln: Köln International School of Design.
Maglio, P. and Spohrer, J. 2008. Fundamentals of service science. *Journal of the Academy of Marketing Science*, 36, 18–20.
Manzini, E. 1993. Il design dei servizi. La progettazione del prodotto-servizio. *Design Management*, 4, 7–12.
Manzini, E. 2008. Collaborative organisations and enabling solutions. Social innovation and design for sustainability. In *Collaborative Services. Social Innovation and Design for Sustainability*, edited by F. Jégou and E. Manzini. Milan: Edizioni Polidesign, 29–41.
Manzini, E. and Vezzoli, C. 2002. *Product Service Systems and Sustainability*. Paris: United Nations Environment Programme, Division of Technology Industry and Economics (DTIE), Production and Consumption Branch.
Manzini, E. and Vezzoli, C. 2003. A strategic design approach to develop sustainable product service systems: examples taken from the 'environmentally friendly innovation' Italian prize. *Journal of Cleaner Production*, 11, 851–7.
Manzini, E., Collina, L. and Evans, S. (eds) 2004. *Solution Oriented Partnership, How to Design Industrialised Sustainable Solutions*. Cranfield: Cranfield University Press.
Marchand, A. and Walker, S. 2008. Beyond abundance. In *Changing the Change Conference*, Turin, 10–12 July.
Meroni, A. (ed.) 2007. *Creative Communities. People Inventing Sustainable Ways of Living*. Milan: Edizioni Polidesign.
Miles, I. 2001. *Services Innovation: A Reconfiguration of Innovation Studies*. Manchester: PREST, University of Manchester.
Miles, I. 2005. Innovation in services. In *The Oxford Handbook of Innovation*, edited by J. Fagerberg, D. Mowery and R. Nelson. Oxford: Oxford University Press.
Mont, O. 2000. *Product-Service Systems. Shifting Corporate Focus from Selling Products to Selling Product-services: A New Approach to Sustainable Development*. Stockholm: Swedish EPA, AFR-report 288.
Mont, O. 2002. *Functional Thinking. The Role of Functional Sales and Product Service Systems for a Function-based Society*. Stockholm: Swedish EPA, Naturvårdsverket Rapport 5223.
Morelli, N. 2002. Designing product/service systems: a methodological exploration. *Design Issues*, 18(3), 3–17.
Morelli, N. and Sangiorgi D. 2006. *Managing Globalisation and Local Issues in Service Design. On the Convergence Between the Opposing Demands of Industrialisation and Personalisation of Service Performances*. Design2Business Conference, Shanghai, 17–19 March.

Morelli, N. and Tollestrup, C. 2007. *New Representation Techniques for Designing in a Systemic Perspective*. Nordic Design Conference: Design Inquiries, 27–30 May, Stockholm, Sweden.

Morin E. 1993. *Introduzione al pensiero complesso*. Milan: Sperling & Kupfer.

Mulgan, G. and Tucker, S. 2007. Scaling up innovation. The ultimate challenge. In *Unlocking Innovation. Why Citizens hold the Key to Public Service Reform*, edited by S. Parker and S. Parker. London: Demos, 156–70.

Nardi, B.A., and O'Day, V.L. 1999. *Information Ecologies: Using Technology with Heart*. Cambridge, MA: MIT Press.

Nesta 2006. *The Innovation Gap. Why Policy needs to Reflect the Reality of Innovation in the UK*. Research report: October 2006. London: Nesta.

Nesta 2007. *Hidden Innovation. How Innovation Happens in Six 'Low Innovation' Sectors*. Research report: June 2007. London: Nesta.

Normann, R. and Ramirez, R. 1993. Value chain to value constellation – designing interactive strategy. *Harvard Business Review*, July–August, 65–77.

Normann, R. and Ramirez, R. 1994. *Designing Interactive Strategy. From Value Chain to Value Constellation*. New York: John Wiley and Sons.

OECD/Eurostat. 2005. *Oslo Manual: Guidelines for Collecting and Interpreting Innovation Data*, 3rd edition. Paris: OECD/Eurostat, France.

Pacenti, E. 1998. *Il progetto dell' interazione nei servizi. Un contributo al tema della progettazione dei servizi*. Ph.D. thesis in industrial design, Politecnico di Milan.

Parker, S. and Heapy, J. 2006. *The Journey to the Interface. How Public Service Design can Connect Users to Reform*. London: Demos.

Parker, S. and Parker S. 2007. *Unlocking Innovation. Why Citizens hold the Key to Public Service Reform*. London: Demos.

Penin, L. and Tonkinwise, C. 2009. The politics and theatre of service design. In *Rigor and Relevance in Design*, IASDR09 Conference, 19–22 October, Seoul.

Pinch, T.J. and Bijker, W.E. 1984. The social construction of facts and artefacts: or how the sociology of science and the sociology of technology might benefit each other. *Social Studies of Science*, SAGE, London, 14, 399–441.

Pinhanez, C. and Kontogiorgis, P. 2008. *A Proposal for a Service Science Discipline Classification System*, 2008 Frontiers of Service, Washington, DC, 2–5 October 2008. Available at: http://www.pinhanez.com/claudio/publications/frontiers08.pdf, accessed 3 January 2010.

Rifkin, J. 2000. *The Age of Access*. New York: Tarcher/Putnam.

Ritzer, G. 2007. *The Globalization of Nothing 2*. Thousand Oaks, CA: Pine Forge Press.

Rullani, E. 2004a. *Economia della Conoscenza. Creativitá e Valore nel Capitalismo delle Reti*. Roma: Carocci.

Rullani, E. 2004b. *La Fabbrica dell' Immateriale*. Roma: Carocci.

Sangiorgi, D. 2004. *Il Design dei servizi come Design dei Sistemi di Attività. La Teoria dell' Attività applicata alla progettazione dei servizi*. Ph.D. in industrial design, Politecnico di Milan.

Sangiorgi, D. and Clark, B. 2004. Toward a participatory design approach to service design. In *Artful Integration. Interweaving Media, Materials and Practices*, Participatory Design Conference, Toronto, 27–31 July.

Schuler, D. and Namioka, A. (eds) 1993. *Participatory Design. Principles and Practices*. Hillsdale, NJ: LEA Publishers.

Singleton, B. 2009. Services as technologies. Service design in new territories. In *Rigor and Relevance in Design*, IASDR09 Conference, 19–22 October, Seoul.

Spohrer, J., Magio, P.P., Bailey, J. and Gruhl, D. 2007. Steps toward a science of service systems. *IEEE Computer*, 1, 71–7.

Spohrer, J., Vargo, Stephen L., Caswell, N. and Maglio, Paul P. 2008. The service system is the basic abstraction of service science. *Proceedings of the 41st Hawaii International Conference on System Sciences.*

Stø, E. and Strandbakken, P. 2008. Social enterprises in modern welfare societies: a bottom-up perspective. In *Collaborative Services. Social Innovation and Design for Sustainability*, edited by F. Jégou and E. Manzini. Milan: Edizioni Polidesign, 137–43.

Tekes 2007. *Seizing the White Space: Innovative Service Concepts in the United States.* Technology Review 205/2007. Available at: www.tekes.fi/en/document/43000/innovative_service_pdf, accessed 3 January 2010.

Tekes 2008. *People – Economy – Environment. Priorities for the Future.* Available at http://www/tekes.fi/en/document/42671/people_economy_environemnt_pdf, accessed 22 December 2010.

Tether, B. and Howells, J. 2007. Changing understanding of innovation in services. From technological adoption to complex complementary changes to technologies, skills and organisation. In *Innovation in Services*, DTI Occasional Paper No. 9, June 2007. London: Department of Trade and Industry.

Thackara, J. 2005. *In the Bubble: Designing in a Complex World.* Cambridge, MA: MIT Press.

Thackara, J. 2007. *Wouldn't it be Great if …* London: Dotto07, Design Council.

Thomas, E. (ed.) 2008. *Innovation by Design in Public Services*, London: Solace Foundation Imprint.

Tukker A. 2004. Eight types of product-service-system: eight ways to sustainability? Experiences from Suspronet. *Business Strategy and the Environment*, 13, 246–60.

Tukker, A. and Tischner, U. 2006. Product-services as a research field: past, present and future. Reflections from a decade of research. *Journal of Cleaner Production*, 14, 1552–6.

Van Halen C., Vezzoli C. and Wimmer R. 2005. *Methodology for Product Service System Innovation. How to Develop Clean, Clever and Competitive Strategies in Companies.* Assen: Koninklijke Van Gorcum BV.

Vargo, S.L. and Lush, R.F. 2004. Evolving to a new dominant logic for marketing. *Journal of Marketing*, 68, 1–17.

Vattimo, G. and Rovatti, P.A. 1998. *Il pensiero debole.* XII edition. Milan: Feltrinelli.

Vergragt, P. (ed.). 2000. *Strategies Towards the Sustainable Households. Final Report. SusHouse Project.* Delft: Delft University of Technology.

Walker, S. 2009. Integration of scales, mass-produced plus locally made parts. In *Design Studies*, Berg, Oxford: Berg, 354–7.

Yee, J.S.R., Tan, L. and Meredith P. 2009. The emergent roles of a designer in the development of an e-learning service. In *Changing the Change Conference*, Turin, 10–12 July.

Zeithamal Valerie A., Parasuraman, A. and Berry Leonard L. 1985. Problems and strategies in services marketing. *Journal of Marketing*, 49 (Spring), 33–46.

Section 2

Design for Services: From Theory to Practice and Vice Versa

2.1
Designing Interactions, Relations and Experiences

This area explores the link between design for services and human experience as it unfolds during service interactions and via the mediation of the service interface. It discusses several approaches through which a service designer can understand and use the experiences of service participants to design better services. It has contributions from authors with a background in communication design, reflecting on design for services from the perspective of the actors' experience and the quality of it.

All the authors of this area consider understanding the experience of people involved in a service interaction the first step in designing or redesigning services. Investigating how a service occurs and how it is perceived individually and collectively helps to evaluate the quality and the very nature of the service itself. As summarised below, this can be relevant in different sectors and can be achieved applying different techniques:

- Szebeko (*thinkpublic*) claims that service design methods can help the UK National Health Service (NHS) get closer to their patients; working with patients as equal and valued partners in their care can inform service improvements while motivating the patients to take more responsibility for their own health and well-being.

- Sancassani and Fabris (Politecnico di Milano) describe how the design of a collaborative e-learning platform was informed by an investigation into cultural differences among students' learning practices. As a consequence, e-tools have been developed with the aim of supporting creative and informal interaction and discussion during distant co-design processes;

- Raijmakers (STBY) describes how empathic conversations with citizens can inspire and inform the regeneration of a large site including an old tin mine in Cornwall;

- Evenson (Carnegie Mellon) focuses on the use of empathic tools, such as storytelling, to give shape to a more human-centred healthcare service environment in the USA. The relevance of designing health information around patient's values, preferences and expectations is emphasised: meaningful health information exchange can nurture more 'empathic' relationships between patients and health staff;

- Vanderbeeken (Experientia) describes how, by understanding the use of mobile phones in emerging markets and in unsafe environments, Experientia ended up designing functionalities for mobile phone services.

These case studies suggest how understanding experience is crucial for design for services; this is because experiences are connected to and affected by all the elements that shape the nature and the quality of a service. As a consequence, the search for methods and tools to build 'empathic conversations' with service participants is at the core of all these projects descriptions. Authors look at and take inspiration from existing design approaches such as human-centred design and from existing fields of research such as ethnography, phenomenology and experience design.

Below we will first reflect on how these inspirations are manifested in the projects to then examine the concept of 'empathy' in more detail.

Human-centred Design

User-centred design has been to date the main framework for research into experiences and interactions (Norman 1988, Anceschi 1993, Shedroff 2001). Nowadays, given the growing complexity of design projects, we are witnessing a shift toward human-centred design (HCD), a research framework that looks beyond a limited definition of 'use' requirements to include the whole range of human experience all its facets and scales. At the beginning of the Millennium Richard Buchanan spoke about this concept as an approach connecting design to human dignity and human rights, 'the first principles of design, the principles on which our work is ultimately grounded and justified' (Buchanan 2001: 36). HCD, in such a context, opens up moral and ethical problems that lie at the core of the design professions, refers to the central place of human beings in design thinking, and proposes a disciplinary reflection on how to support and strengthen the dignity of human beings in their lives.

With respect to innovation processes, IDEO (2009) considers HCD (human-centred design also described as Hearing, Creating and Delivering) as an approach that, aimed at enhancing the lives of people, can help organisations to better connect with their existing network of stakeholders, while discovering new opportunities for change. The starting point of the HCD innovation process involves exploration of the needs, dreams, and behaviours of the people that will be involved in a solution: providers, final users and those inadvertently involved. HCD looks at the people in their context within their community, considering the experience of all the actors, and trying to provide a response to their expressed or latent needs. Both Vanderbeeken and Raijmakers propose a similar approach in their projects; by collecting and sharing experiences within a community, they better understood the multiple and sometimes conflicting behaviours, needs and desires of people; these stories were then used to collaboratively envision and explore possible future solutions. This way of designing, including wider communities of practice, tends to naturally surpass the focus on products and more toward generating ideas for services and systems that reconnect resources and people in unseen ways.

Design for Experience

Traditionally focused on user-centred design, design for experience brings into services the challenge of understanding and designing for the emotional aspects of people's interaction with objects, environments and other individuals; in this it relates to the philosophical stream of phenomenology or 'science of experience' and the ethnographic practice of understanding people's culture and behaviours (Bate and Robert 2006).

As a subjective phenomenon that cannot be observed directly, experiences can only be explored indirectly through stories, as a reflection and reconstruction of something past. The use of ethnographic methods, storytelling, video-blogs and emotional mapping as described in the case studies of this area, all aim to gain a deeper understanding of people's experiences in order to inform the design for services. Storytelling, in its different forms, is described by Forlizzi and Ford (2000) as a process that helps generate meaning out of experiences, moving from the *experience* (the constant stream of 'self-talk' that happens while individuals are conscious) to *an experience* (something that could be articulated or named and has a sense of completion) to *experiences as a story* (stories as vehicles to reflect and communicate the meaning we give to our experiences).

Moreover, particularly interesting for design for services is the concept of *co-experience* (Forlizzi and Battarbee 2004). Co-experience is described as user experience in social contexts, where experiences are created together or shared with others. As service experiences are often shared, co-produced and influenced by a wide number of actors, Szebeco and Evenson describe how their use of collaborative storytelling techniques helped directing and enhancing co-design activities.

Experience-based design (EBD), illustrated by Szebeko in her case study, represents the development and application of these considerations into the practice of design for healthcare services (Bate and Robert 2006). EBD is a methodology which helps front-line health teams work with patients in order to identify and make service improvements, based on observations and a collective reflection about people's experiences. Evenson describes a similar approach for the University of Pittsburgh Medical Center in the USA. Here the aim of the project was to maximise the users' positive emotional responses toward their healthcare experience. Both these projects also show, through the process, how patients learn to take more responsibility for their own health and well-being instead of acting as a mere passive recipient of care. In both cases, EBD proves to be an excellent way of introducing incremental innovations in the services by developing empathy between staff and patients, identifying key priority areas for improvement and eventually co-design solutions.

Another interesting example of designing for co-experiences is the project presented by Sancassani and Fabris, of an online environment (a virtual desk) and offline environment to enable teachers and students to creatively interact and co-design in an e-learning context. Aimed at the effectiveness of face-to-face learning experiences in design labs, designers had first to identify the elements of offline learning that contribute most effectively to creative collaborations; they then orchestrated those elements to create the right set of conditions for their replication in an online setting. For example they shared and created content in a friendly and informal way, stimulating students' participation and intrinsic motivation (Csíkszentmihályi 1990, Inghilleri 2003) by developing a similar atmosphere and work style to that which students are used to during face-to-face design workshops.

Finally, these three cases clarify the distinction between *tasks* and *actions* in service behaviours. Assuming that a precondition for a successful design for services is the correct interpretation of the nature and kind of experience desired, this distinction, first conceptualised by Hassenzahl (2003) and then adopted by Forlizzi and Battarbee (2004, Battarbee and Koskinen 2005), helps to differentiate between task-based interactions and fun-based modes of behaviour which lie between two diverse kinds of expected experiences. The first are goal-oriented, practical and effective, the latter action-oriented, driven by enjoyment and emotions. In open and collaborative service models these two behaviours are often mixed, so that designing and suggesting an adequate mental model for a service is a major challenge. When introducing more collaborative models of behaviours in a traditional provider–user environment such as the healthcare sector, this complex kind of experience become a crucial factor for design. Indeed, both Evenson and Szebeko attach a crucial importance to understanding the complex stakeholders' experience throughout the entire service journey, in order to define the meaning and nature of interactions embodied in the service touchpoints.

Linking Field Observation with Co-creation

Field studies are a fundamental stage for any kind of design project. In design for services, however, understanding the intersubjective values of user's behaviours and experiences and linking the individuals to the community seem to be a key focus of investigation (Battarbee 2004). Beside 'borrowing ethnographic techniques' (Wolcott, 1999), such as observation, participant observation or interviewing, service designers are amplifying their research tools to link field studies with co-creation and grass roots innovation. Direct observation of behaviours while recording sophisticated user's requirements can open up completely new opportunities for innovation, revolutionising the traditional ways of thinking about a problem, as well as offering new forms of collaboration. The projects presented by Experientia show a different range of methods as applied in the emerging markets, in order to understand how easy-to-use technology can foster co-creation, grass roots innovation and enable people to create and design their own services. Raijmakers suggests that 'empathic conversations', an approach to field research, help to link the phase of analysis with that of design, and to create a collaborative context for the project. He concludes that the establishment of new relationships between the design team and a wide range of future users is perhaps the most important result, because the project participants all tried to step into the shoes of the others. Directed storytelling, introduced by Evenson, is a tool for the designer to explore user behaviours without having to do long-term ethnographic research, yet still developing empathy with the people they are designing for and with.

Co-creation and Empathy

As explored in this introduction, all the case studies in this area suggest the importance of empathy and related design research tools to support and guide the design for service process in all its phases and to foster different forms of collaborations. Thus the design of interactions in services appears to be affected by two interlinked concepts: co-creation and empathy. Co-creation resonates with the contemporary phenomena of open-source communities (Leadbeater 2008), diffused creativity (Manzini 2007) and democratised innovation (Von Hippel 2005); it is also linked to the need to develop the potential of 'sociability' (Crampton Smith 2007, Norman 2008) of technologies, to create conditions for people to empathise and humanise these kinds of mediated relationships. Empathy, on the other hand, being the way emotions move from a person to another through contagion, is a fundamental skill for designers in general

(Brown 2009) and for design for services in particular; this because design for services mainly consists in designing for social interactions.

As a first conclusion designing for services seems to move designers from user-centred to human-centred design, from designing for experience to designing for co-experience and from field studies to enhancing empathy and on co-creation.

References

Anceschi, G. (ed.) 1993. *Il progetto delle interfacce. Oggetti colloquiali e protesi virtuali.* Milan: Domus Academy.

Bate, P. and Robert, G. 2006. Experience-based design: from redesigning the system around the patient to co-designing services with the patient. *Quality and Safety in Health Care*, 15, 306–10.

Battarbee, K. 2004. Co-experience: understanding user experiences in social interaction. Available at https://www.taik.fi/kirjakauppa/images/2be572c773f32c5b5450d0b313a02c65.pdf, accessed 31 January 2010.

Battarbee, K. and Koskinen I. 2005. Co-experience: user experience as interaction. *CoDesign*, 1(1), 5–18.

Brown, T. 2009. *Change by Design.* New York: HarperCollins.

Buchanan, R. 2001. Human dignity and human rights: thoughts on the principles of human-centered design. *Design Issues*, 17(3), 35–9.

Crampton Smith, G. 2007. Foreword: what is interaction design? In B. Moggridge, *Designing Interactions.* Boston, MA: MIT Press, vii–xx.

Csíkszentmihályi, M. 1990. *Flow: The Psychology of Optimal Experience.* New York: Harper and Row.

Forlizzi, J. and Battarbee, K. 2004. Understanding experience in interactive systems. Paper to the conference: DIS – Designing Interactive Systems: Processes, Practices, Methods and Techniques, 2004, Cambridge, MA, 1–4 August.

Forlizzi, J. and Ford, S. 2000. The building blocks of experience. An early framework for interaction deginers. Paper to the conference: DIS – Designing Interactive Systems: Processes, Practices, Methods and Techniques, 2000. New York City, 17–19 August.

Hassenzahl, M. 2003. The thing and I: understanding the relationship between user and product. In *Funology: From Usability to Enjoyment*, edited by M. A. Blythe, K. Overbeeke, A. F. Monk and P. C. Wright. Dordrecht: Kluwer Academic Publishers, 31–42.

IDEO 2009. *HCD Human-Centered Design, Toolkit.* Available at http://www.ideo.com/work/featured/human-centered-design-toolkit, accessed 31 January 2010.

Inghilleri, P. 2003. *La 'buona vita': Per l'uso creativo degli oggetti nella società dell'abbondanza.* Milan: Guerini e Associati.

Leadbeater, C. 2008. *We Think: The Power of Mass Creativity.* London: Profile Books LTD.

Manzini, E. 2007. Design research for sustainable social innovation. In *Design Research Now*, edited by R. Michel. Basel: Birkhäuser, 233–50.

Norman, D. 1988. *The Design of Everyday Things.* New York: Basic Books.

Norman, D.A. 2008. Sociable design. Available at http://www.jnd.org/ms/1.1%20Sociable%20Design.pdf, accessed 31 January 2010.

Shedroff, N. 2001. *Experience Design.* London: New Riders.

Von Hippel, E. 2005. *Democratizing Innovation.* Cambridge, MA: The MIT Press.

Wolcott, H.F. 1999. *Ethnography: A Way of Seeing.* Lanham, MD: AltaMira Press.

DEBORAH SZEBEKO

CASE STUDY 01 CO-DESIGNING SERVICES IN THE PUBLIC SECTOR

This case study claims that service design methods can help the UK National Health Service (NHS) to get closer to its patients; working with patients as equal and valued partners in their care can inform service improvements while motivating the patients to take more responsibility for their own health and well-being.

Design and Public Services

As public services face substantial challenges with demographic, social and environmental trends, along with the challenging economic times, it has never been more important to work together to design and improve public services for all. We argue that design can help address the complexity of such challenges through harnessing collaborative approaches to public service innovation and improvement. By doing so, we can not only design better services, but also develop lasting skills and capacity within service providers and users.

This is at the heart of how *thinkpublic*, a multidisciplinary social innovation and design agency, works. Our aim is to support and develop the human side of services by working alongside managers, front-line staff and patients to understand, improve and redesign services.

We believe that the people who use and deliver public services have the experience and ideas to make them better. We have adapted methods from the design sector[1] and combined them with cutting-edge thinking in innovation to put the ideas and aspirations of policy-makers into practice at the front line.

The common perception of design in the public sector is that it is expensive, flashy and something that has little to do with healthcare management and service improvement. In 2005, the Cox Review on Creativity in Business reported that creativity cannot be viewed as a skill possessed by the gifted few – creativity needs to pervade the thinking of whole businesses and be embraced within public services (Cox 2005).

Over the last six years at *thinkpublic* we have seen that design processes and methods can help gain deep insight into what people really think about public services, and, in doing so help, identify ways to improve them. Our work and projects, highlighted in the case study in this chapter, has confirmed that members of the

1 Approaches include observation, experience prototyping, ethnographic research and creative thinking tools.

public and public sector professionals can apply design thinking, enjoy the process and the benefits it produces and build their skills and capacity to identify issues and design improvements to address them.

We apply a co-design methodology where members of the public and public sector staff come together to share their experiences, challenges and ideas. Together they agree on key priorities, opportunities and areas for improvement. Co-design teams are then formed, made of up service users and service providers who then engage with and use design tools and process like storyboarding, idea generation, future scenarios and prototyping, to visualise their ideas and create tangible forms.

A PRACTICAL CASE STUDY: TAKING DESIGN TO HEALTH CARE

thinkpublic was commissioned by the National Health Service Institute for Innovation and improvement (NHSi), a national NHS organisation set up to help NHS Trusts[2] improve and innovate the delivery of public health services. The NHSi was keen to learn more about design-led tools and methods of designers and how they could be adapted to improve health services.

The Department of Health's *Creating a Patient-led NHS* (2005), says there needs to be a fundamental shift in the relationship between the NHS and patients. They outlined that this shift needed to move away from a service that does things *to* and *for* patients, towards one that works *with* patients as equal and valued partners in their care (Department of Health 2005). The outcome of this shift would to encourage and empower the patient to take more responsibility for their own health and well-being, rather than just be a recipient of health services.

The diagram in Figure 2.1.1 identifies the degree to which patients have influence and provide feedback about their healthcare experience (Bate and Robert 2007). It illustrates that the development and improvement of health service needs to extend toward experience based design (EBD) in order to understand better the patient experience to effectively improve healthcare.

Experience based design is a way of capturing and understanding how users feel each time they come into contact with a process, product, person or even a building or environment. It then uses that knowledge to redesign all or part of the process in a way that maximises the positive emotional responses of the user. The concept and use of EBD is rooted in design disciplines such as architecture, computing, product and graphic design. In all these disciplines the idea is to focus on the human experience (not just function, aesthetic, quality, safety and efficiency) and make the user integral to the whole design process (Bate and Robert 2007).

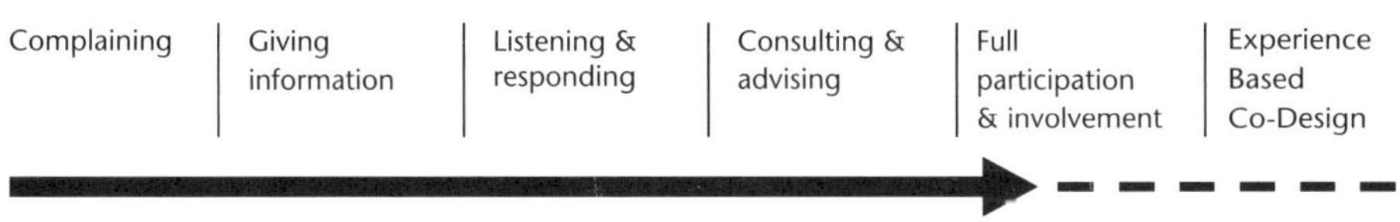

Figure 2.1.1 The continuum of patient influence
Source: Bate and Robert (2007).

2 A National Health Service Trust provides services on behalf of the National Health Service (NHS) in England and NHS Wales including hospitals and GPs.

thinkpublic has worked extensively in the area of EBD to adapt design-led processes and tools to healthcare. One such project involved working with the Head and Neck Cancer Service at Luton and Dunstable Hospital.

Luton and Dunstable Hospital is one of the most innovative and forward-thinking hospitals in the UK. This provided positive supporting culture in which apply EBD processes. Being innovative and forward thinking, Luton and Dunstable Hospital also had a patient satisfaction rating of 97 per cent (Picker Institute 2006). The NHS also wanted to see if 97 per cent satisfaction equalled a positive patient experience and *thinkpublic* puts this to the test.

The pilot project, which *thinkpublic* co-produced, ran over the course of twelve months and was the first project to test and demonstrate the value of EBD in the NHS.

CO-DESIGNING WITH PATIENTS AND STAFF: AN OVERVIEW OF THE CO-DESIGN PROCESS

Figure 2.1.2 shows the time-based process of a co-design project and how members of the co-design team interact and work together. Details of the process are given below and key aspects of our methodology, such as the use of insight tools, are highlighted.

THE GROUPS

- *Core group*. This is the design team at thinkpublic who worked on developing and designing the process together with two organisation development researchers and evaluators, two internal hospital improvement specialists and the national sponsor of the project. This group was also in charge of overseeing the project management, and working with the patient and staff groups separately at first, to understand their current experiences.

- *Advisory group*. Advisory groups were set up to oversee each of the co-design projects. They provided helpful check-in points throughout the project process providing, for example, guidance on ethics and aligning the project with the internal management and monitoring systems.

- *Co-design group event 1*. Bringing together patients and staff, we used their experience stories to identify key priority areas for improvement. Each of these priority areas became a co-design project. Smaller co-design teams were then formed to explore and develop these priorities.

- *Co-design group event 2*. At the completion of the smaller co-design projects, the entire team reconvened to share and reflect on their projects.

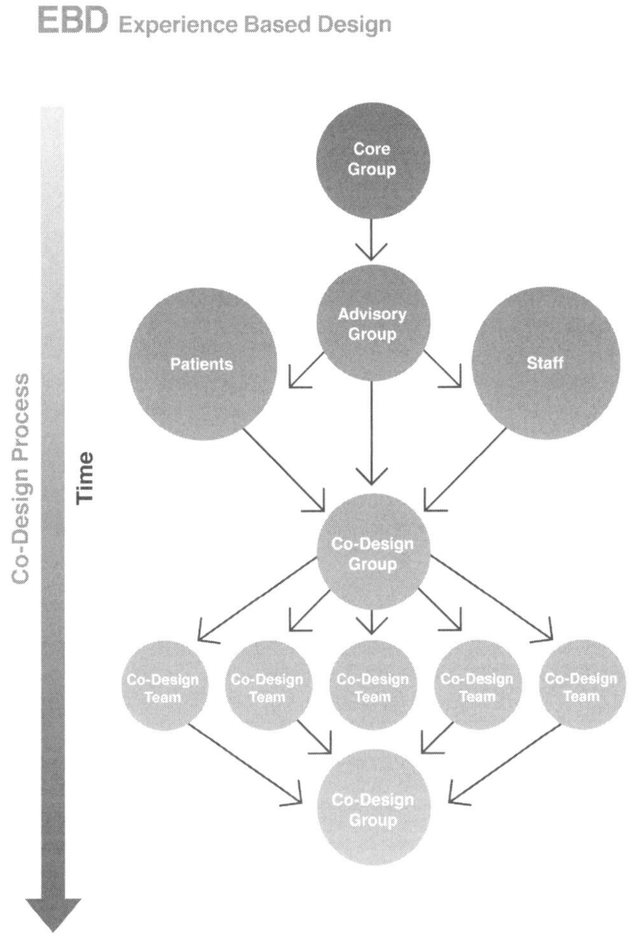

Figure 2.1.2 Representation of the co-design process

Key Aspects of Our Methodology

PREPARING PEOPLE

thinkpublic needed everyone at the Head and Neck Cancer Service to be engaged in the project and with the concept of EBD.

From the patient point of view, we wanted to overcome cynicism about 'patient engagement' exercises. We did so by working with the patients and staff as early on in the project process as possible. Our first task was to brand the project together and create posters and newspapers to enhance its presence and celebrate the project in the hospital (Figure 2.1.3). We also planned milestones in the project together, so that deliverables were reasonable and achievable in relation to the hospital's staff workload.

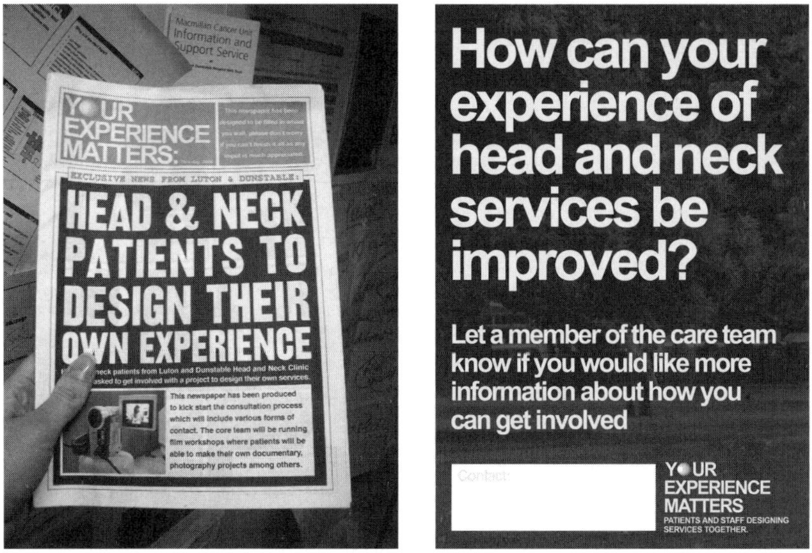

Figure 2.1.3 Posters and newspapers to enhance and celebrate the presence of the project in the hospital

We also involved the participation from a wider group of hospital stakeholders including senior clinicians and ward nurses, and reinforced the project's ties within the management structure of the hospital.

GAINING INSIGHT: INSIGHT TOOLS

Our research into the patient experience at Luton and Dunstable Hospital took a very different approach to traditional research surveys such as questionnaires. We used a wide range of research tools and techniques we collectively call *insight tools*. These insight tools are adapted from the design discipline and include patient diaries, film diaries, observation, storytelling and emotional mapping. They helped us gain a deeper understanding of the patient experience by opening up the process for people to share their experience in a range of accessible ways. The insight tools helped us capture stories about lived experiences, pinpoint emotional touch points[3] and create a map of where patients could be involved in co-designing improvements. Below are some key tools we used with Luton and Dunstable Hospital.

- *Identifying unarticulated actions: participant observation.* Observations were conducted as though we were patients sitting in the waiting room. We recorded observations by taking notes and photographs. These documentations were later used to help explain the context and illustrate service improvement areas to the co-design team (Figure 2.1.4). Being a participant observer provided insights into experiences that weren't articulated through patients and staff interviews. Some of these observations included:

3 An emotional touchpoint is a point in the patient or staff experience that provokes an emotion. It could be a high or low point in the overall experience.

- Issues with getting on weighing scales. The scales were placed in a side corridor in full view of the waiting room. Patients were asked to take their shoes off and stand on the scales before seeing the consultant. We observed that patients, due to age, frailty or obesity, were unable to remove their shoes and weigh themselves.
- An overlooked 'wait here' line. A line drawn on the floor was meant to help direct patients when queuing to check in. In our observations we saw that not one person saw this line and everyone approached the reception desk. When they did they were told to stand in line.

- *Capturing the experience: storytelling by film diaries.* There is a challenge in defining 'experience'. We are surrounded daily by 'experiences' that may include: 'the ultimate driving experience'; 'near-death experience'; 'holiday experience'; or 'the classic dining experience'. Where 'Experience can mean anything (and) is rarely defined in a systematic way' (Skeggs 2001) we had to begin talking about experiences with patients and staff in a subjective, unstructured and open way. We used a 'clean language' approach to storytelling meaning that, to elicit honest responses that ensured little to no steering from the interviewer, we followed a general interview spine that mainly probed the description of the chronology of events.

  We recorded the storytelling by filming the interviews with staff and patients while asking them about their stories from diagnosis to recovery of head and neck cancer. We aimed to expand the service experience to experiences before, after and around the service pathway, to gain a more holistic view of how patients and staff deal with head and neck cancer.

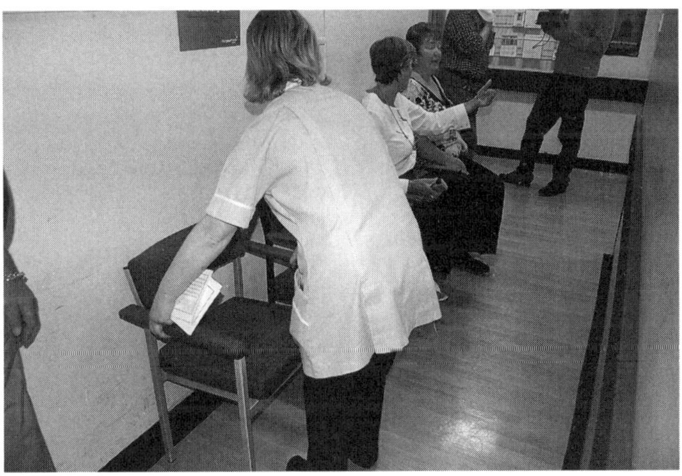

Figure 2.1.4 A picture of the observation phase aiming to identify the unarticulated actions of patients

By interviewing patients and staff about their experiences, we also found touchpoints that were, in their experience, more memorable than others. It was these touchpoints that defined the overall service experience and helped us assemble the main output from the interviews: a short film. We edited the over 30 hours of storytelling footage by the patients and staff to create a succinct 30-minute film to capture the most commonly spoken about themes in head and neck cancer experiences.

While the initial intent of the film was to facilitate a conversation around head and neck cancer experiences, we found that the film could extend to other uses with the permission of the patients. This particular film became a staff training tool and, with added footage, it also became a promotional tool within the NHS to raise awareness of head and neck cancer, demonstrating the value of EBD in healthcare.

- *Understanding the experiences: emotional mapping.* In the next stage of the process, *thinkpublic* facilitated a workshop to bring together staff and patients to share experiences, decide on priorities and design solutions (Figure 2.1.5). We began by showing the film from the previous stage to help patients understand their common challenges; enable staff to understand the patient's challenges; and initiate discussion points to work toward key priorities.

A key part of the two workshops was asking patients to map and then describe emotional touchpoints along their journey through the service (see Appendix 2). This helped everyone understand where priorities for improving the experience lay and gave everyone an opportunity to vote on those priorities.

When mapping the patient and staff experience, we chose to focus on the interaction that happened within the hospital and other areas that the hospital had control over. In doing this, we became aware of missing touchpoints in the patient experience. However, mapping does not have to be limited to the boundaries of the hospital. It can be extended beyond the hospital, for example to the patient's interactions with other NHS services. Beginning with the hospital system helps kick-start the project on a manageable scale.

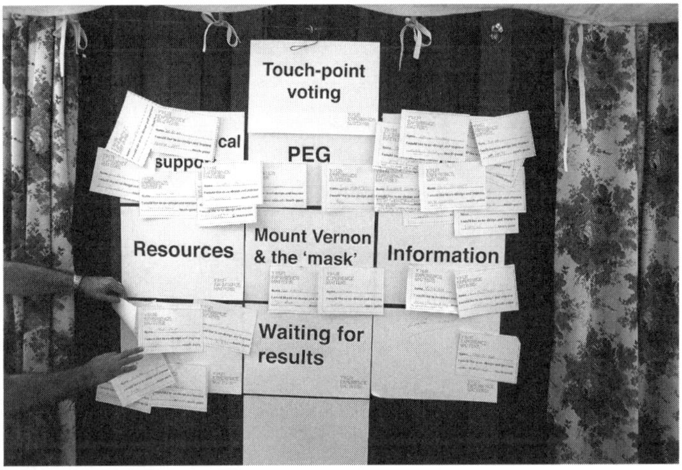

Figure 2.1.5 The emotional mapping of the experience of patients and staff on their journey through the service

FOSTERING OWNERSHIP AND WORKING TOGETHER TOWARDS IMPROVING EXPERIENCES

thinkpublic believes that if people can identify with the problem, they are more likely to become part of the solution. Staff and patients at Luton and Dunstable Hospital immediately felt ownership of the priorities for improvement that they had identified themselves. Some of these priorities for improvement included:

- the delivery of communication and the quality of information given to patients;
- development of a staff training programme that focused on delivering better patient experiences;
- redesigning aspects of the clinical environment such as the waiting spaces and considering the use of rooms;
- rescheduling of clinic times to ensure all patients in the waiting area were able to take a seat.

Through experiencing the process, patients and staff also felt confident that they could work together to implement these solutions. Away from their everyday roles as carer and cared-for, they began to see each other as equals, with a shared goal of improving the Head and Neck Cancer Service.

PROJECT RESULT: 43 LOW OR NO-COST IMPROVEMENTS

The project resulted in a total of 43 separate improvements to the Head and Neck Cancer Service. These improvements addressed efficiency, patient safety, and the overall patient experience of the service. All of the improvements were low or zero-cost, despite the fact that no budget limits had been set for the project.

The project demonstrated that a 97 per cent patient satisfaction figure does not necessarily equate to a positive experience. With 43 low or no-cost improvements in Luton and Dunstable's Head and Neck Cancer Service, there is still lots of room to improve (Figure 2.1.6).

Figure 2.1.6 A co-design event involving patients and staff

Since the project ended, many of the improvements have since been adopted by other services at Luton and Dunstable and shared with other NHS Trusts.

PROJECT IMPACT AND THE CONTINUING WORK OF THINKPUBLIC WITH THE NHS

The project delivered tangible results but it also had a deep impact with the people involved. This included:

- addressing the individual human dignity of the service user;
- fostering a new, collaborative relationship between frontline staff and patients at Luton and Dunstable's Head and Neck Cancer Service;
- reinvigorating the staff in their daily work;
- patient and staff empowerment – some even spoke of the therapeutic effect of the project.

We believe that such deep impact stands in contrast to other attempts to empower and involve patients in a meaningful way. The NHS Institute for Innovation and Improvement were delighted with the results of the Luton and Dunstable pilot project and, *thinkpublic* has continued to work closely with the NHS. After the project, we were engaged to produce guidelines and tools for other NHS services that wanted to explore EBD. This produced The Experience based Design Approach toolkit (see http://www.institute.nhs.uk), which was officially launched in 2009.

Reflections on the Pilot Project

The Luton and Dunstable project sits at the far end of the spectrum in the area of EBD, but the profession of design has not always positioned itself here. At *thinkpublic* our reflections on projects like Luton and Dunstable have demonstrated to us that there is a growing role for design in the public sector and that the profession of design is changing as design moves along the Bate and Robert's spectrum toward experience based co-design (2007). In our case study we have highlighted many positive outcomes, but for the design profession, shifting toward experience based co-design is not without its challenges.

The Design Council's former RED Unit presented in their *Transformation Design* paper (Burns et al. 2006) the challenges facing the design profession as they work in areas that seek to engage people more and more in the design process. Some of these key challenges are about changing the way we have traditionally worked as designers. Those that we believe are important to illuminate include:

- the loss of personal creative authorship of the designer: designers working in EBD move toward harnessing the creativity of others, as well as contributing creativity of their own;
- the need to expose our design process to permit others to participate in design activity;
- the need for designers to understand more consciously what they do to appropriate tools and processes in the design process. We also believe that this reflection not only permits non-designers to participate in our process, but can also identify more opportunities for design;
- the difficulty in communicating the value of design in such projects;
- the need for more design leadership to help further carve out this area of design;
- a minority of designers working in this way;
- the need for encouragement among designers to use their skills to design public services.

This case study reveals many of these challenges but also the benefits of using EBD to improve public services.

References

Bate, S.P. and Robert, G. 2007. *Bringing User Experience to Health Care Improvement: The Concepts, Methods and Practices of Experience-based Design*. Oxford: Radcliffe Publishing.

Burns, C., Cottam, H., Vanstone, C. and Winhall, J. 2006. *Transformation Design. RED paper 02*. London: Design Council.

Cox, G. 2005. *Cox Review of Creativity in Business: Building on the UK's Strengths.* HM Treasury. Available at http://www.hm-treasury.gov.uk/cox_review_creativity_business.htm, accessed 28 January 2010.

Department of Health 2005. *Creating a Patient-led NHS – Delivering the NHS Improvement Plan. System Reform Policy*. London: Department of Health.

Skeggs, B. 2001. Feminist ethnography. In *Handbook of Ethnography*, edited by P. Atkinson, A. Coffey, S. Delamont et al. London: Sage, 426–42.

SUSANNA SANCASSANI AND LUCA MARIA FRANCESCO FABRIS

CASE STUDY 02 DEVELOPING COLLABORATIVE TOOLS IN INTERNATIONAL PROJECTS: THE POLIDAIDO PROJECT

This case study describes how the design of a collaborative e-learning platform was informed by an investigation into cultural differences among students' learning practices. As a consequence, e-tools have been developed with the aim of supporting creative and informal interaction and discussion during distant co-design processes.

PoliDaido project is a case study on the use of e-learning in intercultural education contexts; it explores the Marshall's idea (2001) that electronic media and multimedia technologies promote communication and interaction between diverse groups with the purpose of helping students learn more about contexts. We also analyse the peculiar dimension of e-learning as a service and the strong relationship between an active and aware role of the user and the effectiveness of the service.

If we consider digital services as systems of integrated operations that can generate an intangible added value to users through the support of digital devices connected to the network, then e-learning can actually be a service. A key point of e-learning as a service is creating the conditions for the user to feel motivated to actually explore and use the service. Promoting users' motivation during all service delivery is the specific area in which successful e-learning services need to concentrate their resources.

Building in the Changing Urban Landscape

PoliDaido is a project developed in collaboration with Daido Institute of Technology (DIT) and Politecnico Building Environment Sciences and Technology (BEST) Department. The project, started on October 2007, involved sixty-one students of the Politecnico di Milano (Italians, foreigners from several countries enrolled in the Architectural Master Degree and Erasmus students), five students of Daido Institute of Technology of Nagoya, as well as five teachers from Politecnico di Milano (two professors and three assistants) and six from the Daido Institute (three professors and three assistants and administrators).

The programme was conceived as a series of distance workshops managed through an e-learning platform that was the context for various kinds of interactions with multifaceted purposes and outcomes, among which stimulating creativity. Its design has been approached as the one of a service to support the kinds of informal relationships helping creative processes. Students were tasked with the design of some new buildings dedicated to artists in a derelict area of Sesto San Giovanni, in the northern outskirts of Milan, where a huge urban transformation is about to start.

The City of Sesto San Giovanni is actually promoting a renewal of most of its former industrial areas. For this site the City of Sesto San Giovanni Planning Office asked for ideas to illustrate how (new) landscape and new housing could interact.

The new development of the former Falck steel industries area has been planned by the Renzo Piano Building Workshop (RPBW) and the site chosen for the training exercise lies just on the northern corner of the RPBW master plan. Starting from the present situation, and according to the Sesto San Giovanni Urban Master plan, students were tasked with the design of some new buildings dedicated to artists in an area that was planned to become a public park. They have been trained in the planning and development of built structures up to the executive design. Leading principles of the project were: balanced relation between green-built and light-massive structures, attention to the cycle of the water, climate control, energy saving and the use of building materials with high innovative performances.

A 'Construction and housing planning' course held by Professor Yasushi Kasajima at the Department of Architecture of the Daido Institute of Technology of Nagoya was run in parallel to the workshop held in Italy, where students worked in small teams involving people of the two nationalities.

SHAPING THE VIRTUAL LABORATORY

Given this background and the purpose of the programme, the design of the PoliDaido digital environment followed these aims:

- to support the creation of a collaborative knowledge in the team adopting the user's perspective;
- to design a 'document-centred' communication, that is, to develop a toolbox helping students to discuss, share and manage online various kinds of documents (videos, images, text documents, slides, diagrams);
- to encourage any kind of informal communication allowing exchange and interaction, and supporting the creation of innovative solutions as in a laboratory.

Beside managing the interactions, the challenge of the project was to explore the potentialities of education in the dynamics of global economy, fostering positive collaboration and mutual respect in diversity.

The first step of the research conducted by the Politecnico's team to design the e-learning platform focussed on the analysis of the different cultures and habits of the students involved, with particular attention to the Japanese context. As a result the features of the technological tool were defined and validated. These activities, among the most important and critical ones of the project, were mainly developed at distance.

At the end of the context analysis, the main idea guiding the design of the e-learning services of PoliDaido was to support the intrinsic motivation of students and teachers in using the platform for different kinds of online exchanges. The solution was to provide a 'virtual desk' where all the participants would have had the opportunity to share contents in a friendly and informal way. The metaphor of a virtual desk guided the design of both the synchronous and the asynchronous e-learning activities, until a final workshop held in Japan when it become a physical desk. To involve the Japanese partners in the designing of the e-learning services, a first prototype environment was shared online before the implementation phases. The evaluations of the digital environment by the Japanese partner were crucial for the following design decisions about the system features and the main graphical aspects. Furthermore a continuous discussion regarding the project development was made possible through a web-conference platform.

This path supported the implementation of a customised environment where didactic materials were available on the virtual desk: students were requested to publish their job progresses to make them visible to the teachers and the other students. The students were then invited, in order to ensure maximum interaction during all the in-room activities of the building workshop, to discuss other people's propositions. The challenge was to sustain participants' motivation to be an active part in the project discussion. In order to achieve this, the design choice was to provide the virtual desk with easy tools for informal criticism and to offer the possibility to discuss materials developed by other participants.

Students adopted easy and comfortable ways to conduct conversations, both using a permanent chat (whose thread was saved to allow asynchronous discussions) and a drawing tool; the latter allowed them to directly sketch lines and text on the virtual project paper, in the same way they would do in a class when interacting with their teacher.

In this way, the virtual desk of PoliDaido (Figure 2.1.7) became the place to share structured resources and academic materials (handouts and readings), to present the architectural projects prepared by the groups and to manage distance communication among people through different media such as text, chat and drawings.

Furthermore, the tools of the virtual desk, together with the project materials, have been essential in reducing the linguistic gap between the participants, by introducing a kind of content-centred communication: the discussion was developed not only about the content but *on* the content itself by manipulating images with sketches, symbols and text.

An interesting effect of the use of means for the visual communication was that the English language was perceived as just a further standard communication convention, almost as a 'graphical convention' among the others used internationally in architectural design (Figure 2.1.8).

Beside motivating to share and collaborate, the virtual desk was also used in a synchronous way, providing instant chat and messaging tools (always very appreciated by 'digital natives' as the Polidaido students are) and organising online lectures by experts; these lectures, about technological, structural, physical-environmental and landscape issues, were aimed to engage students with discussions and reflections on the contemporary concepts of city landscape.

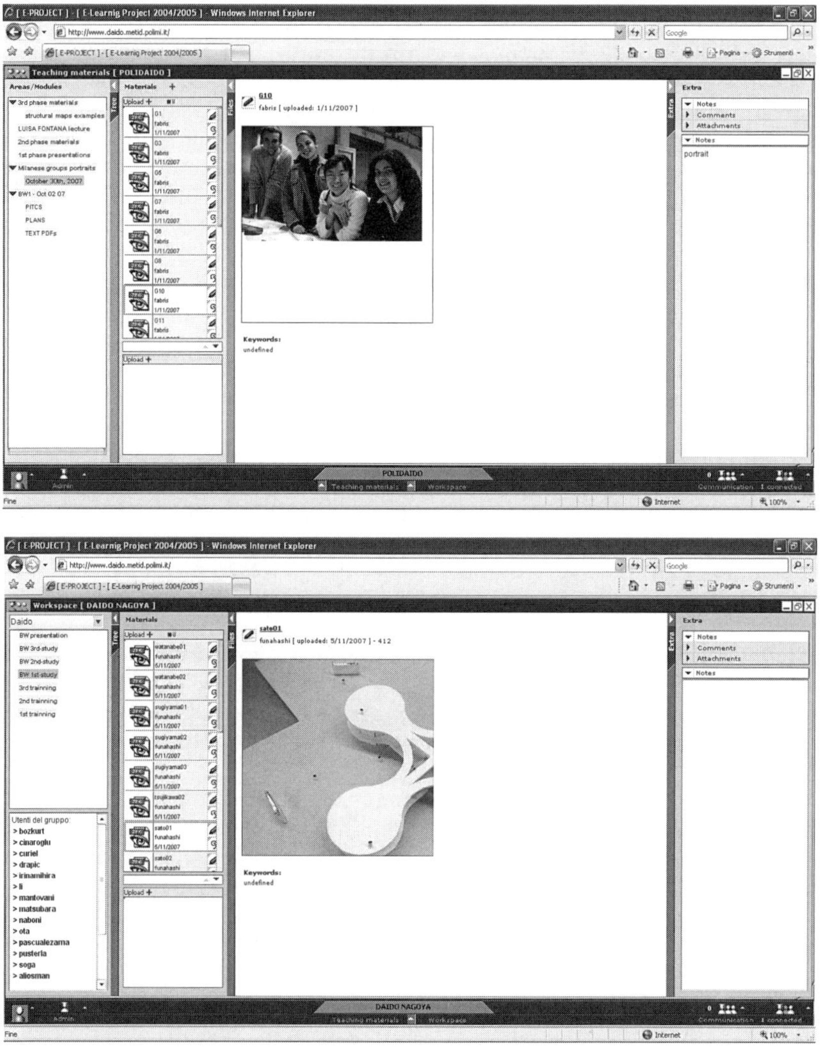

Figure 2.1.7 The PoliDaido 'virtual desk': the area for the teaching materials
Source: Politecnico di Milano.

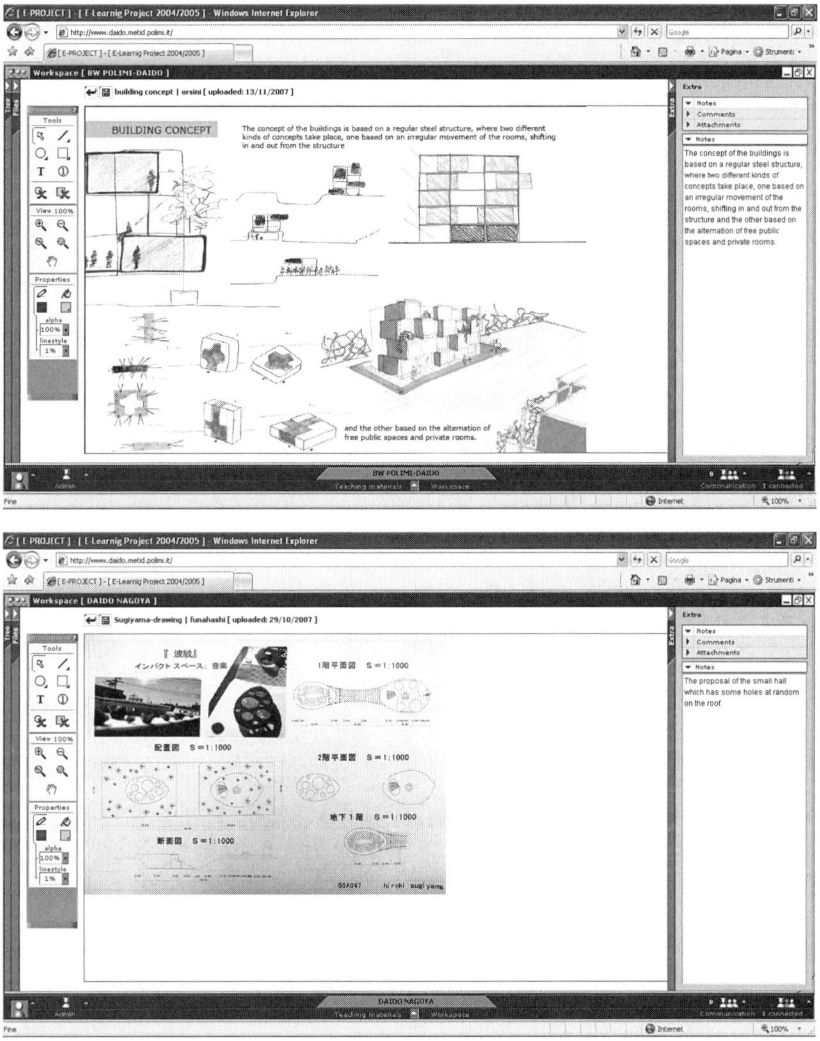

Figure 2.1.8 The PoliDaido 'virtual desk': Italian and Japanese workspaces
Source: Politecnico di Milano.

Conclusions

The PoliDaido project was developed with the aim of providing an e-learning experience focused on users' active participation and motivation. The main research work was devoted to the creation of a virtual environment in which students and teachers, belonging to different countries and with different cultures, could meet and interact, sharing information and ideas, discussing and cooperating with the aim of developing new ideas and innovative solutions. Through on line collaborative environments students and tutors can share an atmosphere similar to the one they are accustomed to in face-to-face design laboratories. Also, thanks to the digital environment, the exchange students of the Erasmus programme that were studying abroad for some months, could stay remotely involved in the workshop activities. The sixty-one students of Politecnico di Milano and the five students of Daido Institute of Technology of Nagoya were active participants in the workshop and interacted intensively via synchronous chat tools despite the local time difference between the two countries. This suggested that the lack of face-to-face interaction may be one of the central factors of success in virtual teams, given that, in a global virtual team context, cues about social influence are missing and participants have a chance to be judged as a function of their performance rather than on more stereotypical cues. The whole experience showed us how digital services are very interesting spaces to explore dynamic forms of support to human interactions: the workshop experience will be repeated and new opportunities of exchanges are now open for the development of further international educational initiatives.

References

Marshall, P. 2001. *Multicultural education and technology: perfect pair or odd couple.* Available at http://www.ericdigests.org/2002-3/odd.htm, accessed 28 January 2010.

BAS RAIJMAKERS

CASE STUDY 03 DESIGNING EMPATHIC CONVERSATIONS ABOUT FUTURE USER EXPERIENCES

This case study describes how empathic conversations with citizens can inspire and inform the regeneration of a large site including an old tin mine in Cornwall.

The Heartlands case study in this section is a design research project that explores possible future experiences of the people that will visit and work at a large regenerated cultural and social site around an old tin mine in Cornwall, UK. This is an area near the centre of Pool village, that encompasses the world's first tin mine and a large open space. Cornwall Council has received funding from the Big Lottery Fund to create a large park with a museum, a community centre, artists' studios, playgrounds and spaces for small-scale retail. As one of the core aims of the project is to include the wider community in the design development phase, ensuring that Heartlands will become a positive and enjoyable experience for all visitors, a series of community involvement activities was initiated. The design research company STBY (Standby) and the Helen Hamlyn Center at the Royal College of Art were asked to advise on how to optimally connect these activities to the design process. Focusing on people's current experiences with similar services in Cornwall proved to be solid ground for speculating about their future experiences in a newly built environment. In 'empathic conversations' (Raijmakers 2007) between the design team and future users these experiences were explored and discussed. For instance, design documentaries were used to explore current experiences of specific groups such as artists, and co-creative workshops were used to inform and inspire the architectural teams of Heartlands. Finding ways of involving people in every stage of the design process is a valued approach in service design. At Heartlands, focusing on people's experiences through empathic conversations helped to move from thinking about buildings to thinking about services.

Heartlands in Cornwall, UK

Heartlands is built on a community-led vision to transform Cornwall's most derelict urban area and the oldest UK tin mine into an inspirational social and cultural landscape.

Characteristics of the design project are the aims of local citizens to realise a vital and dynamic set of environments and services for local and regional communities. The ultimate success of Heartlands depends on its popularity and its use, so it really must offer what local people as well as tourists appreciate, need and dream of.

THE TEAM AND THE PROGRAMME

The team responsible for setting up the empathic conversations included design researchers with backgrounds in social research, user-centred design and architecture. They worked closely with the client and management team of the local council. STBY in collaboration with Yanki Lee of the Helen Hamlyn Centre at the Royal College of Art in London, developed three different types of activities for the multidisciplinary team at Heartlands:

1. Social research to create insights and understanding
2. Co-creation workshops to generate and explore ideas
3. User forums to discuss concepts and prototypes.

In total twelve different activities were organised over the course of a year, with different participants at different times during the design process. Two of the activities are discussed in detail below. All twelve were focused on the future uses and experiences of services, buildings and environments of Heartlands and deliberately avoided more formal aspects of the designs. Even though we organised co-creative workshops, we did not design buildings or parks with local citizens. Instead, we explored, designed and evaluated possible uses and experiences of these places with them and the design teams, through empathic conversations. The design of physical artefacts was left to the experts: the design teams. Local citizens are experts in a different area: the use of their current environment and how they experience all types of local services. We explored these with them, to inform and inspire the design teams.

PARTICIPANTS

Creating a connection between designers and the people they design for is a key aspect of service design. For Heartlands we used the concept of empathic conversations to describe that connection. Empathic conversations build on disciplines older than service design, such as user-centred design and inclusive design, which position the user at the centre of the design process. The UK Department of Trade and Industry (DTI 2005) defines inclusive design as a process whereby designers ensure that their products and services address the needs of the widest possible audience. In large projects such as Heartlands, this becomes rather complex because so many different people are potential future users of what is designed. In addition, the built environment usually lasts generations. This makes 'the widest possible audience' a very large and diverse group.

Residents from local communities, representatives from organisations that may offer social and creative services, people who will work at Heartlands, visitors from all over the UK and abroad, school children, older people and people with disabilities are all expected to be future users. Obviously, one cannot set up small-scale in-depth conversations (a key aspect of empathic conversations as we will see), with all these stakeholders at the same time. In every one of our activities, we deliberately brought together a selected mix of perspectives. Designers and the client team at the local council were active participants in these conversations too.

We also collaborated with local artists during several steps in the project. They were involved in the social research and the co-creative workshops, as participants and contributors to workshop programmes and materials. Being locals, they were able to understand the considerations of fellow participants more easily than the London-based research team: being creative, they were also able to translate these considerations into visual and engaging materials that could do part of the talking in the empathic conversations. In the (architectural) design context we were working in, making the conversations more visual and experiential meant making them richer.

ACTIVITIES AND METHODS

Some activities were triggered by specific stages in the design process. Sometimes designers requested input on the future use, dreams and concerns of particular groups (such as the Cornish diaspora, or local youth) or explorations of particular parts of the designs (the marketplace, community centre, or artists' studios for instance). Sometimes topics for the empathic conversations also emerged from the research we did at the initial stages of our involvement. The methods we used are all considered to be part of the design research toolkit that is also used in service design: in-depth interviews, observations, video ethnography, cultural probe studies, co-creation workshops and user forums. All the activities we organised took place in the village of Pool and most at the actual site which was still derelict at that stage. Below are two examples using design documentaries (a specific way of doing video ethnography), and co-creation.

THE COMMUNITY CENTRE

Our main goal at the early stages of our involvement was to collect stories and create insights through these stories. We were keen to preserve the richness of individual stories when we created the insights and developed ways to communicate these. We found several highly visual ways of doing this, using different media from slideshows and video-blogs to performances and artistic objects.

When we started to look at the community centre for Heartlands, we found that many different local organisations will be using this space, for a large number of activities. All of them already organised activities in different places near Pool, offering a broad mix of services, from child care to social clubs, music to photography. From conversations with these service providers gradually themes emerged. We involved visual artist Jeremiah Krage of Wild Works in these conversations and commissioned him to create four different objects in relation to the themes that emerged from the conversations. For instance, for the theme 'Separate' Krage made a series of wooden boxes that can be opened and let you experience different reasons why some groups want to separate themselves from others in the community centre (see Figure 2.1.9). The objects were used as conversation pieces in the co-creation workshop on the community centre, in order to generate scenarios for the future use of the community centre. We brought future users and future service providers of the community centre together with the architects. We devised tasks in small groups, that each had a set of conversation pieces from the artist to 'kick-off' the empathic conversation and sometimes also guide, structure, or document it. The groups were deliberately kept small and mixed, to create in-depth conversations.

Figure 2.1.9 Conversation pieces by Jeremiah Krage based on interviews with future users
Source: STBY.

THE ARTIST STUDIOS

In some of the empathic conversations, we went a step further and generated ideas about future services and experiences, with future users (both individuals and organisations) and design teams. We applied typical workshop dynamics such as a combination of plenary meetings and break-out groups. The materials we used (Krage's objects for instance) and the situations we created were rather different however. A good example of this is the artists' co-creative workshop we organised.

The workshop itself had been preceded by individual visits to the studios and workshops of five artists in Cornwall, working in different disciplines. These visits were each empathic conversations in their own right, and videotaped by the researcher. They took the form of a guided tour of the space in which stories about how they see and experience their working spaces were told through objects or situations that were shown. These stories were made available to the design team via a video blog[4] that allowed both access to very practical information about floors or lighting, and also more narrative access on pages that connected video clips into stories about how the spaces provided 'services' to their users. The narratives are an example of the design documentaries method, which moves beyond using video clips as evidence to support insights towards using video to tell stories and relate empathic conversations.

For the co-creative workshop, we moved with the architects into the actual site, then still a brownfield site, the artists' spaces they had designed in the Heartlands master plan. Four artists were invited to bring some of their materials, tools and work to take possession of an imagined studio for an afternoon. We asked them to take ownership of these spaces before they were actually built. They had no problems in speculating about their own work practices, because they obviously knew them very well. The starting point of the workshop was that each artist, in a different location at Heartlands, teamed up with an architect, bringing drawings and sketches of the space, and set up his or her own studio (see Figure 2.1.10).

Then we invited four different groups of future visitors of Heartlands, for instance students, art lovers and people with disabilities, to visit the makeshift studios and have conversations with the artists about their work, and how they felt about working at Heartlands. This gave us 16 stories, or scenarios, of how artists and visitors would like to meet and communicate, or not, with each other, presenting therefore the interaction from a service perspective.

Figure 2.1.10 Furniture maker Tristan Harris (far left) talks to guests in his imagined studio at the Heartlands brownfield site

Source: STBY.

4 Accessible at http://bas.blogs.com/artatheartlands/, accessed 8 June 2009.

Characteristics of Empathic Conversations

Perhaps the most important result of the activities we organised were the new relationships that we built between the design teams and a wide range of future users of their designs. The activities were explicitly aimed at setting up empathic conversations between the design teams and future users, about future experiences of specific aspects of Heartlands. As such they connect well to co-creation (Aarts and Marzano 2003), where design teams and participants co-create future experiences, outlining forms of interaction but not actual buildings or parks. We call these conversations empathic because the participants in the discussion all try to step into the shoes of the future users and create insights into future experiences from that perspective. Setting up such a conversation starts with identifying the stakeholders that need to take part in it, and learning about their current and past relationships. Then a context and starting points for the conversation need to be designed. Contexts can for instance be a workshop, or a visit. Starting points can be simply a series of questions, or specially made artistic objects, or a performance. Results of the conversations need to be documented in detail in preferably visual and narrative reports, for instance a slide show of the artistic objects, a DVD of a performance, or a (video) blog. The easiness of sharing this documentation with designers and client teams who are the primary audience for them is the premise for the further co-design activity aiming to create insights for future service concepts. Beside this, at Heartlands some designers had already acquired their most important insights and understanding themselves during the workshops. Our documentation was mostly aimed at helping them to share these insights with other people in their design or client team, and at creating shared, attractive references.

Reflection

The activities we organised for Heartlands were aimed at outlining new roles for users in a future built environment. We wanted to move beyond public consultation and design workshops. Instead, we aimed for setting up empathic conversations between design teams, future users and the local council. The goal of the Heartlands regeneration project is to contribute to the sustainable innovation of Cornish society. We believe that sustainable social innovation can be supported by design research through focusing on people's experiences and being involved in them. It is however not a result we can design by ourselves. As John Thackara says to designers:

> *We need to foster new relationships outside our usual stomping grounds. We have to learn new ways to collaborate and do projects. We have to enhance the ability of all citizens to engage in a meaningful dialogue about their environment and context and foster new relationships between the people who make things and the people who use them. (Thackara 2005: 8)*

The activities we organised can be understood as explorations of what these 'meaningful dialogues' that Thackara mentions could be. Obviously they can be a simple, good conversation over a nice cup of tea, but they can also be much more and very different. People have many more means than words alone to express themselves. In particular for designers, but also for many citizens, different ways of visualising these conversations can be very successful as we have experienced with, for instance, the objects of the artist Jeremiah Krage and the video-blog created by Bas Raijmakers. Leadbeater (2008: 55) recognises this opportunity too as he writes 'Innovation does not come down a pipeline, but from the interaction of all players together. The context for that to happen needs to be designed appropriately.' Or, perhaps more philosophically: 'Design does not take place in a situation – it is the situation' (Thackara 2005: 99). The empathic conversations we set up for Heartlands were part of the design process. They were designed to make a start with fostering a socially sustainable Heartlands that develops over time rather than aiming for a fixed end result. This role for design is relatively new but has started to surface more and more recently, in particular in service design. For the further development of this new role of design, service design can take inspiration and learn from a focus on people's experiences of designed products, environments and services and empathic conversations as a way to explore and communicate these experiences in a multidisciplinary design team.

References

Aarts, E. and Marzano, S. 2003. *The New Everyday*. Rotterdam: 010 Uitgeverij.

DTI 2005. *Department of Trade and Industry Survey on Inclusive Design*. London: DTI.

Leadbeater, C. 2008. *We Think: The Power of Mass Creativity*. London: Profile Books. Available at http://www.wethinkthebook.net/home.aspx, accessed 28 January 2010.

Raijmakers, B. 2007. Design documentaries. Ph.D. thesis, Royal College of Art, London. Available at www.designdocumentaries.com, accessed 28 January 2010.

Thackara, J. 2005. *In The Bubble; Designing in a Complex World*. Cambridge, MA: MIT Press.

SHELLEY EVENSON

CASE STUDY 04 DRIVING SERVICE DESIGN BY DIRECTED STORYTELLING

This case study focuses on the use of empathic tools, such as storytelling, to give shape to a more human-centred healthcare service environment in the USA. The relevance of designing health information around patient's values, preferences and expectations is emphasised: meaningful health information exchange can nurture more 'empathic' relationships between patients and health staff.

Directed storytelling draws on the approach used in narrative inquiry to help designers explore services so they can begin to understand them without having to do long-term ethnographic research. Services are activities or events that form a service product through interaction between the customer, any mediating technology and representatives of the service organisation. In designing for service we need to understand people's expectations when they co-produce their service experiences. Directed storytelling is a method that can quickly reveal consistent patterns in people's experiences. Knowledge of these patterns can help designers produce ideas for services that have the best potential for resonating with their intended audiences. This case study will describe the method and explore how directed storytelling has contributed to the design of healthcare-related services.

The Story

On 19 December 2002 a woman took her husband to the local hospital so that he could have a colonoscopy. The couple left the hospital with the shocking diagnosis of colorectal cancer.

Two efficient sentences and you understand what happened that day. Contrast those two sentences with the following description:

> *One morning in December 2002 a woman sat in a hospital waiting room not unlike most waiting rooms in America that people encounter today. The overall size wasn't very large – maybe 10 feet by 14 feet wide, with a windowed reception desk. There were lots of chairs for people to sit in, but there was no place for the woman to hang her coat. She had planned on*

using her laptop to pass the time, but it was a bit uncomfortable to have the computer and papers in her lap and the chair next to her holding her coat. The TV was on with Katie Curic of the Today *show smiling and joking with Matt Lauer. As she continued to work she noticed many pairs of people arriving, checking in with the front desk, and as they did the pair would split, with one person going off through a door to have a colonoscopy, just as her husband had done after they had arrived. The other half of the pair sat down in the chairs around her. More time passed and she was engrossed in her tasks, but in the periphery she saw people coming and going. As the TV show neared its end she saw couples that arrived at reception after she and her husband had arrived already leaving. She didn't think much of it at first, but as more pairs left, she began to wonder why her husband was taking so long. She thought of going to the desk to check, but she didn't want to have to pack up her stuff to approach the desk and tap on the window, so she went back to looking at her laptop. Soon a man in a white coat approached her, introduced himself and asked her to come with him. As she rushed to pack up her things, she felt the eyes of everyone in the room on her. The 'doctor' approaching her broke the pattern of activity that was the routine in the room that morning. She was suddenly nervous and felt flustered grabbing her computer, handbag and coat. She followed him to a room that was dark and cold. The hospital's environmental system was efficiently controlling energy use so the lights and temperature settings were not adjusted until she entered. She remembered the table was rather large and she had lean across it to hear what the man was saying. He said, 'Your husband has cancer.' She said, 'No, that's not possible. We were told this was just a formality to check to make sure nothing was wrong.' He said, 'You need to go in there with me and tell him he has cancer.' She was stunned.*

This is a simple healthcare experience. It can be told in a single sentence or as a story.

Services are activities or events that form a service product through interaction between the customer, any mediating technology, and representatives of the service organisation (Fitzsimmons and Fitzsimmons 2004, Bitner and Zeithaml 1999). The husband was the recipient of the colonoscopy service, but the wife was also a participant in the service experience. In service, people interact with producers via touchpoints that foster product or service experiences. These touchpoint experiences form a larger arc or path: the journey. Most colonoscopy service experiences have different outcomes, but each one has the potential to unfold in the way this experience did. In the end, the colonoscopy journey touched off a larger journey of treating the man's cancer.

The series of experiences aggregate to form an impression of the product or service in its context – before, during and after the central service experience – developing an idea of what it does, what it means, its worth, and what the person thinks of the brand of the organisation providing the service.

Ideally, the experiences build a strong relationship between customer and producer. Csíkszentmihályi (1990) introduced the concept of 'flow' to explain how people can be completely involved in an activity for its own sake – the ultimate in seamlessness. How Michael Jordan played basketball is an excellent example of someone in the flow. In peak flow experiences, people are engaged in discovery, transported to a new reality.

In most experiences we cannot expect flow, where people 'become so involved that nothing else matters', but what is more involving to the woman than her husband's medical crisis? Nothing could change the results of his procedure, but perhaps if the facets of experience in the cycle had been addressed more carefully her experience could have been different – and better?

THE CONTEXT

Healthcare services in the United States are undergoing radical changes. Recent McKinsey research with hospital patients found that '75 per cent would consider switching hospitals' if they could be better informed (Grote, Newman and Sutaria 2007). Clearly information matters to people. The SPARC Innovation Program at the Mayo Clinic has identified three era shifts in healthcare. The first is pursuing medical knowledge; the second is improving quality through process innovation and reducing costs, errors and time, while the third is an era where the goal is to develop human knowledge to inform values, preference and expectation. The Mayo group sees this shift as a movement to real conversations delivering translated information (Breslin 2007). If this description is accurate then service design in this setting means that the job of the service designer is to design the resources for setting expectations and facilitating conversations with a delivery organisation throughout a customer journey.

Clearly we need to better understand what happens when the service model changes in this way – from passive recipient of medical care, to active participant in the service delivery experience – in this context where the stakes are so high. In designing for service we need to understand people's expectations when they co-produce their service experiences.

Pittsburgh Pennsylvania has emerged as a health research and healthcare centre. UPMC (University of Pittsburgh Medical Center) is a very highly rated and well-respected healthcare system in the United States. Yet in Pittsburgh (as in most places) the healthcare experiences (the healthcare as a service) – are not always consciously designed.

In the fall of 2006, students from Carnegie Mellon University began to work with UPMC's Center for Quality Improvement and Innovation (CQII). We worked on projects in the centre ranging from reducing no-show rates at a local lower-income clinic to optimising the family and patient experience at a neurosurgery clinic, from emergency rooms to a cardiac catheterisation lab. Student teams range in size from two to six people and they came from many different disciplines including computer science, business and design. In each project, the students were paired with a specialist from the CQII. The pairings were effective because the CQII staff brought medical knowledge and the students brought human-centered design methods and fresh eyes to the healthcare environment.

In designing for service students begin by immersing themselves in the context. Often this effort starts with the team taking photographs of how they see the environment. This is because they have learned that great services communicate what affordances they provide before you encounter them (and then ultimately deliver on the promise) (Norman 2009). In many cases the images are very revealing of a point of view the staff or management rarely sees – the view from the patient or family member's eyes.

Empathetic Connections

Another method we employ is called 'directed storytelling'. In designing for service (or any other design context) it is critical to develop empathy with the people one is designing for. It is critical to understand stakeholder needs and the patterns in people's everyday experience. Dev Patnaik suggests that when companies create an empathetic connection to the people they serve, they are focused on what really matters and as a result can be more nimble in servicing them (Patnaik 2009, Schmidt 1999).

Anthropologists and social scientists have long understood this need. The problem is that most ethnographies – the description of a particular culture or group usually produced by an anthropologist – can take one or more years to produce. In design, we rarely have much time. Designers are usually asked to provide ideas for solutions in weeks or months. Additionally in design, we are usually looking at a very particular aspect of an experience to impact not every aspect of every experience. The directed storytelling method was developed as response to a designer's need to find ways to get to the heart of the experience very quickly.

The method draws on the approach used in narrative inquiry to help designers conduct research on an experience so they experience it without having to do long-term ethnographic research – or in this case intrude on an often very personal situation (Evenson 2006). It is a method that can quickly reveal consistent patterns in people's experiences. Knowledge of these patterns can help the design team produce ideas for service design resources that have the best potential for resonating with their intended audiences and provide fodder for good conversations. Directed storytelling is useful for conducting research when the design team really has no other viable option for getting information, or when a team seeks a starting point for developing a more comprehensive a research plan.

There are usually three people engaged in a storytelling session. First, you need a person that had an experience that is central to the experience (for example, a patient, family, or staff member from the cardiac catheterisation lab). They act as the storyteller. Second, you need a person to lead the storyteller in their story (a student leader) and finally you need a third person to act as the documenter in the session (a student documenter). If more people are available, they can also act as documenters. The more stories you document (through a series of storytelling sessions), the richer the data is for interpretation and pattern analysis. It is also helpful to develop a rough guide for the session that consists of an opening line such as 'Tell us about your day in the lab, starting when you woke up this morning'. The guide should address the journalistic who, what, when, where and how framework.

As the story unfolds, the documenters write ideas on Post-it notes. Ideas are elements of the story that seem to be important either through the emphasis that the storyteller has given, or through their own interpretation of the information from the storyteller. Storytellers are encouraged to reference props in the space if they are related to the experience and if they have them at hand.

After all the sessions the data is clustered into an affinity diagram or map (Beyer and Holtzblatt 1998). At first, the team lays out all the important ideas generated from the documenters on a wall. Next, the team works together to group the ideas into clusters or patterns and name each cluster. Through the process of negotiating and naming the clusters the team defines the most common themes related to the particular experience. Often a model or framework that reflects and documents the categories or themes, as well as the relationships between and among themes, is created. The framework can become a kind of shorthand for the knowledge of what people commonly experience in the situation. The themes and the model drive the design team's choices about what to do and what to make.

In addition to getting to what is most important about the experience quickly, the directed storytelling effort serves another related purpose. When a service design team is called in, they may or may not have any personal knowledge of the service experience that they are attempting to address. They are 'outside' the situation. Directed storytelling quickly brings them into the centre of what people are doing, saying and thinking – immersing them in the service experience, as if they were the ones engaging in the service. By creating an affinity diagram that looks at the component parts from the story, the designers gain a first-hand understanding of the elements in the service design language – the resources that people are interacting with to 'design' or produce the experience for themselves. Categorising or clustering the elements allows them to 'abstract up' as a way of getting to the service essence. This can be as simple as finding that a registration process includes 'approach–interact–confirm/update expectation'. They can then use the framework to think of other situations that might have the same process, but provide better outcomes to inform the design.

The Generative Phase

After these more exploratory methods, the students move on to utilising more generative methods, which actually engage the patients, family and staff in participatory activities such as describing their experiences in journals, or using images to map their feelings. The findings from these methods are compared with the frameworks or 'meanings' the team made from storytelling to validate that it is really what is meaningful to the patients, family and staff in order to begin to design the most meaningful resources for people to use in their future experiences.

Returning to the colonoscopy story, clear themes can easily be drawn from an analysis of the story. For example, though the facility may have been designed to support conducting the colonoscopy procedure, little thought was given to the design of the facility to support waiting for a patient having a colonoscopy procedure. Greeters were behind glass putting a physical wall between producer and user, creating a barrier to information seeking and support. Chairs in the waiting area offered a place to sit for two to three hours, but there was little support for anything else. There were no tables for people to sit and work, and no place to even hang coats in the middle of winter. There were no updates on patient status and the design of the space made any disruption of the pattern of patient/support person flow obvious to the entire population of the waiting room. When the difficult conversation had to happen, the room was cold, dark and at an inappropriate scale for a one on one conversation.

Example resulting themes from the story:

- reduce physical or social barriers between patients, caregivers and information sources;
- embrace wait time and provide resources for work, relaxation and entertainment;
- provide personal spaces for safe storage of coats, bags and other valuables;

- provide continuous updates on patient status whenever possible;
- design flexible space configurations that can be reconfigured for privacy;
- provide warm, intimate, and comforting spaces for difficult conversations among staff, patients and caregivers.

One conversation creates empathy for colonoscopy stakeholders and a place to start for more investigation or design research. With the big picture or service ecology in mind, and an understanding at the resource level of what's important to people, service designers can work with architects, interior designers and communication designers to provide an integrated set of resources for the service experience. For orthopaedic surgery the need for a preview of the journey that provided better information about what the patient and family might expect during the process was identified. Imagine how much better for the patient, friends and family and staff if the space and communication materials did double duty – supporting understanding the potential healthcare journey (like a museum stages a story for visitors) – and, at the same time, delivers the best medicine has offer for orthopaedic care.

In the course of our work, student team conversations have revealed many similar needs. Through directed storytelling, embracing wait time was identified as a clear challenge for patients and caregivers waiting in a neurosurgery clinic. For friends and family waiting for cardiac catheterisation patients continuous updates on patient status and flexible waiting room configurations were patterns of need that were quickly revealed through directed storytelling. Different experiences and different healthcare facilities, yet very similar needs remain unmet.

Conclusion

Our work in several different healthcare contexts confirms that clear opportunities for innovation lie in providing resources for people to become more active participants in their healthcare service experiences – with more information for the service conversation (Breslin 2009). Directed storytelling is one method for quickly getting to the heart of the service experience. The benefits of the method include quickly identifying patterns in service experiences that can be addressed or further researched and, at the same, time it provides designers with the opportunity to become immediately empathic with the audiences they are designing for.

References

Beyer, H. and Holtzblatt, K. 1998. *Contextual Design: Defining Customer-centered Systems*. San Diego, CA: Academic Press.

Bitner, M. and Zeithaml, V. 1999. *Service Marketing*. New York: McGraw Hill.

Breslin, M. 2007. 'Conversations' Designing for Social Change. Paper to the Conference Transform: A Collaborative Symposium on Innovation in Health Care Experience and Delivery, Mayo Clinic Center for Innovation, Rochester, Minn. 13–15 September.

Csíkszentmihályi, M. 1990. *Flow: The Psychology of Optimal Experience.* New York: Harper and Row.
Evenson, S. 2006. Directed storytelling: drawing patterns from memories to inform design. In *Design Studies: Theory and Research in Graphic Design*, edited by A. Bennett. New York: Princeton Architectural Press, 231–40.
Fitzsimmons, J.A. and Fitzsimmons M.J. 2004. *Service Management: Operations, Strategy and Information Technology*. London: McGraw-Hill.
Grote, K., Newman, J. and Sutaria, S. 2007. A better hospital experience. *McKinsey Quarterly*, 30 November, Available at http://sloanreview.mit.edu/the-magazine/articles/2009/summer/50407/designing-waits-that-work, accessed 23 December 2010.
Norman, D. 2009. Designing waits that work. *MIT Sloan Management Review.*
Patnaik, D. 2009. *Wired to Care: How Companies Prosper When They Create Widespread Empathy*. Upper Saddle River, NJ: FT Press.
Schmidt, B. 1999. *Experiential Marketing: How to Get Customers to Sense, Feel, Think, Act, and Relate to Your Company and Brands*. New York: The Free Press.

MARK VANDERBEEKEN

CASE STUDY 05 EXPLORING MOBILE NEEDS AND BEHAVIOURS IN EMERGING MARKETS

This case study describes how, by understanding the use of mobile phones in emerging markets and in unsafe environments, Experientia ended up designing functionalities for mobile phone services.

The massive impact of mobile phones and services on the livelihoods of more than one billion people in emerging markets has been extensively covered in the media (Garreau 2008, Clavin 2008, International Telecommunication Union 2009, McGreal 2009, Rudebeck 2009).

Much of the most recent mobile innovation within emerging markets has taken place on the service side – for example mobile activism (FrontlineSMS,[5] Global Voices,[6] Ushahidi[7]), mobile banking (m-Pesa[8]), mobile health (Masiluleke[9]), mobile chat (MXit[10]), and mobile information platforms (Nokia's LifeTools[11]) – and we can now safely state that in terms of key services (m-health, m-banking, m-development), many emerging markets are now more advanced than the developed world. This transformation has not come about accidentally, but illustrates the power of design research, participatory design and service design on a global scale. Therefore, understanding what services matter to people and how they should be designed are the keys to effective innovation in emerging markets.

Design Research Methods

Over the last five to eight years, many major technology and communication companies, including France Telecom, Google, HP, Intel, Microsoft, Nokia, Philips, Samsung and Vodafone, have developed sophisticated qualitative design research

5 www.frontlinesms.com, accessed 28 January 2010.
6 http://globalvoicesonline.org, accessed 28 January 2010.
7 www.ushahidi.com, accessed 28 January 2010.
8 www.safaricom.co.ke/index.php?id=745, accessed 28 January 2010.
9 www.poptech.org/project_m, accessed 28 January 2010.
10 www.mxit.com, accessed 28 January 2010.
11 http://europe.nokia.com/A41393072, accessed 28 January 2010.

tools to analyse the needs of people in emerging markets and their contexts of living and working – insights which are then developed, often in co-creation with the people involved, into new culturally relevant products, applications and services.

Broadly speaking there are five methods that these companies use to create more relevant products and services for emerging markets: long-term observation and ethnographic research, local design centres, participatory field design, grassroots innovation and remote research via Web or user panels.

In this chapter we will briefly introduce all five methods, describe some of the research done by my own company Experientia in this field, and outline possible future implications for service design.

ETHNOGRAPHIC RESEARCH

The most common methodology is on-the-ground observation, honed into a fine craft by Nokia's former design ethnographer Jan Chipchase[12] and his team, who have done research in Afghanistan, Brazil, China, Egypt, Ghana, India, Iran, Mongolia, Nepal, Pakistan, South Africa, Tajikistan, Thailand, Turkey, Uganda, Uzbekistan and Vietnam.

Chipchase is not only a daring traveller and a keen observer of the role of mobile phones globally (Chipchase 2008), but is also a great analyst and storyteller, as is obvious from his blog and often demonstrated by his mesmerising presentations at international conferences.

Nokia has been at the forefront of the development of many new culturally relevant products – for example the torchlight phone – and mobile software – for example Nokia Life Tools (a range of innovative agricultural information and education services designed especially for rural and small town communities in emerging markets) (Banks 2008b, 2008c). Not surprisingly, the many innovations that Nokia launched based on its design research have had a dramatic impact on the company's market share (an estimated 70 per cent of mobile phones used in Africa are made by Nokia) and profits (emerging markets were the main reason for Nokia's 25 per cent increase in profit during the first quarter of 2008[13]) (Meyer 2009, Dev Sood 2006).

This long-term commitment to on-the-ground observation is an approach also taken by technology giant Intel. Intel's focus is on understanding deeper issues that can affect the future uptake of technology, and on better understanding the various cultural and social paradigms in order to avoid forcing a Western concept of technology on societies and cultures that have different viewpoints (Chavan et al. 2009).

Genevieve Bell[14] and other Intel anthropologists are keenly interested in researching concepts such as the use of technology to support religious practices, cultural differences in storing and archiving, the concept of the home, and what sharing might mean in the social and cultural context of Asia. This has led to many of Intel's innovations, including the Classmate PC and the Community PC.

LOCAL DESIGN CENTRES

Contextually relevant design is often better practised by local designers from within the countries themselves. In 2005, Intel set up four new offices in Bangalore, Cairo, São Paulo and Shanghai that are staffed with anthropologists and engineers to help design computers with features for emerging markets (Krazit 2005). This led to the company's release of software in China and Brazil for instance, which makes it easier to manage PCs in Internet cafes.

12 www.janchipchase.com, accessed 28 January 2010.

13 www.nokia.com/A4136001?newsid=1210364, accessed 28 January 2010.

14 www.intel.com/pressroom/kits/bios/gbell.htm, accessed 28 January 2010.

HP's design research on emerging economies[15] is done from Bangalore, India, where they tackle issues that impact the effective spread of information technology, such as the access divide, the communications divide, the need for contextual design, the language divide and the lack of sustainable business ecologies. Technologies developed by HP based on this research simplified Web access for the next billion customers and for pen-based interfaces.

Microsoft also runs all their activities for emerging markets from India. The research in the 'Technology for Emerging Markets'[16] group consists of both technical and social science research. They do work in the areas of ethnography, sociology, political science and economics (Vance 2008). All of this helps form an understanding of the social context of technology, together with technical research in hardware and software to devise solutions for emerging and under-served markets, both in rural and urban environments. The theme of mobile services in emerging markets is the focus of a software development centre that a software development centre that Google opened in Nairobi. According to a *New York Times* article (Zachary 2008) 'enhancements to basic phones can be experimented with cheaply in Nairobi, and because designers are weaned on narrow bandwidth, they are comfortable writing compact programs suited to puny devices'.

Typically these design centres employ local resources and collaborate with local design institutes and universities, thereby assuring a mutual knowledge exchange, beneficial for both parties. For instance the Nokia design studio in Bangalore, which does work in industrial design, user interfaces and ethnographic research, is in fact housed within the Srishti School of Art, Design and Technology.[17] This enables students from the institute, Nokia's designers and external designers to work together, and achieve 'co-creation', or collaborative design with users of mobile phones.

PARTICIPATORY FIELD DESIGN

In fact, co-creative approaches are becoming increasingly popular. To create locally relevant products and services, designers from the global headquarters or from one of the local design centres work directly with people in their own communities to build a shared understanding of their needs and context of living.

In 2005, Philips Electronics had the idea of creating a simple voice-email handset and cheap audio services for urban shanty towns and isolated rural areas in the developing world, which would overcome problems of illiteracy or minority languages (Faludi 2005). Field research in the favela of Recife, Brazil led them to conclude that real-time connectivity was not the biggest issue; the solution was essentially a modified mp3 player that could be occasionally connected to the Web from a telecentre. Allowing people to send and receive voice and text messages, this device was good enough (and much cheaper than mobile phones at that time).

The Nokia Open Studios (Jung and Chipchase 2008) are an exploratory design research method for engaging communities in shanty towns. According to Nokia's Jan Chipchase,[18] 'the most valuable output of the Open Studio lies in providing an alternative way for people to articulate their wants and needs – within the context of their community'.

15 www.hpl.hp.com/india, accessed 28 January 2010.

16 http://research.microsoft.com/en-us/groups/tem/default.aspx, accessed 28 January 2010.

17 http://srishti.ac.in, accessed 28 January 2010.

18 www.janchipchase.com/blog/archives/2008/10/nokia_open_stud_2.html, accessed 28 January 2010.

GRASS ROOTS INNOVATION

People in emerging countries are often not just consumers but, by necessity, invariably also producers, with every household acting as a small entrepreneur. The lack of established service ecosystems in these markets – banks, transportation, broadband internet, public services, etc. – makes people even more likely to come up with ad hoc solutions, in this way leapfrogging more developed countries, especially in creative mobile phone use. Indeed, some of the more exciting and innovative technology-based services actually stem from bottom-up innovation within emerging markets and ingenious indigenous use of technology. *Business Week* calls this 'trickle-up innovation'.

Examples are plentiful: micro-credit solutions from the Bangladeshi Grameen Foundation; mobile banking systems derived from the m-Pesa service, originally developed in Kenya (Banks 2008a); enhanced mobile phone speakers that allow for easy music sharing, originally observed by Nokia in Ghana and Morocco; or the crowd-sourced news reporting on Ushahidi, a website that was developed to map reports of violence in Kenya after the post-election fallout at the beginning of 2008. MobileActive08,[19] an important Johannesburg conference was entirely devoted to showcasing African bottom-up innovation in mobile phone use.

Many of these service innovations are focused on development, crisis management, media distribution, education and healthcare, with international organisations and private foundations stimulating the grassroots innovation. Some major companies have now begun working with the non-profit sector to help support these initiatives with more adequate technologies.

REMOTE RESEARCH

Remote research allows companies with smaller budgets and fast development cycles to get quick input from users in emerging markets without the investments that ethnographic research and local design centres require.

A classic example of remote research is the beta lab (e.g. Nokia Beta Lab, Vodafone Betavine,[20] and Vodafone Betavine Social Exchange[21]) where developers and users can test software but also share their own software, or rate that made by others.

Finally there is remote ethnography, observing people from afar using the mobile phone itself as the tool. Although this method doesn't allow for the contextual sensitivity of on-the-ground observation, it allows a small team of researchers to interview people in emerging markets by phone, or provide them with mobile devices, which they use to complete simple tasks by SMS or MMS.

Cheaper than on-the-ground observation, this technique – which has been used by Vodafone, in a project done in collaboration with our company Experientia – does require the involvement of local recruiters and junior ethnographers to identify and support the people in completing their tasks, or to provide translations.

What Drives People in Emerging Markets?

So what have these companies learned from all this research? This question is too complex to answer in this case study, just as emerging markets are simply too varied and too vast to be summarised quickly with a few conclusions. However, we at

19 www.mobileactive08.org, accessed 28 January 2010.

20 www.betavine.net, accessed 28 January 2010.

21 http://crowdtalk.wordpress.com/bsx/, accessed 28 January 2010.

Experientia have been involved in various design research and experience prototyping projects in India, Senegal, South Africa and Egypt.

A mobile ethnographic research study that Experientia conducted for Samsung in South Africa and Senegal involved extensive ethnographic observations by teams of local researchers (Figure 2.1.11). Our Turin, Italy-based analysts and design researchers subsequently interpreted the contextual observations and structured them all in a number of high-level insights that Samsung could act upon.

Uncertainty and some chaos are a given in the informal economy that supports the majority at the bottom of the economic pyramid (BoP) (Bhan and Tait 2008, Bhan 2009; Corbett 2008, de Silva, Zainudeen and Ratnadiwakara 2008, Heeks 2009). Our contextual observations and insights led us to the definition of six key user requirements: ease of use, services for resource sharing, tools for budget management, low power usage, durability (as natural conditions are much harsher), and security.

Figure 2.1.11 Four photos from field research in Africa (Senegal and South Africa)
Source: Experientia.

The Experientia design team then summarised these requirements – simplicity, survival and commitment – and articulated them in a number of design concept prototypes.

Our research highlighted that the need for security was especially high in South Africa. Due to a variety of social and economic factors, including high unemployment, endemic poverty and increasing disparity between incomes and cost of living, crime is widespread, and the mobile phone has become a popular item for theft (Donner and Gitau 2009). With a high value to size ratio, it is easily disposed of or sold. However, since the cost also represents a significant proportion of the owner's income, this is a major loss of investment.

Not only is the physical device an expensive investment to lose, but from a frequently used phone, there is also a considerable loss in terms of data – each time your phone is stolen, you must begin again.

These observations contributed to the product design and were seen in the product service configuration.

Samsung's Safety Phone, a Service Inside a Product

In late 2008 Samsung launched two new phones in India (Figure 2.1.12) with two unusual service features directly informed by the Experientia research and its insights on security: the mobile tracker tool allows people to track down their phone if they forget it or if it is stolen. If someone tries to use the phone by changing the SIM card, the phone will automatically send an SMS to up to two numbers preset by the owner, giving the contact number of the new users without their knowledge. The mini-site lossproofmobiles.com explains in detail how it works.

The emergency SOS alert ensures that help is at hand when people are in trouble. By pressing the 'C' key four times, the phone will automatically send out an SOS message to up to ten numbers that the user can preset.

Although these services were created at minimal cost (in essence they are software that is added to the device), their value for the end-user cannot be overestimated, especially in the environments for which they were designed. However, these services could be adapted for developed world environments too.

FUTURE SERVICE DESIGN AS AN ENABLER OF GRASS ROOTS SERVICE DEVELOPMENT

We at Experientia expect that with the greater diffusion of easy to use, powerful technology, the value of co-creation and grassroots innovation will become increasingly self-evident.

After all, people in their local communities are much better placed than any company to create the solutions that serve them best (Jagun, Heeks and Whalley 2008, Ramey 2008, Jana 2009). The MIT Fab Labs[22] – a technical outreach for ordinary people in places such as India and Ghana to learn not just about science and engineering but actually design machines and make measurements that are relevant to improving the quality of their lives – have been demonstrating this for years. But until now, the tools have not been available for people to design these solutions themselves.

This is now starting to change. The future therefore lies not only in centralised participatory service design, but also in a radical decentralisation of technology, with

22 http://fab.cba.mit.edu/, accessed 25 Feb 2010.

Figure 2.1.12 Five photos illustrating field research and participatory design in India
Source: Experientia.

major businesses providing the tools to people in emerging markets to create and design their own services.

Ethnographic research, participatory workshops and remote research will still be needed but will no longer be focused on conventional end-to-end service design, but rather on the creation of service ecosystems or contexts, in which grassroots service development can take place.

Acknowledgments

This case study has been written with the collaboration of Erin O'Loughlin.

References

Banks, G. 2008a. Mobile finance: indigenous, ingenious or both? *PC World*, 20 November. Available at http://www.pcworld.com/article/154274/.html, accessed 28 January 2010.

Banks, G. 2008b. Mobile phones and the digital divide. *PC World*, 29 July. Available at http://www.pcworld.com/article/149075/mobile_phones_and_the_digital_divide.html, accessed 28 January 2010.

Banks, G. 2008c. Nokia: from technical development to human development? *PC World Business Center*, 5 November. Available at http://www.pcworld.com/businesscenter/article/153349/nokia_from_technical_development_to_human_development.html, accessed 28 January 2010.

Bhan, N. 2009. The 5D's of BoP marketing: touchpoints for a holistic, human-centered strategy. *Core77*. Available at http://www.core77.com/blog/featured_items/the_5ds_of_bop_marketing_touchpoints_for_a_holistic_humancentered_strategy_12233.asp, accessed 28 January 2010.

Bhan, N. and Tait, D. 2008. Design for the next billion customers. *Core77*. Available at http://www.core77.com/blog/featured_items/design_for_the_next_billion_customers_by_niti_bhan_and_dave_tait_9368.asp, accessed 28 January 2010.

Chavan, A., Gorney, D., Prabhu, B. and Arora, S. 2009. The washing machine that ate my sari – mistakes in cross-cultural design. *Interactions Magazine* 16(1). Available at http://interactions.acm.org/content/?p=1205, accessed 28 January 2010.

Chipchase, J. 2008. Small objects travel further, faster. *Vodafone Receiver Magazine* (20). Available at http://www.receiver.vodafone.com/small-objects-travel-further-faster, accessed 20 February 2010.

Clavin, C. 2008. Mobile communication in the developing world – a design challenge. *Vodafone Receiver Magazine* (20). Available at http://www.receiver.vodafone.com/mobile-communication-in-the-developing-world, accessed 20 February 2010.

Corbett, S. 2008. Can the cellphone help end global poverty? *New York Times Magazine*, 13 April. Available at http://www.nytimes.com/2008/04/13/magazine/13anthropology-t.html, accessed 28 January 2010.

de Silva, H., Zainudeen, A. and Ratnadiwakara, D. 2008. Perceived economic benefits of telecom access at the bottom of the pyramid in emerging Asia. *LIRNEasia* May. Available at http://www.scribd.com/doc/3105489/LIRNEasia-ICApc-Benefits-at-BOP-v2-1, accessed 28 January 2010.

Dev Sood, A. 2006. *The Mobile Development Report: The Socio-Economic Dynamics of Mobile Communications. Rural Areas and their Consequences for Development, Center for Knowledge Societies*. Available at http://www.nokia.com/NOKIA_COM_1/Corporate_Responsibility/Sidebars_new_concept/Related_topics_Society/Mobile_Development_Report.pdf, accessed 28 January 2010.

Donner, J. and Gitau, S. 2009. New paths: exploring mobile-only and mobile-primary internet use in South Africa. Paper submitted to the Workshop Africa Perspective on the Role of Mobile Technologies in Fostering Social Development. Maputo, 1–2 April. Available at http://www.w3.org/2008/10/MW4D_WS/papers/donner.pdf, accessed 28 January 2010.

Faludi, J. 2005. Betting on the next billion: 'voices in your hand'. *World Changing*, 5 October. Available at http://www.worldchanging.com/archives/003636.html.

Garreau, J. 2008. Our cells, ourselves. *Washington Post*, 24 February. Available at http://www.washingtonpost.com/wp dyn/content/article/2008/02/22/AR2008022202283.html, accessed 28 January 2010.

Heeks, R. 2009. IT and the world's 'bottom billion'. *Communications of the ACM*, (4), 1 April. Available at http://cacm.acm.org/magazines/2009/4/22950-it-and-the-worlds-bottom-billion/fulltext, accessed 28 January 2010.

International Telecommunication Union 2009. *Measuring the Information Society – The ICT Development Index*. Available at http://www.itu.int/ITU-D/ict/publications/idi/2009/material/IDI2009_w5.pdf, accessed 28 January 2010.

Jagun, A., Heeks, R. and Whalley, J. 2008. The impact of mobile telephony on developing country micro-enterprise: a Nigerian case study. *ITID Journal*, 4(4), 47–65. Available at http://www.itidjournal.org/itid/article/view/310/142, accessed 28 January 2010.

Jana, R. 2009. Innovation trickles in a new direction. *Business Week*, 11 March. Available at www.businessweek.com/magazine/content/09_12/b4124038287365.htm, accessed 28 January 2010.

Jung, Y. and Chipchase, J. 2008. Nokia open studio: engaging communities. Available at http://younghee.com/wp/wp-content/uploads/2008/10/nokiaopenstudio_final_20081030.pdf, accessed 28 January 2010.

Krazit, T. 2005. Intel opens China, India design centers. *InfoWorld*, August 1. Available at http://www.infoworld.com/t/hardware/intel-opens-china-india-design-centers-114, accessed 28 January 2010.

Meyer, P. 2009. Bridging Africa's digital divide. Unite. Nokia Siemens network, 29 April. Available at http://unite.nokiasiemensnetworks.com/adwords/article/view/id/126, accessed 28 January 2010.

Ramey, C. 2008. From favelas to townships: mobile use in low-income populations. *MobileActive.org*, 15 July. Available at http://mobileactive.org/favelas-townships-mobile-use-low-income-populations, accessed 28 January 2010.

Rudebeck, C. 2009. Closing the digital divide, sustain IT supplement. *The Independent*, 10 March www.independent.co.uk/news/business/sustainit/closing-the-digital-divide-1640433.html, accessed 28 January 2010.

Vance, A. 2008. Microsoft goes far afield to study emerging markets. *The New York Times*, 26 October. Available at http://www.nytimes.com/2008/10/27/technology/companies/27microsoft.html, accessed 28 January 2010.

Zachary P.G. 2008. Inside Nairobi, the next Palo Alto? *The New York Times*, 20 July. Available at http://www.nytimes.com/2008/07/20/business/worldbusiness/20ping.html?_r=2&adxnnl=1&adxnnlx=1267426855-bl13UH6Jh7OijtWRZb9S4g, accessed 28 January 2010.

2.2 Designing Interactions to Shape Systems and Organisations

This area of contributions explores how service designers often start (re)designing service interactions to then enter into deeper transformational processes of service systems, cultures and organisations. It has contributions from authors working traditionally in interaction design and information science that have explored the area of service design, transferring their existing knowledge from their original field into the one of design for services.

All the projects reported in this area have in common an interest and focus on developing and applying methods to evaluate and/or (re)design interfaces and interactions as a starting point for their design interventions. They apply methods mainly from interaction design and human-centred design such as participant observation, interviews, shadowing, storyboards, notational tools, experience prototype, interaction design guidelines, expressive blueprinting and customer journey to suggest improvements in existing services, and to enable the implementation of new service models (see for example, the case study of Dote Lavoro by Domus Academy Research Centre).

The case studies illustrate how service designers, starting from their interaction design focus, deal with wider organisational dynamics and issues related to organisational culture, stakeholders' collaborations and configurations, work practices and business models:

- Holmlid (Linköping University) investigates the Swedish Customs service, showing how service designers need to deepen their understanding of the system behind user–service interactions; he does so by introducing the issues of multiple service channels navigation and the concept of 'service ellipses';
- Pacenti (Domus Academy Research Centre) reflects on how applying interaction design guidelines (such as trust, transparency, and coherence of identity) at the service operation level, requires a deeper transformation process of the public service culture;
- Kimbell (Oxford University), observing service design professionals at work with science-based service companies, suggests how designers work across boundaries of knowledge domains reframing business models and service configurations;

- Spraragen and Hickey (IBM) explore service design methods to understand employee's behaviours and inform internal service processes in order to increase awareness of information security rules, policies and guidelines in a financial service company.

All these examples are the manifestation of the fact that service interactions don't happen in a vacuum: the individual service encounter 'is nested within broader managerial issues of organisational structure, philosophy, and culture that also influence service delivery and ultimately customer perceptions of service quality' (Bitner 1990: 69). With this in mind, service designers can use their interaction and human-centred design approach to have wider transformational impacts (Junginger and Sangiorgi 2009) into service organisations; in so doing designers can facilitate the development of new delivery modes and the generation of new service ideas and business models whilst stimulating organisational changes.

In this sense service designers apply an 'outside in' approach to service innovation (Tekes 2007) that starts from observing and understanding users behaviours and experiences (see Chapter 2.1) to then suggest incremental changes to service delivery or proposing completely new service ideas and business configurations. A further step is when the service designers enter an organisation to help them embed the 'outside-in' approach in their existing innovation processes.

As it has already been mentioned and discussed elsewhere (Sangiorgi 2009, Holmlid 2009) one of many focuses of design for services is about designing service interactions. Interactions can have a wide meaning; Buchanan asserts how 'interaction' refers to how 'human beings relate to other human beings through the mediating influence of products' (2001: 11); he also suggests how 'products' can be interpreted as physical artefacts but also as experiences, activities or services. Starting from this wide interpretation of interaction and looking at the case studies, we have observed three main levels at which design for services operates: user–service interaction; service staff–service system interaction; and interactions among different service systems. A detailed description of these three levels of interventions follows as an introduction to the case studies.

User–service Interaction

The user–service interaction area and the moments of interaction have been referred to in different ways, for example, service interface, service evidences, touch-points, service encounters, customer journey and moments of truth. Design for services uses interaction design discipline as a source of principles and design tools to evaluate service interactions, but at the same time, in a conscious or unconscious way, is linking and overlapping to a longer tradition of research in marketing on the service encounter. Service encounters are defined by Shostack as 'a period of time during which a consumer directly interacts with a service' (1985: 243); they are the context where, as Klaus suggests, 'the system configuration for a certain quality experience becomes empirically observable' (Klaus 1985: 25). The same epiphenomenal approach to quality is emphasised in the design literature; Parker and Heapy (2006) suggest service designers do not see services as commodities: designers 'focus on how people actually experience services, in order to understand how large service organisations can create better relationships with their users and customers' (Parker and Heapy 2006: 15).

Pacenti (1998) defined service design as the design of the area, ambit, and scene where the interactions between the service and the user take place. She describes how the 'service interface', as the tangible and visible part of a service that a user can experience, has a double role: to support and orient the action and the interaction (interface as a tool) and to vehicle the service identity and values (interface as a shop window). In the following case studies, service designers and researchers use methods such as shadowing, situated interviews, blueprinting and customer journey to map out and evaluate these two dimensions of service interaction:

- *Service interface as a tool*: through shadowing and participant observations (Sperschneider and Bagger 2000) designers observe how the user interacts with the service, looking for any evidence of breakdowns or discomfort. In Human–Computer Interaction (HCI) design 'breakdowns' are 'situations in which some unarticulated conflict occurs between the assumed conditions for the operations on the one hand, and the actual conditions on the other' (Bødker 1991: 27). Within a service these conflicts can be originated by the fact that a service is new to the user or because the service process is not transparent enough thus generating disorientation or false expectations (see for example Dote Lavoro or Swedish Customs projects). In both these cases designers operate by redesigning the service evidences to support the creation of a clearer mental model of how the service operates and develops, 'making it clear' as Pacenti describes it. Holmlid talks for example of 'service progress evidences' as communication devices that can provide the user with timing information about the undertaken steps and the coming ones, in particular when moving from one 'service ellipse'[1] to the other. In HCI this is the design principle of 'feedback', while in service marketing literature studies have shown the relevance of the development of a clear 'service script' for both the user and the provider. A script is a 'coherent sequence of events expected by the individual, involving him either as a participant or as an observer' (Abelson 1976: 33). The way people interact with services is based on previous experiences with similar services; these experiences are then compared thus influencing the satisfaction with the encounter. Clarifying scripts means also clarifying roles in the interaction as 'service encounters can be characterised as role performances' (Solomon et al. 1985: 108) and 'discrepant roles expectations decrease efficiency' (ibid. 109). Pacenti's 'notational tool' (a simplified visual script to guide staff's actions) is a response to this need of clarity on staff's role; it is designed to support the situated social negotiation of role behaviours among users and staff.

- *Service interface as shop window*: every visible element of the service works as a 'clue' for users to get oriented amidst the service interface, and to evaluate the service quality and coherence in relation to its claims and promises; for this reason designers pay particular attention to the overall orchestration of service identity and appearance. Dote Lavoro project works on this aspect. DARC (Domus Academy Research Centre) was called to study the communication strategy for a new service called Dote Lavoro

1 Service ellipses are the main interaction sequences users encounter through the whole service interaction process.

(a service aiming at orienting and supporting unemployed people to look for training opportunities): this project evaluated the unity of identity and the uniformity of style of delivery among the service providers' network, while considering the most effective way to communicate the novelty of the service to users. In this sense the role of designers become the one of a 'director' able to manage the integrated and coherent project of all the aspects that influence the interaction quality (Pacenti 1998). At the same time building up a coherent service interface and identity is used as a strategic 'glue' to keep different stakeholders together. The understanding of service experiences and identity in a holistic way is a key contribution of designers within service projects. In service marketing Bitner (1992) uses the concept of 'servicescape' to show how the quality of the service performance can be evaluated by looking at the sum of single characteristics (such as ambient conditions, layout, signs, symbols and artefacts). Designers apply instead broad design guidelines (see for example the service interaction design guidelines, Appendix 2), generally described as 'heuristic' methods, that lack in precision and predictability, but that capture well the epiphenomenal emergence of service quality.

Staff–service Organisation Interactions

Service staff has been defined by service marketing literature as boundary-spanning roles 'resulting in their being as close psychologically and physically to the organisations' customers as they are to other employees' (Bowen and Schneider 1985: 127). They are described as both 'gatekeeper of information' and 'image maker' (ibid.). This boundary role is a critical one, as their behaviour cannot be simply driven by strict 'service scripts' or controlling measures as, apart from personal characteristics, their behaviour embodies and manifests the overall organisational culture. A human-centred design approach to design for services necessarily doesn't stop to understanding users, but includes service staff and their work environment to generate change.[2] For example DARC soon realised the need to participate actively to a longer transformational process of the service culture in the Regione Lombardia offices in order to make their intervention work in the longer term. This focus on work practice and environment emerges also in the projects described by Stefan Holmlid, Lucy Kimbell, Susan Spraragen and Valerie Hickey where designers use their ethnographically inspired methodologies or collaborative approaches (see expressive blueprinting session) to go beyond service encounters and question service processes and internal interactions. A step further for this kind of interventions is when design realises how design thinking needs to become part of staff mindset and routines. This transformation would require not only integrating design approaches within existing innovation processes, but also affecting the way staff interact with spaces, with customers and with ambiguity and risk. As Mulgan and Albury (2003) confirm, public sector innovation needs to create the space, time and capacity for creative thinking as well as to learn how to handle risk and uncertainty. Moreover, Suchmann and Trigg emphasise 'work practice is fundamentally social ... it is the community rather than the individual, that defines what a given domain of work is and what it means to accomplish it successfully' (Suchman and Trigg 1991: 73). These often

2 See the interview with Sabine Junginger at http://www.servicedesignresearch.com/interviews/?profile=722.

implicit social dimensions and their interdependence with the material artefacts are becoming increasingly a central object in the practice of design for services and in designers' conversations with service organisations and user communities.

Interactions Among Service Systems

Vargo and colleagues (2008) suggest that companies generate 'value propositions', meaning that value is not exchanged, but is 'co-created, jointly and reciprocally, in interactions among providers and beneficiaries through the integration of resources and application of competences' (ibid. 146). As an example DARC understood the need to look at the overall providers' network to verify if the 'value proposition' was really recognised and co-produced through their collective efforts or if the network connections were too loose for the final users to recognise the 'value' of the new service model. It seems that in both cases designers work to verify and co-create the agreement around the new service formula; they do so by observing current practices and creating the necessary tools (such as Web tools, manuals or corporate identity elements) to support the convergence of interests and visions; at the same time designers work to coordinate stakeholders' efforts toward a unified service experience. Stefan Holmlid claims coordination among service systems as a way to get a better integration of back office and stakeholders' activities to deliver a coherent and seamless experience to the final users.

Designers also take the role of reconfiguring existing networks based on new service ideas: this emerges in Kimbell's research project. She describes how designers seem to view the service as a fluid arrangement of human and non-human artefacts, rather than a fixed intangible entity. This capacity of thinking in terms of solutions and not in terms of organisations helps to break existing barriers for novel collaborations, creating spaces for new businesses to emerge. Or, as Normann and Ramirez would say (1993), consider value at the centre and build the necessary constellation around it.

The combination of these three kinds and levels of interventions summarises how designers can work with and within organisations, as illustrated by the following case studies.

References

Abelson, R. 1976. Script processing in attitude formation and decision making. In *Cognition and Social Behavior*, edited by J.S. Carroll et al. Carnegie-Mellon University, Hillsdale, NJ: Lawrence Erlbaum Associates Publishers, 33–45.

Bitner, J. 1990. Evaluating service encounters: the effects of physical surroundings and employees responses. *Journal of Marketing*, 54, 68–82.

Bitner, J. 1992. Servicescapes: the impact of physical surroundings on customers and employees. *Journal of Marketing*, 56 (April), 57–71.

Bødker, S. 1991.*Through the Interface: A Human Activity Approach to User Interface Design*. Hillsdale, NJ: LEA Publishers.

Bowen, D.E. and Schneider, B. 1985. Boundary-spanning-role employees and the service encounter: some guidelines for management and research. In *The Service Encounter*, edited by J. A. Czepiel, et al. Lexington, MA: Lexington Books: 127–47.

Buchanan, R. 2001. Design research and the new learning. *Design Issues*, 17(4), 3–23.
Holmlid, S. 2009. From interaction to service. In *How Designers Can Deliver Better Services: Designers' Role and Working Methods in the Service Design Processes*, edited by S. Miettinen and M. Koivisto. Helsinki, Finland: TAIK, 78–97.
Junginger, S. and Sangiorgi, D. 2009. Service design and organizational change: bridging the gap between rigour and relevance. *Conference Proceedings of the IASDR09 Conference*, Seoul, 18–22 October.
Klaus, P.G. 1985. Quality epiphenomenon: the conceptual understanding of quality in face-to-face service encounters. In *The Service Encounter*, edited by J.A. Czepiel, et al. Lexington, MA: Lexington Books, 17–33.
Mulgan, G. and Albury, D. 2003. *Innovation in the Public Sector*, Strategy Unit, Cabinet Office.
Normann, R. and Ramirez, R. 1993. Value chain to value constellation – designing interactive strategy. *Harvard Business Review*, 71, July–August, 65–77.
Pacenti, E. 1998. Il progetto dell'interazione nei servizi. Un contributo al tema della progettazione dei servizi. Ph.D. thesis in Industrial Design, Politecnico di Milano.
Parker, S. and Heapy, J. 2006. *The Journey to the Interface. How Public Service Design can Connect Users to Reform*. London: Demos.
Sangiorgi, D. 2009. Building up a framework for service design research. *Conference Proceedings of the 8th European Academy of Design Conference: Design Connexity*, Aberdeen, Scotland, 1–3 April.
Shostack, G.L. 1985. Planning the service encounter. In *The Service Encounter*, edited by J. A. Czepiel et al. Lexington, MA: Lexington Books: 243–53.
Solomon, M., Supnant C., Czepiel, J. and Gutman, E. 1985. A role theory perspective on dyadic interactions: the service encounter. *Journal of Marketing*, Winter 85, 49(1), 99–111.
Sperschneider, W. and Bagger, K. 2000. *Ethnographic Fieldwork under Industrial Constraints: Towards Design-in-Context*. Stockholm: NordiCHI.
Suchman, L. and Trigg, R. 1991. Understanding practice. In *Design at Work: Cooperative Design of Computer Systems*, edited by J. Greenbaum and M. Kyng. Hillsdale, NJ: Lawrence Erlbaum, 65–89.
Tekes 2007. *Seizing the White Space: Innovative Service Concepts in the United States*. Technology Review 205/2007, Available at www.tekes.fi/en/document/43000/innovative_service_pdf, accessed 3 January 2010.
Vargo, S.L., Maglio, P.P. and Akaka M.A. 2008. On value and value co-creation: a service systems and service logic perspective. *European Management Journal*, 26, 145–52.

STEFAN HOLMLID

CASE STUDY 06 THERE IS MORE TO SERVICE THAN INTERACTIONS

This case study, an investigation into the Swedish Customs service, asserts that service designers need to deepen their understanding of the system behind user–service interactions: it does so by introducing the issues of multiple service channels navigation and the concept of 'service ellipses'.

Several service analytical frameworks highlight the interactive nature of services. In this case study, the idea of designing services as interactions between actors and service systems will be explored. It is argued that service designers need to develop a deeper and more articulated understanding of what makes a good service interaction, going beyond the focus on individual encounters and connecting these to the wider service system.

The interactive nature of services has been investigated, from a marketing perspective, by Zeithaml, Parasuraman and Berry (1990), among others (Sasser et al. 1978, Edvardsson et al. 2000); in their studies they describe four main characteristics of services. Two of these are: 1) services are *heterogeneous*, meaning that they are hard to standardise and are variable in performance, due to their dependence on human judgement and interaction, and 2) service production and consumption are *inseparable*, meaning that the value of a service is co-created in the service experience by the producer and the consumer. Recently Vargo and Lush (2004, 2008) introduced the concept of a Service-Dominant Logic (SD logic) as a way to challenge the current goods-dominant economy. Two of the ten foundational premises of SD logic claim that firms can only offer *value-propositions* and that *value is co-created* with customers in a service performance through interaction.

Interactions have also been studied within the different fields of design research. Buchanan talks about four orders of design, each representing a 'place for rethinking and reconceiving the nature of design' (2001: 10), moving from 'symbols' and 'things' to 'interactions' and 'environments'. These can be viewed as perspectives on the design object. In particular 'interaction design' focuses 'on how human beings relate to other human beings through the mediating influence of products' (2001: 11). As part of this order, digital interaction design has turned its attention to the design of usable, desirable and effective interactions (Bannon and Bødker 1991, Löwgren and Stolterman 2005).

If one views services as co-constructions of value through interaction between provider and client, or customer and service system, service design would also be part of the interaction order. One focus of service design, as an emergent discipline, has been on service interactions (Shostack 1984, Mager 2004, Holmlid and Hertz 2007, Sangiorgi and Pacenti 2008 and Sangiorgi 2009) gaining knowledge and expertise from digital interaction design (Holmlid 2007, 2009a).

The case study presented here adds to the knowledge already developed in the area of service interaction design by exploring the issue of multi-channel integration in a service performance. It does so by illustrating service 'sequencing' and 'distribution' and introducing two main concepts, those of 'service ellipses' and 'service progress evidence'.

Swedish Customs

This case study reports on an investigation into the Swedish Customs' services related to the area of efficient trade, especially services to support the import of goods. The research team from Linköping University collaborated with the Customs Agency, three importing companies (one dealing with electronic equipment, a sports store chain and a confectionery company) and a logistics company.

The two main research interests were: 1) to understand how the different actors interacted, through which channels and with what evidence, and 2) to formulate design directions identifying 'what if' statements based on the analysis. In order to achieve this, data was collected through interviews, participant observation and documentation. Notes and documents were analysed qualitatively, identifying common as well as differentiating themes. The research also helped design researchers to deepen the understanding of multi-channel service interactions identifying two significant design issues, *sequences of service interactions* and *distributed service experiences*, which will be discussed in the following sections.

SEQUENCING SERVICE INTERACTION

The tangible evidence and touch-points that make up the obvious parts of service interactions are often connected with each other in sequences and chains. The Swedish Customs Office aims to make trade efficient, facilitating the overall import process. This happens mainly through a series of interactions between the importer and the Customs utilising different service channels. The research team identified three main interaction sequences through the whole service process that we called *service ellipses*: application, import and payment. Each ellipsis has its own trigger and closure actions, as well as its own structure of service evidences, and differently negotiated roles among service performance participants (Figure 2.2.1).

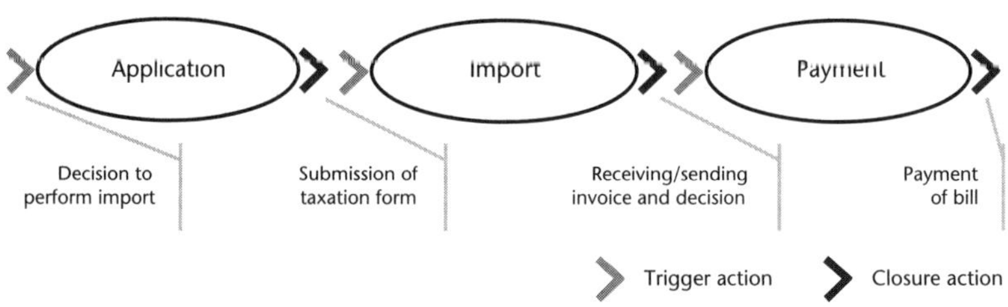

Figure 2.2.1 The service ellipses with trigger and closure actions
Source: Stefan Holmlid.

- *Application*: at the beginning of the process the importer interacts with the customer service department of the Customs Office in order to fill out the necessary forms correctly. These service interactions are *triggered* by the importer's decision to import goods to Sweden and are mediated by phone calls to customer service in case of need for assistance. Customer service has no access to the taxation form or to the preparatory work that the importer has done. These conversations often require the importer to start each interaction from the beginning, generating delays and potential misunderstandings. This 'service ellipsis' has its *closure* when the importer submits the taxation form to the Customs Office. During this first interaction sequence the Customs Office is perceived as an 'expert' (see Figure 2.2.2).

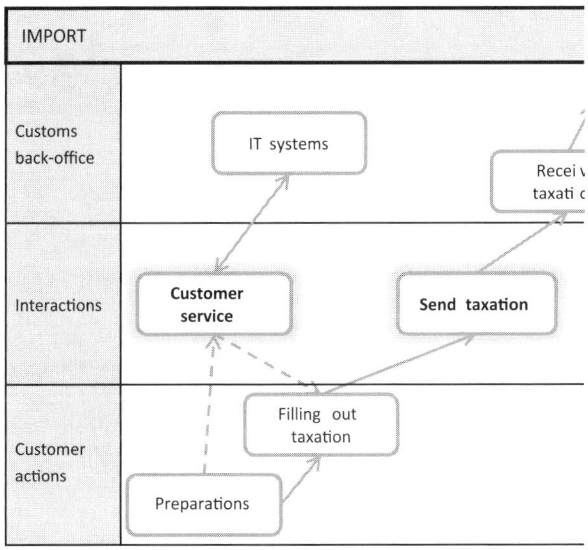

Figure 2.2.2 Simplified blueprint of the first service ellipsis: the application
Source: Stefan Holmlid.

- *Import*: sending the taxation form is the trigger for a new sequence of interactions. If there are any problems with the taxation form the Customs Office sends it back, often together with a definition of what needs to be clarified. During this period the importer also handles the practicalities with the logistics of importing, and finally receives the goods. When the goods arrive the import documents are given to a customs officer at the border. The effect of this is that the Customs Office sends an import taxation decision and invoice to the importer. Receiving the invoice defines the closure for the second ellipsis of the import process. During this stage the importer views the Customs Office as a government office (see Figure 2.2.3).

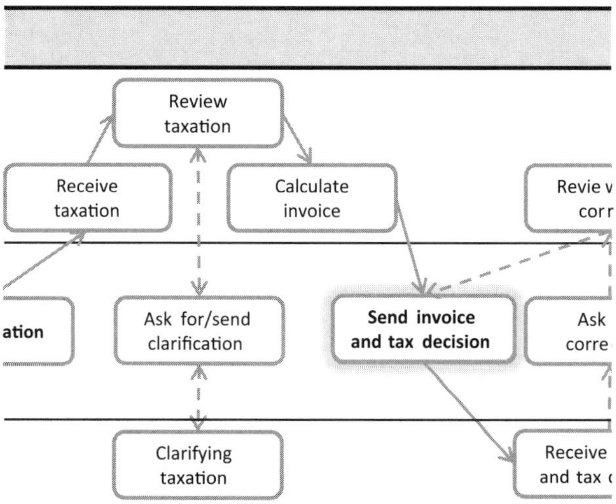

Figure 2.2.3 Simplified blueprint of the second ellipsis: the import
Source: Stefan Holmlid.

- *Payment*: receiving the import taxation decision and the invoice is the trigger of a third set of interactions. The importer checks that the invoice states the correct goods and the correct amount of goods that have been received. If there are discrepancies the importer contacts the Customs Office in order to deal with these differences in the invoice. Having done this, the importer pays the bill. This defines the closure for the third chunk of interactions of the import process. During this part of the process the importer views the Customs Office as a recipient of payment (see Figure 2.2.4).

As described above service interactions and service evidences are ordered in a sequence through the whole service process, utilising different channels for the performance. They are also sequenced in three distinct chunks, or service ellipses. These ellipses have their own trigger actions and closure actions.

Each ellipsis represents a closed meaningful activity; and these could be designed as separate units. Designers need to identify for each of them the aim, the service participants, their roles and the service evidence as these might change in each ellipsis.

For example, the importer's view of the Customs Office role in relationship to the import process changes between the different ellipses: from expert, to government agency to payment recipient. The changes in role are related to changes in terms of the objective of each sequence of action; when the objective changes, the actors renegotiate their roles toward the agreed outcome. The value network is dynamically codetermined for situated value co-production. These changes in role can have an impact on the design of a service; service interactions with a taxation expert might have different requirements and expectations from those with a government agency.

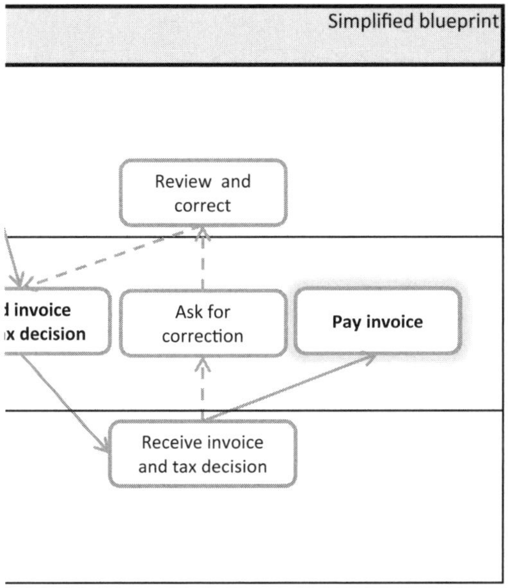

Figure 2.2.4 Simplified blueprint of the third service ellipsis: the payment
Source: Stefan Holmlid.

These differences in 'archetypical roles' should be reflected in the way the service interactions are designed, in the same manner as with personas or 'archetypical users'.

Even if intended as closed meaningful activities the single service ellipsis needs to be integrated with the overall service performance. There is a need to consider how the individual sequence fits with the other sequences and how the service organisation coordinates itself. Missing this bigger picture can reduce the effectiveness and the quality of the service experience.

Based on these considerations, and especially on the role of the Customs Officer as an 'expert', the research team suggested, as a way of connecting the different ellipsis to each other while keeping their independent nature: what if customer service had access to the online taxation form in preparation? Or, what if the customer service representative had access to all earlier import files for that specific importer? Or, what if the importer had their own phone number to customer service, with a set of dedicated customer representatives?

DISTRIBUTED SERVICE EXPERIENCES

Another aspect that emerged from the analysis was the *distributed nature of service experiences*. The experience of the Customs Office is, for example, distributed over time, over channels, media and over people. This requires well-developed design and customer relationship management systems (Holmlid 2008, 2009b) and to work with other design objects, such as the coordination between complex systems (Sangiorgi 2009).

The person in customer service may not be the same person that checks the taxation forms as received in the second ellipsis. The person filling out the taxation form might not be the same one that receives the taxation decision and invoice.

Import permits are paper-based documents while the taxation forms are digital. Human decision making and behaviour is not an individual process, but it is based and 'distributed' over a combination of goals, tools, people and settings (Hutchins 1996, Hollan et al. 2000). Thus service designers need to pay attention to how service experiences are developed and supported during the overall service performance. For example it can be hard for participants to understand the service process and to have confidence in the overall service offering, especially where the dependency on several actors for the progression of the process is strong. In such cases, a set of service process instructions and progress evidence could be designed to make the process more visible and understandable.

Based on these considerations the research team asked the following questions: *what if* a piece of service evidence was sent to the importing company upon reception of the taxation form in the second ellipsis, stating what the next steps in the taxation process would be? Such *service progress evidence* adds a way-showing experience to the service process, and directs and destines the service experience. Such evidence can harness both feedback and feedforward information (Holmlid 2002). When delivered several times during a service performance, one piece of evidence could make earlier service progress evidence obsolete, which should influence its design. Precisely because this is a distributed service experience, service design should support coordination between complex systems and provide clear-cut service interactions.

Concluding Remarks

This case study has provided a closer look at the structure and qualities of multi-channel service interactions. On a general level, services should be regarded as the activities and events that make interactions meaningful. Given that service interactions are sequenced and distributed, a few design considerations have been identified.

Service interactions are made up of *service ellipses* that, with their trigger and closure actions, represent the local context and structure of events within which customers interpret and get oriented through the service experience. Thus, each ellipsis contributes to the building of the overall meaning of the experience, and vice versa, the service provides a meaningful context for each interaction. This represents a perspective on the design object that should guide service designers. It also has potential to help designers create design languages and service semantics. A prerequisite for these ellipses is that archetypical roles are taken or construed by clients and service providers.

Based on the case study, we suggest that service experiences are distributed over time, over people and different channels. For service customers, *service progress evidence* facilitates such an experience. In order to achieve that, service designers need to orchestrate all the elements and conditions that guarantee the continuity and coherence of this distributed performance. For the service organisation, it becomes fundamental to position and interlink each interaction in the wider system.

All in all, the ability as a service designer to shift perspective between interactions, service systems, complex actor networks and the functioning of these within and among even wider systems is therefore crucial.

Acknowledgements

The author wishes to acknowledge the companies participating in the study, as well as the government offices and the partners, for sharing their experiences. Mia Living, Stefan Nygard, Fabian Segelström, Jonatan Wentzel and the other students participating in developing the case studies. This research was made possible by a research grant from VINNOVA, the SERV project, *Service design, innovation and involvement*, ref no 2007-03444.

References

Bannon, L.J. and Bødker, S. 1991. Beyond the interface: encountering artifacts in use. In *Designing Interaction: Psychology at the Human–Computer Interface*, edited by J.M. Carroll. Cambridge, MA: Cambridge University Press, 227–51.

Buchanan, R. 2001. Designing research and the new learning. *Design Issues*, 17(4), 3–23.

Edvardsson, B., Gustafsson, A., Johnson, M.D. and Sandén, B. 2000. *New Service Development and Innovation in the New Economy*. Lund: Studentlitteratur.

Hollan, J.D., Hutchins, E. and Kirsh, D. 2000. Distributed cognition: toward a new foundation for human–computer interaction research. *ACM Transactions on Human–Computer Interaction: Special Issue on Human–Computer Interaction in the New Millenium*, 7(2), 174–96.

Holmlid, S. 2002. *Adapting Users: Towards a Theory of Use Quality*. Linköpings Studies in Science and Technology, Dissertation No. 765.

Holmlid, S. 2007. Interaction design and service design: expanding a comparison of design disciplines. Paper to the Nordes conference: Nordes 2007, Design Inquiries, 27–30 May, Stockholm, Sweden. Available at http://www.nordes.org/data/uploads/papers/143.pdf.

Holmlid, S. 2008. Towards an understanding of the challenges for design management and service design. Paper to the International DMI Education Conference, Design Thinking: New Challenges for Designers, Managers and Organizations, 14–15 April, ESSEC Business School, Cergy-Pointoise, France. Available at http://www.dmi.org/dmi/html/conference/academic08/papers/Holmlid/Holmlid.pdf.

Holmlid, S. 2009a. From interaction to service. In *How Designers Can Deliver Better Services: Designers' Role and Working Methods in the Service Design Processes*, edited by S. Miettinen and M. Koivisto. Helsinki: TAIK, 78–97.

Holmlid, S. 2009b. Managing interaction design and business innovation: understanding interaction design as a key activity of the operating core. *Aesthesis, International Journal of Art and Aesthetic in Management and Organizational Life*, 2(3), 99–105.

Holmlid, S. and Hertz, A. 2007. Service-scape and white space: white space as structuring principle in service design. Paper to the European Academy of Design conference: Dancing with disorder: Design, discourse and disaster, Turkey, 11–13 April.

Hutchins, E. 1996. *Cognition in the Wild*. Cambridge, MA: MIT Press.

Löwgren, J. and Stolterman, E. 2005. *Thoughtful Interaction Design: A Design Perspective on Information Technology*. Cambridge, MA: MIT Press.

Mager, B. 2004. *Service Design: A Review*. Köln: KISD.

Sangiorgi, D. 2009. Building up a framework for Service Design research. Paper presented to the 8th European Academy of Design Conference, Aberdeen, 1–3 April.

Sangiorgi, D. and Pacenti, E. 2008. Emerging practices of service design-driven innovation. Paper persented to the Service Design Network conference, Amsterdam, 24–26 November.

Sasser, W.E., Olsen, R.P. and Wyckoff, D.D. 1978. *Management of Service Operation*. Boston, MA: Allyn and Bacon.

Shostack, G.L. 1984. Designing services that deliver. *Harvard Business Review*, 62(1), 133–9.

Vargo, S.L. and Lush, R.F. 2004. Evolving to a new dominant logic for marketing. *Journal of Marketing*, 68 (January), 1–17.

Vargo, S.L. and Lush, R.F. 2008. Service-dominant logic: continuing the evolution. *Journal of the Academy of Marketing Science*, 36(1), 1–10.

Zeithaml, V.A., Parasuraman, A. and Berry, L.L. 1990. *Delivering Service Quality: Balancing Customer Perceptions and Expectations*. New York: The Free Press.

ELENA PACENTI

CASE STUDY 07 HOW SERVICE DESIGN CAN SUPPORT INNOVATION IN THE PUBLIC SECTOR

This case study, the redesign of a public service communication model, illustrates how applying service interaction design guidelines (such as trust, transparency and coherence of identity) at the service operation level necessarily requires a deeper transformation process of the public service culture.

This case study describes a service design project developed in collaboration with an Italian regional authority; it reflects on the use of service interaction design guidelines to introduce a new service formula to citizens and to promote a user-centred service culture within public organisations.

In Italy the public sector has little experience and understanding of the practice of service design and of its focus on user experience; as a reflection of this citizens have a generally low expectation with respect to the quality and effectiveness of public services.

Within this context, the contribution of service design has been to highlight the importance of improving communication and interaction with users as a fundamental part of the overall service design process. The case study shows how bringing a user-centric view at service operation level created the premises to introduce a design culture at higher political tables.

The New Service Model: Dote Lavoro

The design group of Domus Academy Research Centre (DARC) has been assigned to study the communication needs and model for a new service of the pilot programme *LaborLab* of the Department of Work and Education of Regione Lombardia.

The new service model, promoted in the Job Placement and Training sector, is called Dote Lavoro*:* it consists of a set of incentives and personalised services offered to individual unemployed citizens willing to find a job. Presented as a 'voucher' to be spent in one of the licensed job centres, Dote Lavoro should enable unemployed citizens to build up a personalised package of training and empowerment services.

Dote Lavoro exemplifies the political principles of 'active policy actions' and 'person-centric services' aimed at supporting and enabling people to be proactive for their placement and not waiting for assistance from the government. Being proactive, in this case, means using the public aid to improve competences and skills to widen opportunities to enter (or re-enter) the job market.

The novelty of Dote Lavoro is that public money is destined to final users instead of being given to job centres; in this way the licensed job centres will use public money to provide those services that are actually asked for by final users. Supporting freedom of choice, the voucher allows citizens to choose what services to buy according to their expectations, competences and employability. This implies a significant cultural and behavioural change both for the service organisation and for citizens.

As part of the LaborLab programme, the regional authority started a pilot project offering two types of Dote Lavoro, one for unemployed over 40 and one to temporary workers; public job centres and private agencies applied for being part of the network of licensed centres while the new service formula was advertised through leaflets and posters (Figure 2.2.5). An Internet-based platform and a guide of more than 50 pages were then given to the operators to help them with the provision of the new service.

Figure 2.2.5 The poster for LaborLab used to promote the new service to citizens
Source: Photo by Domus Academy Research Centre.

The On-site Analysis

Given the ongoing pilot project the design team started an analysis among a sample of job centres and private agencies to observe how the service was promoted, presented and offered to their users.

The analysis and the selection of the agencies was organised in strict synergy with a national programme aimed at identifying the procedural quality standards for the licensed job centres in order to improve the minimum quality levels for the services to be provided (QUES programme 2006–2008). While the colleagues of the national programme where dedicated to checking the service provision quality standards (through interviews on predefined diagram flows and blueprinting tools), the design team focused on the observation and the evaluation of touchpoints, communication evidences and interaction supports.

The analysis was based on an evaluation grid made up of six interaction design guidelines (see Figure 2.2.6): identity, visibility, accessibility, usability, personalisation and transparency. Some of the findings were:

- *identity and visibility of Dote Lavoro network*: citizens found it difficult to perceive the job centres they interacted with as part of the network; a catalogue of the licensed job centres, available in the centres, was insufficient to build up the perception of the network;

- *visibility of the service opportunity*: most of participants knew about the service by word of mouth, just a few by the advertising campaign; the novelty of the service offer made it difficult for people to understand the opportunity through traditional leaflets and posters;

- *accessibility and usability for service staff*: the operators were not given enough support to provide a high-quality service as the information system managing users' data was still unstable and had some usability issues, while the training manual was too long and complex to be used;

- *personalisation and interaction quality*: the way the service was provided and supplied to citizens varied a lot according to the professionalism, organisational procedures, user targets, sensitivity and the relational quality of each provider.

Through the on-site analysis, it became clear to the regional authority that the job centres could represent the weakest point in the programme. Beside the urgency of solving all the operational and procedural problems (that is the IT system or mode of payment), they also understood the necessity to start a closer dialogue with the operators to:

1. grow consensus about Dote Lavoro and strengthen their sense of belonging to a network;

2. make the service model clearer and more visible;

3. provide clear parameters and effective supporting tools to perform the service to the desirable quality standard (Figure 2.2.6).

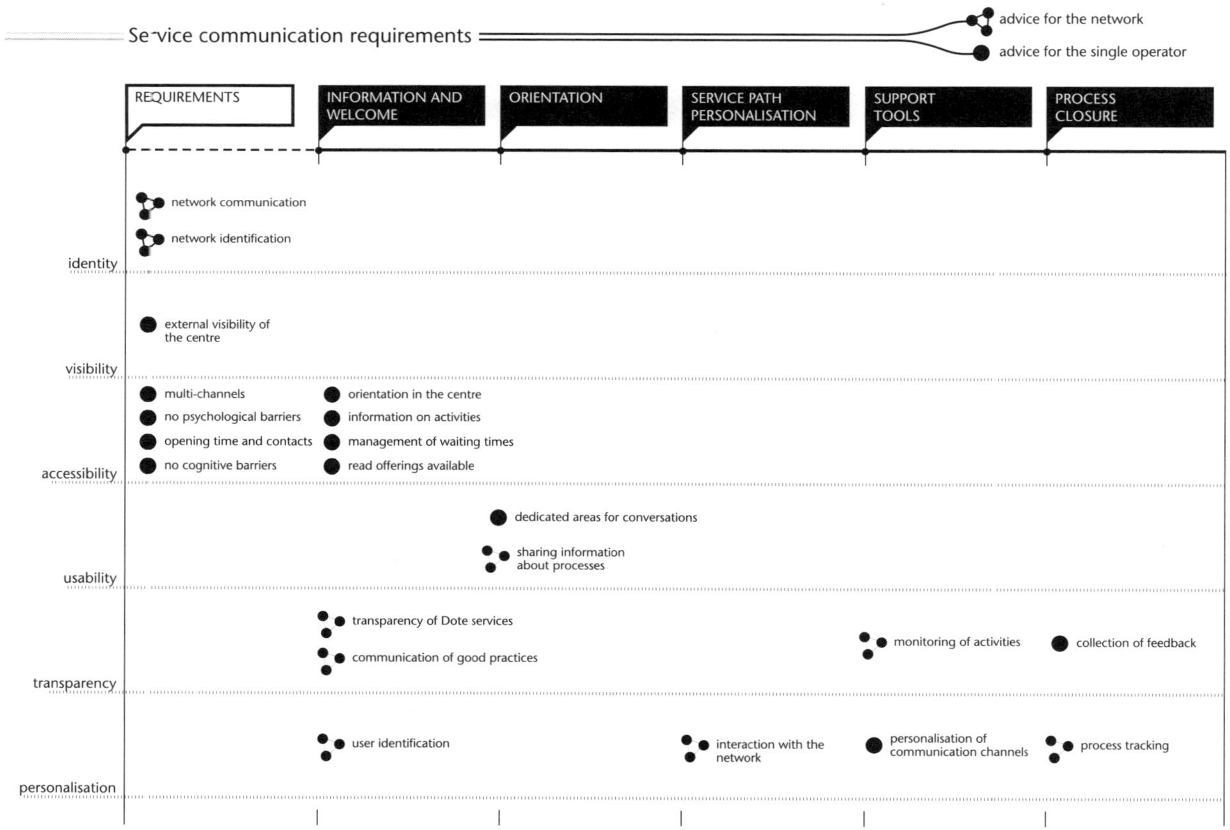

Figure 2.2.6 Evaluation grid for the analysis of service touchpoints
Source: Domus Academy Research Centre.

Design Interventions

The design intervention has been developed based on the interaction design guidelines and summarised as follow: 1) 'make it visible', working on service identity and visibility, 2) 'make it clear', working on service accessibility and usability, 3) 'build the trust', working on transparency and personalisation.

1: MAKE IT VISIBLE

- *Identity and the visibility of the Dote Lavoro service system*: the network of private and public job centres entitled to provide the new service should be perceived as part of a unique system, although it would still respect their own individual identity. DARC suggested the creation of an umbrella brand of Dote Lavoro, to be exposed as an identification mark in each centre of the network, as well as a series of communication tools explaining what the network is and listing the participants and their vocation (job, training, private temporary work centres);

- *Visibility of the service offer*: Dote Lavoro should be presented and explained in a clear and unique way by all the job centres and explained as an additional offering beside their normal service offering. The overall offer of incentives should be clearly explained through a specific tool (an offer map) and given in consultation to all people coming into the centres; it should be promoted through different media (to reach the widest audience as possible) and it should be continuously updated to reflect its vitality.

2: MAKE IT CLEAR

- *Accessibility and usability of the service*: in order to be accessible for all potential users, Dote Lavoro should be displayed and presented in a simple language, using the simplified guide and offer map as visual support (Figure 2.2.7), that doesn't exclude people because of their language, cultural, social or education background. The entitled centres should also guarantee a standard level of accessibility (service hours, sign on streets and on dedicated personnel, accessible entrance).

3: BUILD THE TRUST

- *Personalisation of the service*: the interaction with each person should be based on a one-to-one dialogue aiming at identifying the best programme of support actions: after welcoming and providing key information about the service, the operator should carry on a preliminary interview and use the 'skills and attitude evaluation' format to co-create the right plan. After this first meeting the centre should maintain a personal relationship between the tutor and the user by recording each encounter (diary) and constantly evaluating how the programme develops (Figure 2.2.8).

- *Service transparency and feedback*: the service offering and the reciprocal commitment should be clearly stated from the very beginning of the process. Each centre should provide the user with a booklet stating values, principles, obligations and quality standard; this together with a constant feedback on the process and the availability of successful users' testimony should help users to build the necessary trust in the service while progressively augmenting the sense of control of their own path.

Figure 2.2.7 The guide and the ID tools provided to the operators to support the consistency of service interactions
Source: Domus Academy Research Centre.

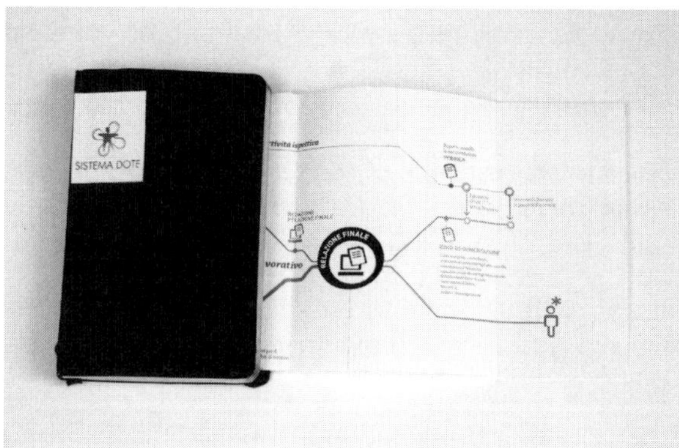

Figure 2.2.8 The user diary can support the recording of service interactions while stimulating user participation
Source: Domus Academy Research Centre.

Figure 2.2.9 An example of a tool to grow transparency and trust: list of service values and principles
Source: Domus Academy Research Centre.

Findings

At the beginning of the project the public authority considered the design of service communication and interface as a marginal aspect of the whole design, engineering and implementation process of the new service. Understanding the key role played by the job centres and service operators in the provision and effectiveness of Dote Lavoro, Regione Lombardia gradually accepted the need to consider the guidelines of visibility, identity, accessibility, usability, transparency and personalisation as part of a new service culture to be developed.

When the institution started redesigning the Dote system to become fully operative (a year after the pilot project started, Dote Lavoro has been launched as a full service) they therefore involved the network of job centres into a series of encounters called 'the agenda of change' aimed at growing awareness and consensus on the new person-centric model of the service. They also involved a sample of operators in focus groups to evaluate the strategic, procedural as well as relational aspects of the service, to feed into the redesign of the overall interface and to implement the new procedure.

This growing awareness in Regione Lombardia of the importance of relational aspects of service provision was a significant outcome of the project collaboration. Designers learned how the success of the redesign of the service interface depended on wider organisational dynamics, touching issues such as identity, learning, motivation and participation. Working on the innovation of the service interface elements, the design team had therefore to deal with organisational change processes.

Collaborating with a highly political and bureaucratic organisation such as Regione Lombardia DARC had to adapt their mode of work as follows:

1. defining scalable design objectives as the service interface is linked to different decisional centres;
2. adopting a flexible service design approach to adapt as the process direction develops;
3. bringing design tools into decisional processes.

Together with the need to plan the scalability and flexibility of design objectives and tools to negotiate design achievements, the service design team had to consider the issue of *participation*, both on the staff and on the user side. This required focusing on 'learning' processes, supporting transparency of service processes and maintaining engagement and interest along the way.

The design approach facilitated this gradual change in the service culture of Regione Lombardia and facilitated a good level of engagement in the project by visualising the elements of the solution. Simulating the appearance and showing the need for some evidences and touch-points that were not considered in advance helped the design team to convince the public authority of the importance of a 'design direction' of all the aspects related to the interaction with users. The ability of the design-driven culture of sketching and making service ideas and processes visible was revealed as the most effective skill to promote and communicate the role and the potential impact of a service design culture in the redesign of public services.

From the initial stages, the design team was progressively involved in strategic phases of the design of the new service, taking part in the encounters with the network, participating in the 'agenda of change' and in discussions about the policies behind the service design. This proves the effectiveness of clearly stated interaction design guidelines to drive and communicate the analysis and design of the new services. It also suggests the need to further develop a service interaction design approach that considers both the users and operators and that recognises the wider organisational and political processes needed to implement the required cultural change.

LUCY KIMBELL

CASE STUDY 08 FROM NOVELTY TO ROUTINE: SERVICES IN SCIENCE AND TECHNOLOGY-BASED ENTERPRISES

This case study, an investigation how service design professionals collaborate with science and technology-based service companies, illustrates how designers work across boundaries of knowledge domains reframing business models and service configurations.

This case discusses the particular circumstances of designing for services in science and technology-based enterprises. Service innovation and the role of design within it are relatively understudied within management disciplines (Chesborough and Spohrer 2006). There is a considerable body of research into technology innovation, but while universities have been spawning science parks in efforts to commercialise science, services based in recent scientific research have received little academic attention.

Drawing on empirical research, the case discusses the distinctive contributions that professional service designers can make to enterprises offering services originating in scientific research. It argues that service design practices have the potential to help newly established service providers rethink and remake their offerings. When science and technologies are novel, service design – itself a novel kind of enterprise – offers managers and entrepreneurs ways to reconfigure services which may lead to further innovation. However, the practices of service design professionals raise further questions for research, suggesting that a discipline of service design that neglects other bodies of knowledge, such as those in management and organisation studies, will not meet the challenges faced by enterprises offering science-based services and perhaps those facing other kinds of organisation.

To explore these questions, three service design consultancies were asked to work for six days over a period of some months with and for technology-based enterprises whose services originated in scientific research, as part of a larger project (Kimbell and Seidel 2008). Each encounter involved an established enterprise paired with a consultancy offering service design. Consultancy IDEO was paired with Prosonix, which offers particle engineering through ultrasonic processing; live|work worked with g-Nostics, which offers personalised medicine based on genetic markers, such as its smoking cessation support service, Nicotest; and Radarstation worked with

Oxford Gene Technology (OGT), offering micro-array services to researchers. All three service providers were knowledge-intensive enterprises, in which their commercial customers had a high level of expertise in order to use and assess the service. Only one of the three cases involved a service in which there were end users who were non-specialists. Data were gathered through video that was then transcribed and participant observation. Drawing on an academic tradition that is attentive to work as embodied and situated practice (Orlikowski 2000, Schatzki et al. 2001, Reckwitz 2002, Shove et al. 2007), the study found distinctive features in the ways the service designers' practices reconfigured services in the enterprises and the idea of service design.

Findings

First, the designers' practices and artefacts suggested they viewed the service from a perspective in which both humans and objects constituted the service. All three consultancies made use of what they called 'customer journeys' resembling the service blueprints that emerged in services marketing (Shostack 1982, 1984, Bitner et al. 2008). For example designers from Radarstation reframed OGT's complex technical service from the point of view of its customers by interviewing three customers and then creating a customer journey diagram making visible customers' engagements with service touchpoints such as emails, phone calls, and other artefacts over time, suggesting that nearly everything to do with a service can be designed (Candi 2007). The designers then reviewed this in a workshop with OGT and created a more accurate version that synthesised the three interviewees' experiences and critiqued several touchpoints (see Figure 2.2.10). In the diagrams created by designers from live|work, attention was paid to representing key elements in the service experience of the person trying to give up smoking and their encounters with it in the pharmacy, at home and on the Web. The designers then created a two-dimensional digital document of this journey to share with g-Nostics, which identified 'issues' and 'recommendations' for the company to consider. While the human-centred (Krippendorf 2006) experience of the service was a key way into understanding and (re)designing the service, the designers were also attentive to the roles of artefacts in constituting it.

Secondly, taking an ethnographic approach, the designers sought to understand the practices of customers and stakeholders in constituting services (Shove et al. 2007). For example, in their work with Prosonix, designers from IDEO wanted to see first hand how this technical business-to-business service was discussed at a first meeting with a potential client. Attending and shadowing this meeting and analysing this experience enabled the designer to generate insights about the service that, together with her colleague and the manager, then enabled them to create what they called an 'opportunity map' for the enterprise. Similarly designers from live|work visited a pharmacy where g-Nostics' smoking cessation service was being trialled, going through at first hand some of the experience of engaging with the service and, importantly, attending to the practices of the assistant, a lead user who helped deliver it.

Thirdly, the designers all discussed existing business models and saw it as key to the success of their project that they understood the enterprise's activities and aims, while not claiming specialist knowledge about the underlying science or technology. But the designers were also involved in critiquing these models. For example, the live|work designers created sketches, some of which proposed new business models, suggesting that it was hard to separate service concepts from service design and service processes (Voss and Zomerdijk 2007) (see Figures 2.2.11 and 2.2.12). Creating the sketches was a way for the designers to generate quick alternatives to problems they had identified, such as issues in the existing trial service, where the application of skills in graphic or packaging design might generate improvements. However, some of these sketches proposed ideas for new service components and also entirely new services, suggesting that the solution-focused practice of the designers was not bounded by a constraint of accepting the existing business model.

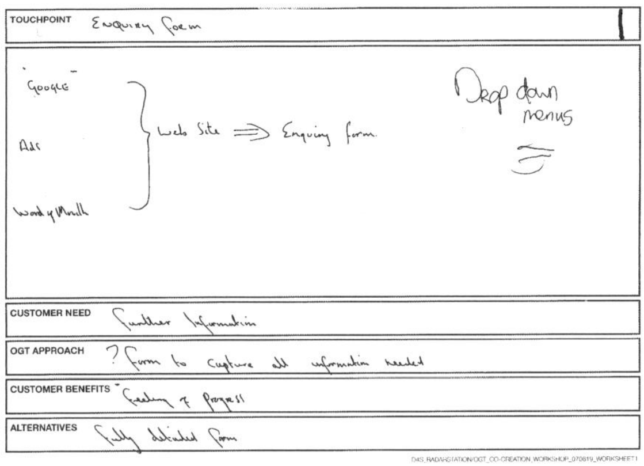

Figure 2.2.10 Analysis of service touch-point created in workshop run by Radarstation
Source: Radarstation. © University of Oxford.

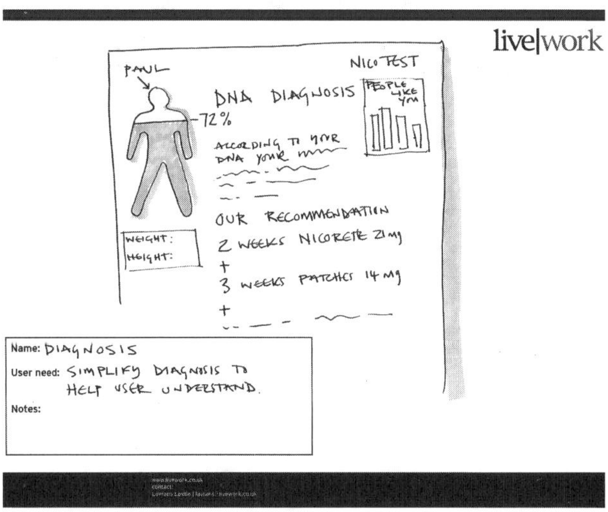

Figure 2.2.11 Sketch by designers from live|work suggesting improvement to an existing service component of the Nicotest service
Source: live|work. © University of Oxford.

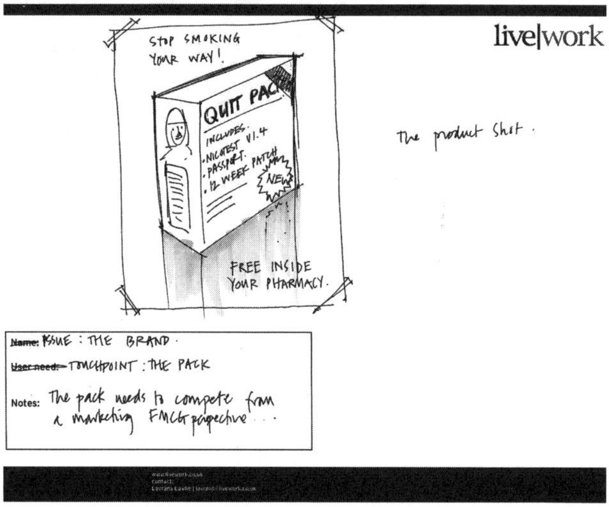

Figure 2.2.12 Sketch by designers from live|work suggesting a new way of thinking about the Nicotest service

Source: live|work. © University of Oxford.

Fourthly, the service designers all applied design criteria as heuristics for judging the effectiveness of a service. For example the IDEO designers repeatedly referred to a framework of 'desirability, viability and feasibility' (Jones and Samalionis 2008) in their work with Prosonix. For these designers, an ideal service would be desirable (consumers would want it), viable (it made sense to the business) and feasible (it could be built). They used this to evaluate the existing service and the opportunity map of innovations they developed with the manager. Within only a few days, managers from Prosonix began to use this terminology too as a way of discussing service opportunities and the designs that were realised to take advantage from them.

Finally, the designers' approach to service design meant that they took on a role as spanners of formal and informal boundaries, negotiating complex knowledge domains including the science on which the service was based; the organisation's strategy, operations and marketing functions; and the practices and concerns of customers, stakeholders and users. The artefacts they created – whether customer journey diagrams or rough sketches – became important 'boundary objects' (Star and Griesemer 1989) used by the designers and the managers for discussing what was involved in the design of services viewed across their different professional boundaries. In two of the three projects, the designers' practices involved co-creating ideas with the managers. Designers from Radarstation organised what they called a 'co-creation' workshop with two managers, saying that they themselves did not – and could never – know as much about the science and the service as the managers. The designers claimed no expertise about the science or technology underpinning the service; their practices were more concerned with (re)assembling artefacts and humans into sets of arrangements which had different meanings for different groups.

So far this case study has focused on the practices observed in the study that, it must be emphasised, was a limited, six-day encounter during which the design consultancies were unable to do much of the work they typically would with clients. A second set of insights are advanced by observing what the designers did not do, based on discussions at five workshops at which the designers and managers presented their accounts of their work together to a multidisciplinary academic audience. The questions that emerged from these conversations drew on management and social science, rather than design literature, and served to raise complementary questions about the design of services in technology-based enterprises originating in scientific research.

From an operations management perspective, one question is how service architectures might be designed so that modules can be arranged into services reducing the need for bespoke services, increasing efficiency and enabling enterprises to scale up. Theories of design management and industrial design, which argue for modularity, offer opportunities for the design of services (Voss and Mikkola 2007). How applicable are these ideas to services such as those involving human contact, which is typically difficult to standardise? What are the implications for small business-to-business enterprises, which may have a few, extremely different types of customers?

From a strategy perspective, one question is how customers, stakeholders or end users are involved in co-creating value and how can designers design for this (Vargo and Lush 2004, Möller et al. 2008). If services are about value co-creation, what are the tools and methods designers and managers can use to represent and, if necessary, quantify where and how value is created? Designers from live|work sometimes add to their customer journey diagrams or blueprints an additional line for these kinds of metrics, but are these representations sufficient when value is co-created over many different times and spaces and in non-binary sets of relations? What representational forms will be created to make these arrangements visible? A further question is how people other than customers, stakeholders or end users are involved in co-creating value and how can designers design for this (Ramirez and Mannervick 2008).

From a perspective that looks at the development of professions, there are questions about the extent to which service design practice will become less novel and more routinised. The development of a 'services science' by the global IT services company IBM (Spohrer and Maglio n.d.), which includes service design as one of its topics, may serve to formalise and standardise bodies of knowledge emerging in service design practice, authorising some methods, tools and artefacts, but not others.

Discussion

In this study, the designers' practices were a novelty for the managers working within enterprises where there was an existing service that had not been self-consciously designed. As examples of 'silent design' (Gorb and Dumas 1987) – design activity undertaken by people other than professional designers – these services were then rethought in the encounters between the designers and managers. In the time available, there were no opportunities for prototyping, testing or implementing the designers' ideas but through their practices and artefacts, the designers were involved in reframing the services in the following ways:

- from an organisation-centred service to a service in which humans and non-humans played important roles in constituting the service;
- from a novelty-based, technically-dense service to a service offering 'handrails' (Weick 2004) to stakeholders;

- from a service in which what contributed to success or a good service experience was unclear to a service in which the roles human and non-human actors played in realising the service were more explicit.

To conclude, a number of themes which pose questions for professional service design as a field as it becomes less novel and more routinised emerged in this project. It found the practices of service design consultants are applicable to many aspects of the design of services in enterprises based in scientific research. Drawing on approaches that owe more to the arts than to the sciences, and to tacit rather than explicit knowledge, these designers made valuable contributions to the enterprises they worked with over only a few days, even without specialist domain knowledge of the science underlying the services. In order to do their designing, the designers had to find ways to negotiate the boundaries between themselves and the managers they worked with. In small, fluid organisations facing high levels of uncertainty, there were limited resources for engaging with the designers, but these design professionals found ways to share an approach to thinking about the design of services that reconfigured the managers' understanding about what it could offer. The practices and artefacts described here raised important questions about the design of services which other bodies of research, including in organisation and management studies, may help answer.

Acknowledgement

With thanks to the Arts and Humanities Research Council and Engineering and Physical Sciences Research Council whose Designing for the 21st Century initiative funded this research.

References

Bitner, M., Ostrom, A. and Morgan, F. 2008. Service blueprinting: a practical technique for service innovation. *California Management Review*, 50(3), 66–94.

Candi, M. 2007. The role of design in the development of technology-based services. *Design Studies*, 28(6), 559–83.

Chesborough, H. and Spohrer, J. 2006. A research manifesto for services science. *Communications of the ACM*, 49/7 (July), 35–40.

Gorb, P. and Dumas, A. 1987. Silent design. *Design Studies*, 8(3), 150–6.

Jones, M and Samalionis, F. 2008. From small ideas to radical service innovation. *Design Management Review*, 19(1), 20–7.

Kimbell, L. and Seidel, V.P. (eds) 2008. *Designing for Services in Science and Technology-based Enterprises*. Oxford: Saïd Business School.

Krippendorff, K. 2006. *The Semantic Turn: A New Foundation for Design*. Boca Raton, FL: Taylor and Francis.

Möller, K., Rajala, R. and Westerlund, M. 2008. Service innovation myopia: a new recipe for client-provider value creation. *California Management Review*, 50(3), 31–48.

Orlikowski, W.J. 2000. Using technology and constituting structures: a practice lens for studying technology in organizations. *Organization Science*, 11(4), 404–42.

Ramirez, R. and Mannervick, U. 2008. Designing value-creating systems. In *Designing for Services in Science and Technology-based Enterprises*, edited by L. Kimbell and V. Seidel. Oxford: Saïd Business School, 35–7.
Reckwitz, A. 2002. Towards a theory of social practices: a development in culturalist theorizing. *European Journal of Social Theory*, 5(2), 243–63.
Schatzki, T.R., Knorr-Cetina, K. and von Savingny, E. (eds) 2001. *The Practice Turn in Contemporary Theory*. London: Routledge.
Shostack, G.L. 1982. How to design a service. *European Journal of Marketing*, 16 (1), 49–63.
Shostack, G.L. 1984. Designing services that deliver. *Harvard Business Review*, 62(1), 133–9.
Shove, E., Watson, M., Hand, M. and Ingram, J. 2007. *The Design of Everyday Life*. Oxford: Berg.
Spohrer, J. and Maglio, P. (n.d.) *The Emergence of Service Science: Toward Systematic Service Innovations to Accelerate Co-creation of Value*. Almaden: IBM Almaden Research Center.
Star, S.L. and Griesemer, J.R. 1989. Institutional ecology, 'translations' and boundary objects: amateurs and professionals in Berkeley's Museum of Vertebrate Zoology, 1907–39. *Social Studies of Science*, 19, 387–420.
Vargo, S. and Lush, R. 2004. Evolving to a new dominant logic in marketing. *Journal of Marketing*, 68, 1–17.
Voss, C. and Mikkola, J. 2007. Services science – the opportunity to re-think what we know about service design. Paper to the Services Science meeting, Cambridge, UK, 14–15 June.
Voss, C. and Zomerdijk, L. 2007. Innovation in experiential services – an empirical view., In *Innovation in Services*, edited by DTI. London: DTI.
Weick, K. 2004. Designing for throwness. In *Managing as Designing*, edited by R. Boland and F. Collopy. Stanford: Stanford Business Books, 74–87.

SUSAN L. SPRARAGEN AND VALERIE HICKEY

CASE STUDY 09 ENABLING EXCELLENCE IN SERVICE WITH EXPRESSIVE SERVICE BLUEPRINTING

This case study, the investigation and redesign of work practices around the information security system of a financial service company, illustrates how the use of service design methods to understand employee's behaviours and practices can inform the redesign of internal service processes and rules.

Organisations are required to maintain information security guidelines and regulations as they manage, share, and repurpose their internal and customer data. This task is becoming increasingly more complex as so many services are enabled to collect more and more data from a wider range of sources. Technology initiatives that enable smarter decision-making while increasing energy efficiencies through the sharing of server resources, invite concerns about the security of the data being exchanged. In this case study, we found the issues of security breaches to be an emerging priority for one of our financial services clients. We learned how vital understanding employee behaviour is for meeting security guidelines. That is where we found a role for service design: we addressed how procedures need to be aligned with the needs of employees and the goals of the institution for which they work.

Service design is a discipline that supports taking decisive and deliberate actions that will promote and sustain positive service experiences. As we strive to advance our service economy and the quality of services being delivered, we look towards employing design thinking for implementing service goals successfully. Design thinking also plays an important role here for informing and structuring internal service processes – even when the process is not visible to the customer during their service experience. This case study is about how design thinking, coupled with using a design technique called *expressive service blueprinting*, was used to improve employees' awareness of information security guidelines.

Expressive service blueprinting is an extension of traditional service blueprinting. Service blueprinting (Shostack 1984, Zeithaml et al. 2006) is a customer-centric approach used to map the customer journey as it is linked to provider actions. This technique is often used by service designers and providers to gain a richer understanding of a customer's perspective on service interactions and organisations. Service blueprinting exposes service gaps and enables the provider to make decisions to mitigate the risk of weakening the customer relationship. To this technique we introduce human quality dimensions – thus making it more 'expressive'. The human elements add insights to the mapping of customer and provider actions by noting customer behaviours and emotional states during the service engagement.

We used expressive service blueprinting on an information security awareness strategy assignment with a major Canadian bank. Our role as consultants was to define a strategy that would increase awareness of information security rules, policies and guidelines, and to thereby influence behaviours. As change consultants we are always seeking empathetic ways to articulate the stakeholder experience. Here we were seeking ways to design awareness interventions that would cut through dull presentations and training fatigue on a potentially tiresome topic. We will review a case study where expressive service blueprinting was employed in three distinct ways: mapped collaboratively to fully identify the client problem, shared with a broader team to better communicate the problem, and analysed to introduce corrective interventions at the appropriate moments during the client experience.

As we began our engagement looking for alternative ways to address security issues, we also looked to use alternative methods for understanding the work environment inside the bank. We took the stakeholder perspective and realised that process maps or data flow diagrams would not reveal the source of frustration being felt by the employees and others who required a more complete understanding and appreciation of information security policies. Topics that required compliance included learning how to use tools that would retain the classification of data, understanding data classification categories, and recognising the regulatory risks of non-compliance. We needed a consistent framework that we could use across all roles to identify and map stakeholder motivations and actions as they encountered enforcement of these policies while they were completing their work task. Expressive service blueprinting provided us with a visual and thoughtful method for understanding the stakeholder experience.

The bank was targeting ten high-risk roles for the awareness strategy, such as people managers, board members, executives and their delegates, business contact centre staff, financial analysts and investor relations. With those roles identified we realised they each have unique information security issues and therefore we would draw separate blueprints for each role. To organise this endeavour and to insure efficient collaboration, we facilitated ten two-hour sessions, one for each of the high-risk roles. The guest of honour at the sessions was a bank enterprise information security consultant who worked with the high-risk role and could represent that role's experience with information security. The meeting room was equipped with a whiteboard that extended the full length of the wall. We took the following steps:

- *Blueprint template*: we began the exercise by constructing a blueprint template, similar to those used in traditional service blueprinting (see Figure 2.2.13). We drew a horizontal line across the whiteboard and labelled the top half 'Onstage' and the bottom half 'Backstage' and then added in various other labels to capture onstage and backstage roles. Onstage roles and activities are those that are visible to the employee. Backstage roles and processes are those that the employee does not see. These areas are separated by the horizontal line – the line of visibility;

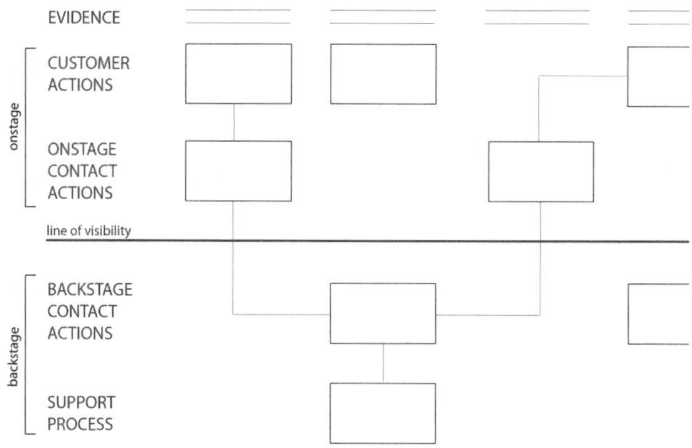

Figure 2.2.13 Template of a traditional blueprint

- *Action profile* and *motivation*: we created a space on the board for noting the action profile and motivation of each role. We worked with an information security consultant who supplied us with valuable insights as to the characteristics and attributes of the roles being mapped out. Motivations, such as the pressure of the job, were shared and served as input for assigning reasonable emotive states of the employees;

- *Service evidences*: we noted that there is a report that is generated regularly listing incidences of non-compliance. This report may serve as an indicator for measuring improved security awareness. When blueprinting a service, such documentation of activities or progress during a service is referred to as evidence, so we mark it in the blueprint accordingly;

- *Scenario building*: we determined what scenario we would map that day. An example was 'the investor relations role repurposes restricted financial data in order to make it public'. The window of time when the data is considered as restricted information is when information security standards on data transport and transmission need to be followed. Another example was when a human resource consultant sends confidential employee data to a third-party vendor and is instructed to encrypt the email, yet does not have the tools to do so. Yet another example was when a human resource role accesses the Internet to conduct work-related research and is locked out of sites that have been blocked due to information security standards (see Figure 2.2.14);

- *Mapping main steps*: through facilitation and discussion, we mapped out the relevant steps that the high-risk roles took to complete their task and drew them on the whiteboard. We were capturing a story that detailed the day in the life of an employee attempting to complete what would seem to be a straightforward task. We linked those steps to the provider steps – the provider steps appeared both in the onstage and the backstage areas. The interactions were noted with vertical lines or arrows linking the customer steps with the provider actions. We transcribed these blueprints into a presentation that could be shared with the client.

Up to this point, we were following the basic approach to service blueprinting for mapping the service activity (Shostack 1984). However, we wanted to do more than chart the steps the employees took to complete their task. We wanted to personalise it and demonstrate how in their attempts to meet security guidelines, their frustrations motivated them to find solutions outside the security protocols. Using the expressive service blueprint, we accentuated the interaction lines and added graphics or icons that corresponded to the observed emotional states (Spraragen and Chan 2008). In this case, we included emotive terms paired with call out 'bubbles' to demonstrate how their emotions affected their behaviour.

As shown in Figure 2.2.14, the employee felt eager, frustrated, angry and resentful as she attempted to conduct research on the Web, in preparation for a work-related conference presentation. The bubbles contained actual empathic remarks made by the employee as the experience unfolded. Step five, the last one, illustrates how the employee circumvented the company restrictions by completing her task at home. It also demonstrates how the decision makers (in this case the director of IT) who are responsible for upholding security guidelines are typically impervious to the emotional state that certain policies might provoke.

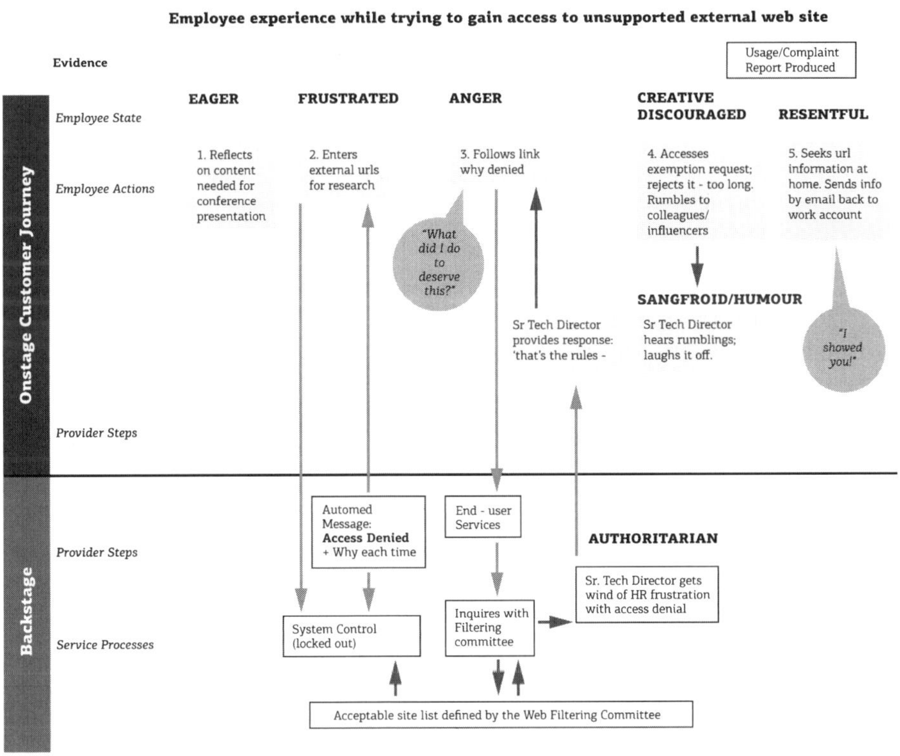

Figure 2.2.14 Example of an expressive service blueprint
Source: IBM.

Findings

Expressive service blueprinting was a highly instrumental technique for fully understanding people's experience with information security as they worked through their day. The technique allowed us to:

- Identify and communicate the human level experience of interacting with information security from two perspectives – that of the information security provider and of the 'high-risk role';
- Gain a deep understanding of the service itself and its degree of complexity, applicability, effectiveness, efficiency, intent and areas for improvement;
- Identify areas of frustration in the service of delivering information security standards and guidelines, which should be expected and managed accordingly. For example the information security unit at the bank required the use of encryption but they were not yet making the tools available for use by the general business population. We understood the frustration that business users were experiencing and responded with: 'We want you to encrypt but we don't provide you with the tools to do so; we hear you, the process isn't perfect yet; thanks for your patience as we improve';
- Reuse the moments of strong emotion and frustration as scenarios and themes relevant to many audiences in the recommended learning and awareness programme;
- Situate the 'high-risk roles' on an awareness maturity scale that defined five levels of awareness of information security: follower, independent, rule-based, entrepreneurial and inclusive thinkers. Ideally, the bank's employees would become rule-based in terms of compliance to information security policies. Expressive service blueprinting enabled us to profile each of the ten roles effectively, and place them accurately on the maturity scale. We were then able to recommend appropriate awareness-building activities that would resonate with our audiences.

Without this design technique we would have followed a more common path of fact-finding and information-gathering, such as interviews, resulting in text-based notes. Blueprinting provides a much richer narrative and visual storyline, completed with process steps, intentions, emotions and facts. It accelerates our ability to produce the final deliverable – a well thought-out awareness strategy that enhances the usual training events.

Customers may not report their satisfaction with a service in a timely or adequate way. Service providers may not understand their client's disenchantment with a service until the contract does not get renewed or extended. Emotional cues exhibited by the client during key moments of the service experience can be used as early indicators for how they may evaluate the service (Mattila and Enz 2002). Expressive service blueprinting enables the service designer to capture those moments by drawing a representative client experience map. Upon completing this exercise, more is learned about the client motivations and intentions than what is typically collected from a client satisfaction survey.

Service blueprinting has been applied to a broad range of service experiences (Bitner et al. 2008). This case study demonstrated how an extended blueprinting approach was applicable in an organisational business service scenario. Here, recognising how people are responding emotionally to a service used internally by employees provided unique insight for understanding behaviours and actions that needed to become aligned with company standards. It is hoped that expressive service blueprinting will continue to provide a proactive, empathetic approach for exploring customer responses in order to unveil areas for service improvement.

References

Bitner, M.J., Ostrom, A. and Morgan, F. 2008. Service blueprinting: a practical technique for service innovation. *California Management Review*, 50, 66–94.

Mattila, A.S. and Enz, C.A. 2002. The role of emotions in service encounters. *Journal of Service Research*, 4(4), 268–77.

Shostack, L.G. 1984. Designing services that deliver. *Harvard Business Review*, 62(1), January–February, 133–9.

Spraragen, S. and Chan, C. 2008. Service blueprinting: when customer satisfaction numbers are not enough. In *Proceedings of International DMI Education Conference: Design Thinking: New Challenges for Designers, Managers and Organizations*, Paris, 14–15 April.

Zeithaml, V.A., Bitner, M.J. and Gremler, D.D. 2006. *Services Marketing*. New York: McGraw-Hill.

2.3 Exploring New Collaborative Service Models

This area explores the role of design for services to imagine more collaborative service models as a way to redesign public and community services. It reports how service designers are working with and within public organisations and users' communities to develop platforms and skills to enable a culture of change, to explore new radical service models and innovative usages of social technologies within these processes.

Society as a whole is facing growing challenges such as an ageing population, the rise in long-term debilitating health conditions, immigration, racism, environmental degradation, climate change and lately the economic downturn. These conditions have forced government and institutions to take innovation in public services more seriously (Mulgan 2007), meaning on one side recognising and supporting the existing resources and innovative practices, and on the other side rethinking the nature, practice and dimension of innovation as a whole. Given the situation, incremental changes are no longer sufficient, while new radical service solutions and approaches to innovation are required (Harris and Albury 2009). The four cases of this area deal with this situation at different scales of intervention, from a small pilot project in a single institution to service prototypes for radical change:

- Bury and colleagues (Lancaster University) observe the emergence of community network-based services and initiatives by providing a rural village with access to broadband, offering Internet access to residents in their homes and at public locations;
- Winhall (Participle) reflects on the application of co-creation principles to rethink the welfare state model; she does so describing a pilot project combining the functions of a concierge service, a cooperative and a social club to provide practical help and social connections to older people in a London Borough;
- Sangiorgi and colleagues (Lancaster University) look at change in the education system conducting a design inquiry into issues of personalisation and participation within a secondary school;
- Pillan, Ferri and Cipolla (Politecnico di Milano) comment on projects developed by master students within four municipalities in the suburbs of south Milan (Italy), exploring more collaborative solutions to issues related to immigration, identity and social inclusion.

Reading the case studies four main characteristics seem to emerge as conditions for the development of more collaborative solutions. These are:

1. an emphasis on co-creation;

2. transformational and experimental approaches, that is design methods that build capacities and win resistances to change by engaging service participants in joint reflection processes, pilot projects and prototyping;

3. new service system configurations that bring in new innovation actors and explore new business models;

4. new media as enabling platforms.

We will explore these characteristics briefly one by one.

Emphasis on Co-creation

The case studies emphasise solutions built around people that become partners and participants in service delivery. Collaborative solutions (Cottam and Leadbeater 2004, Jégou and Manzini 2008) aim to break up the paternalistic and top-down approach to public services, transforming the conception of people as passive receivers of services to the one of active participants and collaborators. In line with this orientation, the case studies by Winhall and Pillan et al. document the potentials hidden behind the 'activation' of people, if and when people are intended as resources instead of as 'problems'. These two case studies illustrate how designers can tap into existing or latent networks of support and technological potentials, answering to needs that traditional public services generally cannot address: for example the needs of older people's daily practical life or the request for inclusion of a growing immigrant population. The traditional 'scripted' sequential services where designers shape foreseeable one-to-one paths of interactions, give here space to more open-ended service models that aim to re-engage people in their communities and networks. The model of fitting people into overwhelmed service provider delivery processes (that are already stretching their limited capacity) is transformed by connecting people to flexible networks; these networks are shaped around people's needs and grow in capacity (instead of reducing) with the numbers of people using and contributing to the service.

A Transformational and Experimental Approach

As Mulgan reports (2007) there is a deep and common disbelief in the inner capacities of public organisations to innovate. Challenging these assumptions is also part of this transformation. He suggests:

> *today, the caricature of public agencies as stagnant enemies of creativity is disproven by the innovation of thousands of public servants around the world who have discovered novel ways of combating AIDS, promoting fitness, educating, vaccinating vast populations or implementing new methods like intelligence-led policing or auctions for radio spectrum. (Mulgan 2007: 4)*

This existing creativity needs to be enhanced, supported, scaled up and protected.

This seems to reflect a general shift in the perception of 'creativity' itself as no longer the province of a few specialisations, but as a capacity that permeates every part of modern life and draws upon the knowledge and skills present in every organisation (Cox 2005). Working with and within service organisations and user communities, designers aim to make people aware and able to use their existing creativity to deal with change and complexity and co-develop innovative solutions.

In this section, all the collected projects rely on and believe in the resources and creativity of service organisations and citizens; at the same time they are all aware of inner potential resistances to change. The participation of service personnel to innovation processes is, for example, key to any transformation as service staff can bring both their expertise, ideas and potentialities for change, as well as resistances and deep-rooted assumptions. A real transformation process, as Junginger and Sangiorgi mention in their case study, rely on a joint reflective process that helps unveil unnoticed fundamental assumptions about 'what' the service and the organisation are. As an example Junginger and Sangiorgi describe a design inquiry in a secondary school that led to uncovering how staff and students' perception of what 'participation' meant to them (from being active in a classroom to become co-designers of the education service) could represent a barrier to the application of radically new teaching and learning modes.

At the same time any transformation, even if developed through participatory approaches, always requires a process of adoption by users that can be innovative in itself. Designers can decide to take advantage of this process of adoption as part of the transformation they are aiming at. The research projects conducted in Wray village, as described by Bury and colleagues, well represent this effort to engage communities in experimenting with new technological possibilities and to 'co-realise' (Hartswood et al. 2002) activities and services that are relevant to the community. This reflects the recent practice in IT systems design (that is also extremely relevant for design for services) to identify user requirements in the context of, and through, use: 'through processes such as "learning by doing" and "learning by interacting", users are able to experiment, share and appropriate innovations of others, mobilising their collective resources to evolve systems, to continue "design-in-use"' (Hartswood et al. 2001: 13). Wray community, by being exposed to new technological potentials, has generated collaborative solutions such as the computer club, the movie club or content and activities for the public displays that have led to the emergence of new community rules and roles.

Moreover, when ideas for new services are highly novel and dependent on people's participation and motivation, design needs to find ways to let people experiment in advance possible future experiences, while testing out their feasibility. Pilot projects, prototypes and living labs (as applied in the case studies) all work as experimenting tools. They enable new behaviours and system configurations to gradually emerge, based on a reciprocal learning process.

Prototypes and living labs try to create, as Winhall suggests, the right thing 'that will crack open a different space in the system' in order to suggest and experiment with a paradigm shift. Winhall describes how, through service prototypes, they have been able to better understand what the service was for and what it meant to people as well as reducing resistances to change, by allowing people to try it out in a 'safe' environment. As collaborative solutions require deep changes in current behaviours and relationship modes, it is fundamental for service designers to explore and create the right conditions to support and motivate new forms of interactions.

Penin and Tonkinwise (2009) suggest ways in which designers should apply and engage themselves in dramaturgical processes and improvisations to explore the 'plausibility' and 'ethicality' of service interactions. In the case studies gathered in this area, designers and researchers constantly probe service situations with new technologies or possibilities to iteratively co-create practices that, while fitting in and making sense to the current activities, generate plausible transformations.

Finally when transformations require organisational change, pilot projects represent 'seeds for change' (Junginger and Sangiorgi 2009): they 'provide insights into new modes to look and work on problems (design thinking), can materialise and share knowledge gained through the joint-reflective process and generate a vision that can guide transformative interventions' (Junginger and Sangiorgi 2009: 7). In this sense 'pilot projects' represent exemplar change projects that can be scaled up, involving wider parts of the organisation provoking deeper cultural transformations.

New Service Configurations

Michael Harris and David Albury in their discussion paper *The Innovative Imperative* (2009) suggest looking beyond the traditional service providers to find new innovation actors. As they phrase it 'the most radical innovations in public services are likely to be developed outside of existing services, rather than within them' (Harris and Albury 2009: 23). Innovation often involves the capacity to reconnect existing and distributed resources in different ways, the role of designers is therefore to identify, connect and motivate different actors to co-create innovative solutions, but also to contribute to find a better working model for them to collaborate in a sustainable way.

Service environments are acknowledged to be highly fluid as an increasing number of innovations come from the reformulation of the so-called value network and business model (Tekes 2007). The 'Circle' project, described by Winhall, brings together a London Borough Council and a media company; in a similar way the projects developed by Politecnico di Milano saw a collaboration among city councils, local citizens groups, academia and Telecom Italia Lab. In these potential new service configurations designers generate the vision, through visualisations and prototypes, that 'build the case' for the partners to collaborate.

The practice of imagining and facilitating convergence among diverse actors is mirrored by the growing literature on business networks. This field of studies is investigating a recent transformation of business management toward a 'network paradigm' as companies increasingly cooperate beyond dyadic relationships creating interorganisational networks (Achrol 1997). A useful way to look at different network models is from the value creation and knowledge exchange perspective. Möller and Rajala (2007) interpret services, citing Parolini's work (1999), as the result of value creating activities delivered by different actors, with a different set of resources and competences. They argue that when new business nets emerge around new opportunities the level of determination of the system and the level of knowledge exchange among potential collaborators are low. The dominant activities in this phase are 'sense making of the emerging opportunities' as well as 'co-creation of knowledge through exploration'. They look at agenda setting as a way to gradually reduce this uncertainty and ambiguity. Design for services therefore seems to take the role of supporting, through field studies, strategic conversations, idea generation, visualisations and prototyping, this sense-making process of potential partners as they frame and interpret the opportunities for radically new service solutions.

Within this sense-making process, the development of a novel business model, or 'net business model', is a fundamental step forward. In highly collaborative solutions, business models need to adopt a net perspective and not focus on individual organisations (Palo 2009). To define a net business model it is necessary to define the product/service, the actors and their roles, and the value-creating exchanges among the actors (Komulainen et al. 2006). When the value creation is not profit-oriented, the system configurations are not immediate and need novel agreements that protect the social value implicit in the solution. Participle engaged, for example, an expert in social enterprise[1] in the design team in order to define the right model to host the new hybrid kind of collaborative solution they were suggesting. Designers can guide and facilitate the generation of these new forms of governance.

New Media as Enabling Platforms

Distributed and collaborative solutions are strictly interlinked with the technological platforms that enable them. Digital technologies have, as Murray recalls, 'provided the infrastructure – or more accurately – the inter-structure – that has transformed the relations of consumers to markets and of citizens among themselves' (Murray 2009: 10). As an example the Wray village reinforced its existing community dynamics, adopting the wireless mesh network into their daily life, developing new community-based solutions that rely on people collaboration and reciprocal help (see the case study on the computer club); they also enhanced storytelling and community identity by photos exchange and content generation for the public displays. The projects by Politecnico di Milano explore the potentialities of combining the capabilities of people with the opportunities offered by mobile and Web technology. The Participle project applies technology as a multiplying factor, an organiser as well as a connector, when the Circle needs to grow or reach remote relatives and resources.

Adopting digital technologies amplifies the possibilities for people to connect, contribute, collaborate, share, plan in an open and less hierarchical way. As Leadbeater suggests in his book *We Think* (2008), the use of, in particular, Web.2 technologies enables old ways of being social and organising (such as in Wray village or through the Circle support neighbour network) to be developed in radically new ways. Self-governance and participation become key constituents of these renewed social groups and a way to break through traditional approaches to public services based on 'professionals delivered solutions to people in need' (Leadbeater 2008: 146).

Bringing together these characteristics, designers can describe themselves as enablers of more radical service transformations, as the following case studies will illustrate.

1 As Leadbeater claims (2007) social enterprises are mostly established to meet needs that the state is unable to answer while providing more responsive, fair, personalised and joined up solutions. In a continuum between profit-driven businesses and voluntarism, social enterprises sit between socially responsible businesses and public services, but often rely on forms of volunteering and of collaboration with profit-driven businesses.

References

Achrol, R.S. 1997. Changes in the theory of interorganisational relations in marketing: toward a network paradigm. *Journal of the Academy of Marketing Science*, 25(1), 56–71.

Cottam, H. and Leadbeater, C. 2004. *Health. Co-creating Services*. London: Design Council.

Cox, G. 2005. *Cox Review of Creativity in Business: Building on the UK's Strengths*. London: HM Treasury.

Harris, M. and Albury, D. 2009. *The Innovation Imperative. Why Radical Innovation is Needed to Reinvent Public Services for the Recession and Beyond. Discussion Paper*. London: The Lab, Nesta.

Hartswood, M., Procter, R., Slack, R., Voß, A., Büscher, M., Rouncefield, M. and Rouchy, F. 2002. Co-realisation. Towards a principled synthesis of ethnomethodology and participatory design. *Scandinavian Journal of Information Systems*, 14(2), 9–30.

Komulainen, H., Mainela, T., Sinisalo, J., Tähtinen, J. and Ulkuniemi, P. 2006. Business model scenarios in mobile advertising. *International Journal of Internet Marketing and Advertising*, 3(3), 254–70.

Jégou, F. and Manzini, E. 2008. *Collaborative Services. Social Innovation and Design for Sustainability*. Milan: Edizioni Polidesign.

Junginger, S. and Sangiorgi, D. 2009. Service design and organizational change: bridging the gap between rigour and relevance. *Conference Proceedings of the IASDR09 Conference*, Seoul, 18–22 October.

Leadbeater, C. 2007. *The Rise of the Social Entrepreneur*. London: Demos.

Leadbeater, C. 2008. *We Think*. London: Profile Books.

Möller, K. and Rajala, A. 2007. Rise of strategic nets – new modes of value creation. *Industrial Marketing Management*, 36, 895–908.

Mulgan, G. 2007. *Ready or Not? Taking Innovation in the Public Sector Seriously. Provocation 03*. London: Nesta.

Murray, R. 2009. *Danger and Opportunity. Crisis and the New Social Economy. Provocation 09*. London: NESTA.

Palo, T. 2009. Examining business models for emerging technology-based services – a network perspective. Paper to the 25th IMP Conference Euromed Management: Euromed Management, Marseilles, 3–5 September.

Parolini, C. 1999. *The Value Net: A Tool for Competitive Strategy*. Chichester: John Wiley & Sons Ltd.

Penin, L. and Tonkinwise, C. 2009. The politics and theatre of service design. *Conference Proceedings of the IASDR09 Conference*, Seoul, 18–22 October.

Tekes 2007. *Seizing the White Space: Innovative Service Concepts in the United States. Technology Review 205/2007*. Available at www.tekes.fi/en/document/43000/innovative_service_pdf, accessed 3 January 2010.

SARA BURY, KEITH CHEVERST, JOHNATHAN ISHMAEL, KEITH MITCHELL, NICHOLAS J. P. RACE, MARK ROUNCEFIELD, PAUL SMITH AND NICK TAYLOR

CASE STUDY 10 SERVICE DESIGN, NEW MEDIA AND COMMUNITY DEVELOPMENT

This case study reports on the emergence of community network-based services and initiatives by providing a rural village with access to broadband, offering Internet access to residents in their homes and at public locations.

In this case we report on our projects in Wray – a small, relatively remote village in the north of Lancashire, UK – aiming at using and developing new media to improve or supplement people's everyday experience of community life. Since our interest is in 'community' and 'new media' we look at service design as the specification and co-construction of technologically networked social practices that deliver valuable capacities for action. We use tangible artefacts (displays, set-top boxes) as a way to elicit and observe less tangible social dynamics such as communication, identity, security and trust that can enhance or inhibit community development processes. We therefore deliberately adopt an approach to service design that is not about designing scripted and sequential interactions, but instead offers open platforms that people can inhabit to generate their own services and activities contributing to the maintenance of a network community. The projects showed how technology was incorporated into everyday work and living, rather than fundamentally changing it, generating new parallel activities and roles that replicated existing ones in the community; thus supporting a collaborative process of learning and transformation initiated by few 'experts' or 'technology literate mediators' (Godfrey and Johnson 2009). This process of co-construction shed light on relevant issues for the building of community network-based services such as the ones of identity, reliability (trust and experience) and explicitness (the tension between trust and privacy). The case study will explore these issues and reflect on the consequences for service design practice, describing two main projects carried out in the village: the Internet security project and the digital display project.

Wray Village: A Community Network

Communities, small-scale social groupings of various kinds, appear crucial to social life, and undoubtedly the word 'community' is a 'feel good' word (Bauman 2001);

however, social, economic and technological changes have altered the nature, importance and influence of 'community' (Wellman 1999), so exactly what the expectations are for a community network is open to some debate. As Sardar (1996) notes, a real community 'generates issues which arise with relations to time and space, history and contemporary circumstances, and require responsible judgement' (1995: 787). As Mynatt and colleagues (1998) suggest, the essential features of community are to do with boundaries, relationships and change, the boundaries of community are not just spatial but also relational, social, technological and institutional. A 'community' is a 'place', 'a space which is invested with understandings of behavioural appropriateness, cultural expectations, and so forth' (Harrison and Dourish 1992: 69). This incorporates some notion of 'membership', of inclusion and exclusion based on meaningful and multilayered relationships that are significant and persistent for members. Such relations become a mutual source of orientation and definition of appropriate behaviours and values. In this way the 'community' establishes expectations and responsibilities as mundane features of everyday communal life. From a service design point of view, our research interest lays in exploring Agre's (1999) comments that a design of community networks can generate positive outcomes only if they understand what they are getting into.

In 2003 a group of villagers from Wray approached Infolab at Lancaster University in order to find a solution to the lack of available Internet connectivity in the area. The result was the creation of a wireless mesh network providing the community with access to broadband, offering Internet access to residents in their homes and at public locations around the village. It operates using infrastructure made of devices hosted in villagers' homes and local communal areas, which communicate using wireless technologies. Wireless mesh networks are increasingly being deployed to provide affordable network connectivity in areas where wired deployment strategies are impossible or unreasonably expensive, for example, in rural areas. Such communities rely on these networks to bridge what is sometimes referred to as the 'digital divide', the separation between those with high-quality Internet access and those without, and they are proving to be particularly valuable to individuals, community activities and local businesses (Annison 2006).

The network in Wray is operated on a day-to-day basis by a committee of villagers and functions as a shared community resource. This gradually raised issues on control, mode and amount of broadband use, security and trust that villagers had gradually to deal with negotiating 'behavioural appropriateness' within the community. Alongside providing conventional Internet access the network facilitated a range of communal activities such as the village blog where local news is published, allowing interested parties to contribute and interact with local events. Also the creation of the network has sparked a number of communal activities related to helping villagers make full use of the resources now available to them; examples are the weekly computer club where villagers are encouraged to drop in and ask questions or volunteer time to help each other out, or the movie club, where movies selected by villagers on their daily interactions or via email are downloaded from Internet and watched in a dedicated space in Wray.

Our research project worked as a Living Lab. A Living Lab is a new and powerful research paradigm for integrating user-centred multidisciplinary research and user/community driven innovation based on real life experiments and situations (Figure 2.3.1). It positions research as part of the lives of participants, facilitating reusable experimentation to explore and evaluate new ideas and concepts within everyday life. The overall impact of this approach is the realisation of more accurate and reliable products/services that better represent usage scenarios as well as bringing science, technology and innovation closer to the individual. This developed into an iterative process that balances interventions with the design of the technological platform and devices. Our work focuses on various interfaces of communal and village life, between the community and the outside world, between individuals and families and within the community itself. It has been informed by a range of ethnographic and qualitative techniques (observation, interviews, questionnaires, focus groups and cultural and technology probes) designed to probe some of those important facets of communal life we found mostly affected by technological change. We now describe two projects with some of the findings.

Figure 2.3.1 A blog posting inviting involvement in a community fair
Source: Infolab21.

Internet Security Project

The Living Lab approach has being used to great effect within the Internet security project. Its aims are to develop an understanding of the security and trust issues that both afford and constrain people's everyday or mundane social interactions over the network. Within a 'user-provided network' there is a vastly different model of service when compared to traditional Internet service provision, offering a more pervasive experience, allowing more freedom and giving users control over their own access. Without the use of the facets which make up the Living Lab – such as people, the places and the technology which make up the community – it would be incredibly difficult to model the interactions between the users, and the effects that the varying levels of technical knowledge and expertise might have on their security related actions. The Web is a prime example of a technology that has been made at home in people's lives, in the sense that people rarely consider, or give more than a passing thought to, the technology. However, this very 'invisibility' means that issues of security and trust need, perhaps, to be made far more transparent, as people need to be aware of the vulnerabilities of the technology they routinely use and designers need to be aware of users' security concerns, not least because of the impact such issues have on people's trust, use of technology and perhaps even their very sense of community.

As part of this research, following initial focus groups, we developed and deployed a technology probe, called the Big Red Button, which allows a user to capture an image of their screen when a security concern arises, annotate and obfuscate the image, and send it to a third party for analysis. We found the submissions from the community to confirm a number of the concerns and threats that were raised in the initial focus group (e.g., evidence of phishing emails/scams). Using the overall results we can begin to identify and develop security policies and mechanisms for and in close collaboration with the Wray community, for example, security tutorials could be held in the village, and consider the introduction of intrusion detection systems to determine the existence of compromised systems. This research forms part of a continuing effort to try and understand the difficult social and cultural aspects of security. Like Dourish and Anderson (1996) we agree that the dominant model of security is overly abstract and neglects social practices. We also believe that formulations of security are relatively unpredictable products of a myriad of social and cultural encounters; and that an emphasis on use, on collective information practice and on an understanding of trust in relation to the flow of information is important. Finally, as a consequence of trying to determine why there was an initial slow uptake on the use of the Big Red Button, we learned of an interesting existing security practice already in place within the village where they exploit their own support groups in place in the form of neighbours, friends and family members. Thus through the research within the Living Lab it has been possible to witness how users deal with their security concerns within the realms of their community, finding that often users consult with the more technical members of the community when they encounter security problems, rather than seek outside help, for example.

Wray Photo Display Project

The project concerned with providing situated displays for the village is interested in how situated displays are used – with the kinds of social interactions they support or inspire. Do villagers use the displays to create new 'collaborative experiences' and bring further enjoyment, exploring, in playful and entertaining ways, new possibilities of 'community'? If so, there are a host of implications for the evolution of content, for user experience and for design. Without over-hyping the technology, we believed that public digital displays, designed with the community in mind and deployed in key social spaces, might support communities by fostering notions of community identity and shared history. To investigate this, we developed the Wray Photo Display (Figure 2.3.2) to investigate how a digital display of photographs may be able to help to support communities through reinforcement of community values and by demonstrating the activities, history and other parts of the community's tapestry. The user-generated nature of this content allowed individuals to impart their own views on community values, serving not just to strengthen the commitment of existing members, but also to advertise the benefits of community to others, including visitors and, most importantly, new residents.

While Wray may already have a strong existing community spirit and high levels of involvement, feedback and observations of the Photo Display application have shown various communal benefits, encouraging interaction between newcomers and established community members. In another case, historical photos that were once kept in private collections are now available to the public, and are now used by local schoolchildren for history research, helping to pass on the community's history to a

Figure 2.3.2 The Wray Photo Display
Source: Infolab21.

new generation. Many of the comments received seem to evoke community features such as the integration of new residents, while the popularity of historical photos strongly supports the notion of change and community history – several residents have commented that the display is a 'living history' of the village. Additionally the user-generated content added to the display offers insights into the community itself, identifying the events and pieces of history that the community sees as important. Above all, the turn to user-generated content highlights the way in which a sense of community is accomplished and achieved 'in the doing', by actively reminding a community of their history and mutual ties and obligations.

The design of the display interface and the development of contents and of the mode of engagement were gradually built up based on the villagers' mode and level of involvement and feedback. This methodology was based on technology probes (Hutchinson et al. 2003), an approach which involves the deployment of a simple prototype to inspire ideas from participants. From a very simple prototype, feedback from residents has been used to iteratively develop the display into a system which meets the community's needs. This has proved to be a particularly effective method for learning about the community and discovering local issues and needs which might not be immediately apparent.

Final Considerations

Each of the different Wray projects is concerned with technologically networked social practices that deliver valuable capacities for action; each is concerned with improving the user experience of a particular service, and each points to particular aspects of village communal life. What then begins to emerge from this work is a set of simple design recommendations for creating and sustaining such communities, based on how such communities exhibit a variety of interaction styles and rhythms; the project showed the importance of boundaries to sustain some notion of belonging or membership of the group and the strong relationship between the technology and real world activities. Another important finding has concerned exactly how technology was incorporated into everyday work and living, rather than fundamentally changing it. Our interest is in exactly how and in what ways the technology gets used and adapted – gets 'domesticated' (Silverstone and Haddon 1996) – identifying the important global properties or factors that shape general adoption and use; looking at issues of reliability (issues of trust and experience); explicitness (the tension between trust and privacy); and coordinating and reconciling information needs and resources. We suggest that these issues are important for understanding and responding to a number of issues in service design more generally.

The research team is further developing these findings into a new project: the Peer-to-Peer (P2P Next) Project. P2P Next extends the notion of a conventional media distribution network by introducing a concept of an on-demand, personalised and social network and enhancing audiovisual media distribution with social networking features to support user communities. This research will enable more research into community networks development by exploring issues related to content distribution such as strong peer authentication, recommendations and reputations.

References

Agre, P. 1999. Rethinking networks and communities in a wired society. Paper presented to the American Society for Information Science conference, Pasadena, 24–26 May.

Annison, L. 2006. *JFDI Community Broadband: Wennington*. Digital Dales Ltd, Available at: http://www.liquidzope.com/digitaldales, accessed: 25 June 2010.

Bauman, Z. 2001. *Community: Seeking Safety in an Insecure World*. London: Polity.

Dourish, P. and Anderson, K. 1996. Collective information practice: exploring privacy and security as social and cultural phenomena. *Human Computer Interaction*, 21, 319–42.

Godfrey, M. and Johnson, O. 2009. Digital circles of support: meeting the information needs of older people. *Computers in Human Behavior*, 25, 633–42.

Harrison, S, and Dourish, P. 1996. *Re-placeing Space: The Roles of Place and Space in Collaborative Systems: Proceedings of Computer Supportive Cooperative Work Conference*, 4–8 November, 67–76.

Hutchinson, H., Mackay, W., Westerlund, B., Bederson, B.B., Druin, A., Plaisant, C., Beaudouin-Lafon, M., Conversy, S., Evans, H., Hansen, H., Roussel, N., Eiderbäck, B., Lindquist, S. and Sundblad, Y. 2003. *Technology Probes: Inspiring Design for and with Families: Proceedings of the CHI 2003: New Orizons,* Fort Lauderdale, Florida: ACM, 17–24.

Mynatt, E., O'Day, V., Adler, A. and Ito, M. 1998. Network communities: something old, something new, something borrowed. *Computer Supported Cooperative Work*, 7(1–2), 123–56.

Sardar, Z. 1996. alt.civilisations.faq. Cyberspace as the darker side of the west. In *Cyberfutures. Culture and Politics on the Information Superhighway*, edited by Z. Sardar and J. R. Ravetz. London: PlutoPress: 777–94.

Silverstone, R. and Haddon, L. 1996. Design and the domestication of information and communication technologies: technical change and everyday life. In *Communication y Design: The Politics of Information and Communication Technologies*, edited by R. Silverstone and R. Mansell. Oxford: Oxford University Press, 44–74.

Wellman, B. 1999. From little boxes to loosely-bounded networks: the privatization and domestication of community. In *Sociology for the 21st Century: Continuities and Cutting Edges*, edited by J. Abu-Lughod. Chicago, IL: University of Chicago Press, 94–116.

JENNIE WINHALL

CASE STUDY 11 DESIGNING THE NEXT GENERATION OF PUBLIC SERVICES

This case study, the design of a new social enterprise providing practical help and social connections to older people in a London Borough, reflects on how the application of co-creation principles is at the basis for a systemic change of the current welfare state model.

We need a new generation of public services! Climate change, chronic disease, an ageing population – these are new problems, they are on the rise, and our existing public institutions are not designed to solve them.

The foundation of the UK's public services was created in the 1940s, when William Beveridge, economist and social reformer set out a vision for how Britain should be rebuilt after the Second World War. The 1942 Welfare Settlement made education and healthcare universally available and free at the point of use under a system of national taxation. The NHS was formed. Pensions and benefits were created through National Insurance contributions. At the time, it marked a step change in thinking and service delivery. And for a time, it worked. Britain experienced significant improvements in health outcomes, social mobility and prosperity, and the welfare state was widely copied internationally. But its time has come. Our delivery models are no longer sustainable. Demand for health and social care as the population ages is set to cripple the economy by 2050. Investing in the existing system is not enough: it's time for radical transformation.

As a society we are facing new types of problems that need solving in new ways. Better hospitals will not stem an epidemic of diabetes, nor cure the loneliness that contributes to dementia. Solutions to problems like obesity cannot be *delivered* by public institutions. You cannot give someone a healthy lifestyle. The answers depend on people *co-creating* those solutions – by changing their own behaviours: using less energy, exercising, stopping smoking, participating – and in society *interacting* in a new way. Towards the end of his life, Beveridge considered a fatal flaw in his design of the welfare state: he both missed and limited the potential power of the citizen.

In this century the role of the public sector will not be to *deliver* solutions to passive citizens. It will be to tap into people's motivations and engage and enable them to live well. We need a new generation of public services – designed not around institutions but people's everyday lives, designed to harness the power of people themselves in co-creating solutions, designed to prevent not react – and we need a new method for creating them that starts from people's own experiences and motivations. In this piece we illustrate that service design is key to that new method.

Participle (www.participle.net) is a social business, set up to develop and build new solutions to the big social issues of our time. Working in partnership with citizens, the private sector, third sector and government, Participle designs innovative, affordable services, and launches new social enterprises that can take those innovations to scale. The aim is to develop and test the principles behind a 'next generation' welfare state.

Participle has a core team of social scientists, policy analysts, entrepreneurs and designers, and brings together domain experts and other relevant professionals (psychologists, economists, etc.) to collaborate on each project. A design-led innovation process underpins the collaboration and, especially for government and commercial partners, is key to enabling transformational ideas to take shape in a creative, de-risked way. The role of service design in Participle's larger-scale projects has not been about improving the experience of existing services. Rather, it has been to provide a structure for developing new solutions: framing the opportunities in twenty-first century ways, prototyping radical change and designing sustainable service models to transform both peoples' lives and the wider system.

A Life Less Ordinary

In 2007, Participle created a partnership between a London borough council, the Department for Work and Pensions, and a leading UK-based media company to develop new solutions for an ageing population. In 2008, Circle was launched, a social enterprise that enables older residents to extend their 'third age', with the intention to scale the service nationally.

Design research in the borough with participants from age 57 to 92 and their families uncovered a range of opportunities (Figure 2.3.3). Taking 'younger old' participants to interview the 'older old' helped participants reflect on how they wanted their own later life to be. This, combined with an investigation of the current ageing economy, led to some broad insights:

- Some people are skipping their 'third age' – of leisure and fulfilment – and slipping straight into a fourth age of dependency, often after early retirement. They had little sense of a more fulfilling later life than their own parents had had;

- Older people's needs are episodic, and their desires – like ours – spontaneous. They want the same social lives we do. And yet social care is inflexible and impersonal, increasingly rationed to 'personal care'. There is little help with the small practical tasks and connections that affect people's ability to maintain a social life, yet those people with good networks of neighbours, friends and family are less dependent on state support further down the line.

There is a resource crisis as the population ages. Councils cut spending. Carers are few and poorly valued, volunteering is down, families are living further away from older relatives. On the other hand, older people want to contribute. Their families, guilty about living further away, are looking for opportunities to support their parents from a distance. Although many struggle on an insufficient state pension, 80 per cent of the UK's wealth is actually in the hands of older people.

The question for the project team was how to frame the opportunity in a new way and unlock these resources? What could be designed that would enable older people to proactively 'consume' a fulfilling third age for themselves? That would inspire demand, stimulate supply and change the system? That would combine the resources of state, families, neighbours, commerce – and older people themselves?

Co-design sessions with groups of older people and families led to the outline of a new proposition (Figure 2.3.4). Circle is a membership organisation for the third age, designed to support its members to stay on top of practical tasks, be socially connected and live life with purpose. By creating practical help and social connections at a hyperlocal level – in 'Circles' of a few blocks – it combines the functions of a concierge service, cooperative and social club. For a membership fee, members can access practical help with gardening, DIY, paperwork, shopping and technology on demand from a choice of non-professional neighbourhood helpers, all with different skills but living nearby. For more professional tasks, a peer-to-peer system recommends tradesmen vetted by other Circle members. Being part of a bigger 'Borough' Circle creates buying power to negotiate deals on services or local activities. Older people's social connections naturally decrease, but Circle's knowledge of the local membership

Figure 2.3.3 Working with older borough residents to uncover insights
Source: Participle.

Figure 2.3.4 Co-design sessions with participants to shape the new service
Source: Participle.

provides the intelligence to connect people socially by matching interests like swimming or routines like shopping. Similarly, opportunities for older people – and neighbours – to contribute by teaching, organising and sharing skills, open up with these connections. Families can 'gift' services, and keep track of their parent's well-being. Eventually, families might contribute time to their local Circle, allowing an older relative living elsewhere to benefit.

At this stage, however, the proposition was just an outline, with many unresolved questions around the offer itself, how proactive older people might be, what mix of volunteered and paid time could work. To resolve these, the design team set up an experience prototype with a number of older people in different situations. For two months they made 'neighbourhood helpers' available on demand to participants to see what they used them for. They tried out life-coaching to find out if it helped participants overcome barriers to doing the things they wanted to. They began to connect participants socially, to share interests or skills. They flyered an area of the borough to find out if neighbours were interested in connecting with older people living on their street or being paid a small amount for a flexible job near their home.

The design team 'ran' the prototype service from Participle's studio, playing different roles required in the service, designing tools and communication materials as the need arose, and starting to formulate the design of the service itself (Figure 2.3.5). The team found that some older people were very high consumers of 'help on demand' while others fared better with regular visits. This helped shape the offer. The neighbourhood helper role developed as the team discovered activities both members and helpers got equal benefit from, for example learning to use a mobile phone or buy something on eBay, and that members were happy with a 'neighbourly' standard of help, e.g. patching up a fence, before professional skills were required. Life coaching didn't work for older people – but the team learnt that families were very keen to have someone to make sure their parent was happy and stimulated. A role for the service as local connector emerged as even within a small number of participants the potential social matches were high, with older people willing to contribute. Neighbours were excited not by formal volunteering but by the idea of re-establishing a sense of community, and doing small things for an older person on their street. This insight from the experience prototype formed the basis of the service design, and in parallel the design team ran workshops with other groups of older people and family members to develop and refine the service proposition, key messages and brand.

With the main principle established, a social entrepreneur joined the team at this stage to develop a business model that would make the service both financially and socially sustainable. Could it be self-funding? Could volunteering, contributions from members and paid help be mixed without confusion? What kind of payment model would work for all members, rich or poor? To collaborate creatively the team had to be clear about which design principles could not be compromised as different business models were proposed, and what could be adapted. The team, business and marketing strategists at the media company and borough council partners worked together over potential user scenarios, the changing landscape of social care, individual spend by older people and local delivery capacity. A business case, a service design and an invitation to invest were put to the project partners at the conclusion of the project.

Circle was launched as a social enterprise three months later with start-up capital from the borough council (Figure 2.3.6). Revenue comes from membership fees, with cross subsidisation from premium packages, payments for one-off services from families and commission from recommended vendors. Members contribute their skills and their time as ambassadors and neighbourhood helpers can choose to be paid or to gift their time to the system. Older people in the borough get new opportunities, flexible practical help and increased social connections. At the time of publication, Circle is live in two London Authorities and one rural Local Authority. The Participle and Circle team ran a short service design process to tailor the Circle offer to a rural context. Circle has a strong business case, with a threefold return on investment, breaking even in three years, with year-on-year savings after that, and a measurable increase in social impact. Ten more Circles are in the pipeline and the intention is to scale nationally.[2] The model is being hailed by the UK government and international press as an example of a new model of welfare provision. The borough council's work with Participle – especially as a council with a low income population and at the sharp end of the social care crisis – has opened up the debate on creating and financing solutions for an ageing population, and allowed government to reconceive a difficult financial position as an opportunity to innovate.

Figure 2.3.5 Prototyping the required skills for the service
Source: Participle.

Figure 2.3.6 Early Circle marketing materials
Source: Participle.

2 Visit http://www.southwarkcircle.org.uk/ for more information on the initiative.

The Role of Service Design

In this project example, the role of service design has been to provide the structure for creating a new service. Participle employs a familiar range of service design techniques, but three aspects have become of particular importance.

1: FRAMING THE OPPORTUNITY

Radical transformation requires a new starting point. Although government has recently become interested in mapping 'customer journeys', this approach tends to lead to a perspective on peoples' lives still in relation to the existing system. To build solutions in a new space we have to start beyond the parts the system currently touches. Participle works with ethnographers, psychologists, psychotherapists and film-makers to understand people's reality and tap into their dreams and latent motivations. Design thinking is opportunity-focused, and applied to systemic issues, leads to solutions framed in the new, not in the old. Combining the perspectives of policy analysts, economists and entrepreneurs with design thinking gives the team space to think creatively at a systemic level. As Bruce Nussbaum said of Davos in 2009:

> *a Third Way was being framed in dozens of little sessions going on in innovation and design at Davos. They were framing problems and solutions in much more 21st-century ways. These conversations used social media, open sourcing and design thinking to promote new ways of thinking about old problems – and new solutions as well.*

Framing the bigger opportunity at the outset means that solutions are more likely to be transformational rather than incremental.

2: PROTOTYPING A NEW EXPERIENCE

The real skill of service designers is to take an opportunity and a vision – and make something real that people can interact with. The skill is to decide what tangible 'thing' can be created that will crack open a different space in the system, that will enable people to behave in a different way, that will demonstrate a paradigm shift, that will get systems and resources operating differently and that will also provide real and immediate benefit to people. Staging the potential experience of using/participating in a new service before it is fully designed has become invaluable for a number of reasons:

- Working out *what* the service is for: experience prototypes are exploratory. They uncover the role a service can play in someone's life as they use it in unexpected ways and shape it to best serve them. By just creating something quickly and trying it out with people, we can tap into latent needs that don't come out in research. This helps us to establish value we didn't anticipate.

- Working out *who* the service is for: in experience prototyping it becomes much clearer which people are responding in which way, and therefore which combination of benefits, messages and approach is more appropriate. This refined segmentation becomes the basis for market analysis and helps the business development side see who the 'early adopters' are likely to be.

- Making system change seem possible: radical innovation demands behaviour changes both in the system and in participants' lives, and can appear impossible at the outset. In the past, our prototypes have tested out giving the public control, shifting the power from professionals to people, creating an open service – all things that seemed very risky to our partners. By staging experience prototypes in a 'safe' context we switch the conversation to 'how' rather than 'whether' something can work. Experience prototypes are also a good way to 'force' change in the system: by mocking up a new experience, other parts of the system have to change to accommodate it. Providers can understand the implications of a new service on the rest of the system and see the opportunities, and believe rather than doubt that something is possible to do. This is key to the process of organisational change.

- Designing from both sides: the act of prototyping an experience quickly uncovers the need for tools, rules, roles and infrastructure[3] to support that experience. In an area like social care that traditionally faces low job satisfaction, prototyping new provider roles has allowed us to establish value and to design the service from both user and provider perspectives.

- Understanding what the service means to people: running an experience prototype teaches us what people think is beneficial about the service, why they think it's different, and how they talk about it to other people. The language used in the prototype evolves naturally in dialogue with participants, as does a 'look and feel' that works, and interactions that mark out a new experience. This understanding of messages and tone is invaluable for developing the customer proposition.

- Uncovering further opportunities: as the service develops through prototyping, further possibilities are uncovered – people use it in new ways or contexts, new partnerships become apparent, new sources of revenue emerge, new value is discovered.

3: DESIGNING THE SERVICE MODEL AND THE CASE FOR INVESTMENT

In developing the model for the service, the designer's role is to hold the thread of what is beneficial to the end users and the transformational principles of the concept. We iterate and shape the service design to accommodate different business models as they are proposed, mediating between social and business value and translating that into a service design that works. It is a healthy and creative battle. These large social issues are often everyone's problem but none's direct responsibility, with no obvious 'provider' for solutions. The aim is to develop new entities – social enterprises – that can deliver or host those solutions. As service designers our challenge is to design transferable structures and components that will allow a service to grow or to be replicated nationally.

The service designer's role is also to communicate the case for investment from a visionary and emotional point of view. Service evidence – in the form of, for example, marketing materials – can encapsulate significant insight developed through the project, and communicate the vision and potential for the live service. Although

3 www.livework.co.uk.

experience prototypes do not intend to 'prove' behaviour change, they often result in small changes that provide anecdotal evidence of success, and using film that captures participants' experience of the service carries real weight. A tangible representation of the service alongside the business case is invaluable for our partners in promoting the proposition to their colleagues.

Collaborative Creativity

Designers have a significant role to play in the creation of new services and social value. Their ability to remain opportunity- rather than problem-focused, to turn innovative ideas into practical, usable realities, to see potential experiences and technologies through the eyes of the end users is invaluable – but not alone. A service design approach creates the structure for other disciplines to collaborate creatively to frame the opportunity differently, to quickly model and test out experiences that will challenge the existing system, to really design around the motivations of people on the ground, and create new, financially sustainable solutions that span public, private and individual spheres. It is this that gives service design the potential to become a core process in creating a new generation of public services.

References

Nusbaum. B. 2009. Davos versus TED. Which conference has the answers to today's crisis? Available at www.businessweek.com/innovate/NussbaumOnDesign/archives/2009/02/davos_versus_ted_which_conference_has_the_answers_to_todays_crisis.html, accessed 26 December 2010.

DANIELA SANGIORGI, JULIA GILLEN, SABINE JUNGINGER AND ROGER WHITHAM

CASE STUDY 12
A SERVICE DESIGN INQUIRY INTO LEARNING AND PERSONALISATION

This case study, a design inquiry into potentials of personalisation within a secondary school, explores requirements and resistances to deeper transformations in the education system toward establishing more participatory approaches to learning.

The UK education system and what it should become in the twenty-first century is the subject of a wide debate. It is now recognised that the person who learns (the learner) needs to be at the centre of this effort. As a result, personalisation is emerging as a key strategy to achieve these future educational goals. Human-centred design, which focuses on developing products and services around people, offers a new path to inquire into the redesign of educational practices.

This case explores the use of service design as an inquiry into the current schooling system. We are a team of three design researchers and one education expert. We report on a participatory design project with a secondary school (ages 11–16) in East Lancashire (UK) and reflect on the consequences of personalisation in educational settings. Despite the national character of our pilot study, many of our findings are relevant to educational design in general.

We begin our case study with a discussion of the challenges and efforts of redesigning education. We then introduce key concepts of organisational change theory. In the conclusion, we highlight the connections between service design practices and organisational change. We explain the links between organisational change and service design that are particularly important for education projects.

The Challenge: Redesigning Education for the Twenty-first Century

In 2004 Education Minister Charles Clarke argued that '*in this changing world we know that education has to put the learner at the centre*' (Leadbeater 2004). In 2005, the Department for Education and Skills articulated its new vision as follows:

> *to develop the skills you need for participating fully in a technology-rich society ... [you need to be] spending more time learning in groups, working with other learners, being creative, learning through challenging, game-like activities and materials ... and with clear personal goals that you help to set. (Department for Education and Skills 2005: 11)*

Yet the transformation of the UK educational system remains extremely challenging today. Among the key reasons cited is its continuing emphasis on narrowly defined targets relating to standardised assessment tests and schools' performance in league tables (Twining et al. 2006, Twining 2009). This situation – the perceived tensions between an attractive new vision for transformation and the real difficulties of a perceived 'straitjacket' of a well-established structure for schooling – seemed to us an exciting opportunity to test the potential of a service design intervention.

Initiatives such as the Building Schools for the Future Programme (BSF), the Learning Environments campaign of the Design Council or the projects developed by the Innovation Unit (see The Next Practice in Education Programme, www.innovation-unit.co.uk), have pointed to the need to radically rethink educational models. These have called for changes that do not stop with the design of buildings but instead take an 'inside-out' approach that is able 'to translate an educational vision into an actual working environment, through research, creative thinking, prototyping and iteration' (Design Council 2005: 22).

In this pilot project we built on Leadbeater's (2004) interpretation of personalisation through students' participation. Participation here is the fundamental ingredient in enabling more personalised education and can be either deep or shallow. Deep participation involves users becoming co-designers and co-producers of their educational services.

One of the key requirements in initiating personalisation of learning is to enable students to speak and reflect on their learning experiences (students' voice). The task involves the creation of a virtuous cycle of engagement–responsibility–independence–confidence–maturity and participation in the co-creation of their education (Hargreaves 2006). This requires commitment from teachers and schools to listen to students and to act upon what they hear. Dialogue has to become a regular pattern of the teacher–student interaction (Ruddock et al. 2006).

Schools and their service provision form part of the expression of the overall education system's fundamental assumptions, values, norms and behaviours. A positive cycle of dialogue and self-reflection on these topics is therefore the basis for deeper and lasting transformations of particular schools, which, together, effect changes in the overall learning system.

Service Design as an Inquiry for Organisational Change

Rousseau (1995) defines organisational transformation as a change where the organisation and its members reflect on their fundamental assumptions, redefine their values and change their behavioural norms and patterns. We argue that service design can facilitate these transformational processes by engaging schools in joint reflective processes through designing to unveil their unquestioned assumptions about what education is.

Buchanan (2004) repositions the activity of designing as an inquiry in line with John Dewey's (1938) definition of an inquiry in general. Junginger (2006) demonstrates how designers working with public service organisations (post offices, tax offices) can generate, implement and institutionalise changes within these organisations, when they follow a human-centred approach that involves people from within and from outside the organisation. In such an instance, product development – here the development of services – can turn into an inquiry into the organisation and a vehicle for organisational change (Junginger 2008).

For this project, we focused on participatory design methods to involve students in the design of their education. In addition, we examined those factors in the school that supported and/or inhibited a deep level of participation.

The Project

The pilot project was developed during three phases:

- *Phase 1* We approached the school and explored the possibility of conducting a pilot study. Following the school administration's suggestion, we set out to work with students and staff on how to make the Personal Development (PD) time more meaningful for students. Personal development time refers to a 20-minute extracurricular student activity that is organised and delivered daily by PD tutors. Among its goals is to instil Social and Emotional Aspects of Learning (SEAL). Yet some tutors struggled with delivering PD and students perceived PD as lacking meaning. PD resides outside the formal curriculum, and therefore granted us space and time for experimentation.

- *Phase 2* We worked with a teacher and her group. We developed and conducted a series of exercises and tools that enabled students to conduct their own inquiries into PD; explore their personal likes and dislikes, and express their own ideas about what could be discovered during PD time. We chose an emerging design approach.

  – *Exercise One* wondered 'What is PD like today?' We grouped students into observers and interviewers, equipped them with digital cameras and familiarised them with observation, interviewing and documentation techniques. We then sent them off to visit other PD groups within the school. Since PD sessions lasted just 20 minutes, this activity had to be performed over a period of several weeks. Importantly, the work the students did with us was interrupted by routine PD activities undertaken by the group's tutor. The students presented their findings in a poster session to their tutor, their fellow students and us (Figure 2.3.7).

Figure 2.3.7 Poster presentation
Source: ImaginationLancaster.

- *Exercise Two* asked 'What matters to us in our lives?' Students received cameras and a personal copy of a semi-structured activity booklet we titled 'Myspace' (Figure 2.3.8). In it, prompting questions encouraged students to 'talk about your life', 'share who you like and why', 'tell us what you like to do' etc. We encouraged the use of images from the Internet or magazines, hand drawings, use of personal photos, stickers, text or whatever else they saw fit. Students were free to include (almost) anything they wanted. They could ignore our questions if they wanted and could come up with their own. The students worked over a period of several weeks on their booklets. The results revealed that many students devoted significant time to their 'myspace' booklets beyond their dedicated PD time in school. In the presence of their tutor, they presented their booklets to their fellow students and to us in small group presentations.

Figure 2.3.8 Example of Myspace booklets
Source: ImaginationLancaster.

In preparation for *Exercise Three*, we collected the booklets and identified common themes (creativity, engagement, passivity, games, idols, physical activity, social belonging and status) to develop initial ideas for new PD activities. We did this with the SEAL objectives like self-awareness, managing feelings, motivation, empathy and social skills in mind (Figure 2.3.9). In the final session, we asked students to formulate examples of how they would envision and implement new PD activities around the themes.

- *Phase 3* The LU team shared these tangible outcomes with the wider school community, including the deputy head teacher and a group of PD tutors. We used these sessions to deepen our organisational insights into PD time as well as to explore their understanding of participation in relation to their daily practice. These insights fed into a final report given to the school head teacher to inform a discussion about the school's vision of its future.

Figure 2.3.9 Key themes as emerged from Myspace booklets
Source: ImaginationLancaster.

Initial Observations

With all the limitations of a small-scale pilot intervention, this project enabled our team to gain first insights into the issues of personalisation in schools. By exploring modes to engage students in the design of their education, we observed that deep participation relied on:

1. Capacity/habit to reflect on their practice. We found it especially challenging to engage students with activities that involved reflection on their own feelings and preferences towards their educational experience. Clearly a set of shared beliefs existed among the students about what their educational experience should be like, but this did not include reflection on the process itself. Students expected activities in a classroom to be highly structured, accompanied by tightly defined standards for achievement assigned to them by an authority figure. This model made open and creative processes difficult to facilitate and made our participatory approach a substantial challenge.

2. Generation and exchange of knowledge. On the other hand, through a semi-structured process, the students themselves managed to discover, explore and question the very service they are being offered. This opened new avenues for their PD tutor to learn about her students and for the students to learn from and about each other.

3. The concept of participation itself. Learning about students is recognised by staff as a means to provide more personalised education, but participation seemed still to be conceived as students being active in the lecture, participating in given activities. Many of the ideas generated by the project were instead based on student-led activities based on their personal skills and interests. Allowing students to have such a role at school requires deep changes in the way the service is organised and how the students perceive themselves, and it requires a longer process of cultural and organisational transformation.

4. Spaces and time for experimentation. Our intervention was made possible and yet at the same time constrained by the positioning of PD as what is in some minds (but not all) a marginal school activity. Had we attempted to create an intervention in a curriculum area, we would very likely have been prevented from doing so owing to the highly structured nature of the stakeholders and influences on classroom lessons. Spaces and time for experimentation and small pilots are therefore vital for change.

5. Differences in age and learning abilities. In the PD group we worked with, students ranged from 11 to 15 years. Some had been diagnosed with significant learning disabilities, others were recognised as 'gifted and talented'. In addition, some of the students struggled with difficult conditions in their homes and families.

Conclusion: What Role for Service Design?

The size of the project did not allow us to develop these insights further into a vision for the school, but allowed the team to engage some of the staff in a conversation about their educational practice. Service design has been traditionally working at the boundary of the organisations, rethinking the user experience and the interface between users and the service system. This role necessarily changes when users become co-designers and co-producers of the service itself that can imply a radical change in the service organisation model.

Service designers can provide and adapt tools to facilitate this process of transformation, by challenging current assumptions through the same process of designing. The focus therefore shifts from providing new ideas for service improvements (focus on service product) to facilitating this learning process that can support and motivate deeper transformations (focus on transformation). Traditional service design tools need to be integrated with tools that allow self and joint reflections to be adapted to the specific design context and participants; at the same time service designers need to extend the time horizon of their design interventions, including and envisioning how to start and foster organisational change in the longer term. An understanding of basic organisational change theories and existing practices can help achieve the desired outcomes.

At the same time we argue that introducing design thinking in education settings, as a subject or as an education approach within other subjects, can create a more favourable environment for participatory education models as well as for more effective learning processes. Design brings its capacity to see problems in novel ways and to generate solutions through an iterative process of inquiry and 'reflective conversation with the situation' at hand (Schön 1983). The students' abilities to reflect on their learning experience and articulate their ideas and needs, contribute not only to their capacity to participate in the shaping of their education, but it is also a foundation for the development of high meta-cognitive skills – skills fundamental to 'learn to learn' and to become an independent learner (Sims 2006, Hargreaves 2005).

References

Buchanan, R. 2004. *Design as Inquiry – The Common, Future and Current Ground of Design*. Key Address to the Design Research Society: Future Ground, Melbourne, Australia, 17–21 November.

Department for Education and Skills 2005. *Harnessing Technology: Transforming Learning and Children's Services*, DfES publications. Available at http://publications.dcsf.gov.uk/, accessed 10 April 2009.

Design Council 2005. *Learning Environments. Campaign Prospectus. From the Inside Looking Out*. London: Design Council.

Dewey, J. 1900. *The School and Society*. Chicago, IL: University of Chicago Press (Reprinted in *John Dewey, The Middle Works*, Jo Ann Boydston ed., Southern Illinois University Press, 1976, 1, 1–110).

Hargreaves, D.H. 2005. *Personalising Learning – 3. Learning to Learn and the New Technologies*. London: Specialist Schools Trust.

Hargreaves, D.H. 2006. *A New Shape for Schooling?* London: Specialist Schools and Academies Trust.

Junginger, S. 2006. Change in the making: organizational change through human-centered product development. Ph.D. dissertation, Carnegie Mellon, Pittsburgh.
Junginger, S. 2008. Product development as a vehicle for organizational change. *Design Issues*, 24(1), 26–35.
Leadbeater, C. 2004. *Learning About Personalisation: How can we put the Learner at the Heart of the Education System?* Nottingham: DfES Publications.
Rousseau, D.M. 1995. *Psychological Contracts in Organizations: Understanding Written and Unwritten Agreements.* Thousand Oaks, CA: Sage Publications.
Rudduck, J., Brown, N. and Hendy, L. 2006. *Personalised Learning and Pupil Voice.* The East Sussex Project. Nottingham: DfES Publications.
Schön, D.A. 1983. *The Reflective Practitioner.* London: Ashgate.
Sims, E. 2006. *Deep Learning – 1.* London: Specialist Schools and Academies Trust.
Twining, P. 2009. Exploring the educational potential of virtual worlds: some reflections from the SPP. *British Journal of Educational Technology*, 40(3), 496–514.
Twining, P., Broadie, R., Cook, D., Ford, K., Morris, D., Twiner, A. et al. 2006. *Educational Change and ICT: An Exploration of Priorities 2 and 3 of the DfES E-strategy in Schools and Colleges.* Coventry: Becta.

MARGHERITA PILLAN, GIORDANA FERRI AND CARLA CIPOLLA

CASE STUDY 13 MOBILE AND COLLABORATIVE. MOBILE PHONES, DIGITAL SERVICES AND SOCIOCULTURAL ACTIVATION

The case study, describing projects developed by university students within four municipalities in the suburbs of south Milan (Italy), illustrates the use of mobile phones and digital services to develop more collaborative solutions to issues related to immigration, identity and social inclusion.

Social Networks, Digital Technology and Service Design

Today it is possible to conceive a new generation of services based on the cultural and social skills and values people are endowed with and on the possibilities technology offers of connecting and enhancing these resources by creating new social networks.

Contemporary society is characterised by great social and environmental problems, as well as by a wealth of social and technological resources, which, if properly valorised, could offer effective sustainable solutions to many of the difficulties we are currently facing. Every human being is endowed with a heritage of skills, be they practical or theoretical, specialised or general; each of us possesses a historical background, an intimate relationship with one or more local areas, a network of interpersonal contacts and at least a partial knowledge of the urban, economic, normative and institutional system we are part of. Every citizen develops personal strategies over time to deal with the problems of everyday life: house, transport, education, health, work and entertainment.

By interlinking the potentials of digital technology and social networks this perspective could lead to results of particular importance for public administrations (at all levels and departments) and for the entire information and communication sector. This because it could offer high value added services to a potentially wider public.

The students' projects we are describing in this chapter explores specifically this possibility of connecting these two great resources: the capabilities of people themselves and the opportunities offered by mobile and web technology. This field of research and design will enable us to:

- strengthen the role of service design in proposing solutions based on the spirit of initiative;

- develop the social function of information and communication technology (Thackara 2005);

- stimulate new approaches for the design of services promoted by public administrations and institutional networks to involve citizens to a greater extent in resolving urban problems.

With these objectives we embarked on a course of study and research with 24 students from the Laurea Magistrale in Design, specialising in service design. They were asked to design services for everyday life making the best use of the users' individual and group capabilities and of the possibilities offered by currently available technology.

The outcome was seven projects that exemplify the potential of mobile phones as tools for social dynamisation and participation. These are locally rooted projects but their basic ideas are replicable in other contexts.

Local Context and Project Partners

In collaboration with the Culture and Integration Office of the Province of Milan, the design group operated in four municipalities in the suburbs of south Milan, collaborating with the town councils themselves and with associations operating locally. The group had technical backing from Telecom Italia Lab experts who enabled proposals, which were both innovative and feasible with current technology, to be further developed.

Research carried out in the suburban area south of Milan, that had been previously commissioned by the Culture and Integration Office, highlighted the need to upgrade towns in the area with an emphasis on enhancing human relationship networks; in the last years social networks had in fact deteriorated because of the impact of construction work – like the building of busy traffic arteries that have reduced mobility between different neighbourhoods – and because of the impact of daily commuting towards the centre of Milan on people's lifestyles. This research had underlined the underuse of public places such as libraries and sports and cultural centres, which had a potential as meeting places for the local population. Given these insights design activities were focused on the creation of collaborative services, based on a combination of activities, new forms of organisations and enabling solutions, i.e. technical solutions and artefacts that enable people to cooperate in achieving a given result in a given context.

Design Methodologies and Proposed Services

The design activities aimed to develop proposals consistent with the particular conditions of each context under examination. Every service sought to promote human relationships and enhance local organisational and physical resources, both in terms of public and private institutions and in terms of local population. Activities took place in the following stages:

1. Local context analysis through contact with the public administrations, local stakeholders and residents: work started with data collected during research carried out by the Province of Milan. This led to the identification of significant areas, institutions and local associations potentially suitable for the creation of collaborative services. Field research was then carried out through interviews with local government representatives, those responsible for relevant public bodies (such as libraries, town council offices and meeting places) and representatives of the local population. Further inquiry, observation and assessment of the design proposals were undertaken *in situ* throughout the design process (Beyer and Holtzblatt 1997, Holtzblatt et al. 2005).

2. Study and analysis of widely used ICT (Information and Communication Technology) solutions, focusing particularly on mobile phone systems: seminars were organised with researchers from Telecom Italia Lab to update knowledge of emerging technology and enable a comparative approach to service design.

3. Detailed service design following the user-centred practices of interaction design (Pillan and Sancassini 2003): projects paid significant attention to elements that might compromise the active involvement of service users, considering aspects of usability and accessibility.

4. Visualisation of design proposals: synthetic and analytical formats were used for the representation of design concepts (for example flow charts, system maps, stakeholder matrixes) to describe the processes, the actors involved and their particular motivations, information flows and ICT-based processes.

5. System evaluation. Assessment activities were created in the laboratory using Alan Cooper's personas method (1999), and *in situ* by involving potential users, to verify and optimise project proposals. Various photographic and video materials were produced to create storyboards useful in the design and communication of the service (Buxton 2007). Special attention was dedicated to interactive processes mediated by mobile phone technology, to check that there were no functional or cognitive obstacles to people's active involvement. These activities were conducted using drama techniques involving teachers and students (Cooper 1999, Benyon et al. 2005).

6. Project communication and formalisation. The initial stage of service promotion and information about access conditions was designed for each project. Representations produced during the project were optimised and backed up by explanatory, promotional film clips about the services designed and the designing process.

Seven different services were designed, each contextualised in a different local situation in the province of Milan. They have been described in a dedicated publication and three are presented below: Agorà, Cantastorie and La Maglia.

AGORÀ – A SELF-RUN INFORMATION SERVICE FOR FOREIGN COMMUNITIES PRESENT IN THE AREA

Students: Rikiya Kishida, Tommaso Lamantia, Marco Lorenzi and Federico Rivera.

The province of Milan has been subject to an important immigration flow bringing people from different cultures and divided by linguistic barriers to live in the same place. Integration policies, which intervene at a macroscopic level, cannot govern the deficit in communications that can cause social uneasiness and in some cases attitudes of closure and distrust towards the rest of the community.

The proposal is to create a mobile phone-based communication channel, working as a notice board or word of mouth, to foster interaction between newly arrived and more integrated foreign nationals and the Town Hall. Every participant is automatically assigned a user-tutor and a user-group who will be the first to receive requests. Users will be able to build ties with user-friends to obtain information more quickly and personally, contributing to the creation of a widespread network. We would expect beginner users over time to become sufficiently integrated and expert to be able, in turn, to become tutors for new arrivals.

CANTASTORIE – A SERVICE FOR THE COLLECTIVE BUILDING OF LOCAL IDENTITY

Students: Stefano Barlocco, Nicola D'Angelo and Vincenzo Fancinelli.

This service addresses the issue of rebuilding local identity in consolidated communities. As time passes communities lose their ability to hand down the history of their inhabitants to future generations and the folk memories at their roots gradually fade. With the economic development of the 1970s the town of Opera, like other communities in the Milanese suburbs, expanded rapidly risking the loss of its historical identity.

The Cantastorie, or storyteller, uses the dynamic, multifunctional nature of mobile phones to transform the town into a sort of hypertext where stories, information and opinions can be up- and downloaded. The service is based on Semacode technology, which is able to create codes that dedicated software can render legible to the mobile phone camera. These codes, printed on adhesive paper and placed in a physical place, are the visible element of the service and its point of access. Users can therefore access information on site, download other information, or place new identification codes for as yet unmarked places.

The project aims to create a diffused local museum whereby the town will be able to pass on its history through the eyes and experience of the people who tell it.

LA MAGLIA – A SERVICE FOR IMMEDIATE COMMUNICATION BETWEEN INTEREST COMMUNITIES

Students: Paola Paleari, Serena Pollastri and Valentina Rivieccio.

As for much of the Milanese hinterland, the urban network in San Giuliano is fragmented and its inhabitants live in the town as separate neighbourhoods rather than as a whole. The perception of physical space reflects that of relational space: the possibility of meeting is decreasing and communication between people is breaking down. This is particularly true in the lives of adult women who often find they are left with only unpredictable snatches of time for social relations, which they are often unable to exploit effectively.

The Maglia, or the Link, is a service that enables each user to see where other users are on a town map, in real time, and exchange instant text messages enabling unplanned meetings among those in the same area, at the same time to turn odd spare moments in a woman's day into quality time to share with other women.

The service was developed for the users of Centro Donna in San Giuliano. The proposal addresses a group of women who already form a network; the added value is to make the network more fluid and adaptable to their rhythms and needs.

Figure 2.3.10 La Maglia toolkit
Source: Politecnico di Milano.

Figure 2.3.11 Maglia service prototype
Source: Politecnico di Milano.

ICT AND COLLABORATIVE SERVICE DESIGN

In our projects the involvement of users as active and cooperative actors is a key factor of the system. This must lead to a full understanding of user experience, far beyond mere usability, including motivation factors, personal constraints, cognitive aspects and inclusion strategies. Since the designed services were based on remote communication, mainly through mobile phone technology, a targeted analysis of user-specific requirements, from the technological point of view, was also required in order to handle access and affordance aspects in the widest sense. The designed services were quite heterogeneous and mobile phone technology was employed with a wide variety of approaches. In most cases, the evaluation activities were performed adapting usability tests employed in system and service user-centred design, to the specific contexts (Pillan and Sancassini 2003, Benion et al. 2005).

The adopted design approach was very effective in guiding the transition from concept design to detailed system design phases. In the design of non-tangible artefacts such as digital technology-based interactive services, students tend to concentrate only on the concept design phase and underestimate the complexity of designing interactive systems.

COLLABORATIVE AND RELATIONAL QUALITIES

The mobile phone services described here are characterised by a collaborative approach, that is participants co-produce a common recognised benefit, answering together problems posed by their everyday life. At the same time, in order to function, they depend on interpersonal relations. Considering these characteristics, this specific service model has been defined as a collaborative and relational service (Jégou and Manzini 2008, Cipolla and Manzini 2009).

Today it is common that a service is designed considering users only in terms of their problems (problems to be solved requiring minimum participation on their part). However, the mobile phone services listed above start with what the participants know, are able to, and want to do. They require active participation and personal engagement to work. They promote conviviality (Illich 1973) intended as the 'autonomous and creative intercourse among persons, and the intercourse of persons with their environment [...] individual freedom realized in personal interdependence' (1973: 11).

For these reasons, in our view, the collaborative and relational service model – exemplified in the services at Agorà, Cantastorie e La Maglia – could promote significant steps towards sustainability. In their diversity these cases increase qualities, such as the quality of physical and social environment (with the rediscovery of commons), the quality of capability (with the rediscovery of individual and collaborative know-how); and the quality of relating (with the rediscover of the joy and the possibilities of being together) (Manzini 2008).

Regarding the crisis in welfare, these services are able to offer solutions, if adequately based on new policies and criteria for the development of public services. Moreover 'activation' has become a key word in European Union programmes on social issues (Barbier 2005).

Conclusions

The individual resources of human beings, in terms of knowledge, practical and manual skills, free time and the willingness to relate and embark on interpersonal exchanges, offer the possibility of designing services that can contribute to improving quality of life and upgrading urban life.

Remote communication technology, especially mobile phone technology, which is widely used throughout the population, is able to support the creation of these services and make solutions based on distance interaction between people in urban environments sustainable. If once the social fabric of small urban centres was maintained by the limited size of the town centre and by the presence of places and habits that facilitated socialisation, today ICT can contribute to rebuilding and upgrading opportunities for interpersonal relations.

Although the main driver of collaborative services is people's active involvement, service design has a fundamental role in proposing new models of aggregation, collaboration and participation. Furthermore, service design also operates by proposing enabling solutions that add quality to collaborative forms and it designs technological solutions that must lie within the reach of all who benefit from the service. User-centred service design methodologies, inspired by those of interaction design, are essential to the creation of services that meet human needs and do not hinder collaboration.

References

Barbier, J.C. 2005. Citizenship and the activation of social protection: a comparative approach. In *The New Face Of Welfare. Social Policy, Marginalization and Citizenship*, edited by Jørgen Goul Andersen et al. COST A13 Book Series, Bristol: Policy Press, 113–34.

Benyon, D., Turner, B. and Turner, P. 2005. *Designing Interactive Systems*. Harlow: Pearson Education Limited.

Beyer, H. and Holtzblatt, K. 1997. *Contextual Design*. San Francisco, CA: Morgan Kaufmann Publishers, Elsevier Inc.

Buxton, B. 2007. *Sketching User Experience*. San Francisco, CA: Morgan Kaufmann Publishers, Elsevier Inc.

Cipolla, C. and Manzini, E. 2009. Relational services. *Knowledge, Technology & Policy*, 22, 45–50.

Cooper, A. 1999. *Il disagio tecnologico* [The inmates are running the asylum]. Milan: APOGEO.

Cottam, H. and Leadbeater 2004. *Open Welfare: Designs on the Public Good*. London: Design Council.

Holtzblatt, K., Burns Wendell, J. and Wood, S. 2005. *Rapid Contextual Design*. San Francisco, CA: Morgan Kaufmann Publishers, Elsevier Inc.

Illich, I. 1973. *Tools for Conviviality*. New York: Harper and Row.

Jégou, F. and Manzini, E. 2008. *Collaborative Services. Social Innovation and Design for Sustainability*. Milan: Edizioni Polidesign.

Manzini, E. 2008. New design knowledge. *Design Studies*, 30(1), 4–12.

Manzini, E. Pillan, M., Buganza and T. Ferri, G. 2008. Mobili e collaborativi. Telefoni mobili, servizi digitali e dinamizzazione socioculturale. *Quaderni di Design dei Servizi*, 2, Milan: Edizioni Polidesign.

Pillan, M. and Sancassani, S. 2003. *Costruire servizi digitali.* Milan: APOGEO.
Thackara, J. 2005. *In the Bubble. Designing in a Complex World.* Cambridge, MA: MIT Press.

2.4
Imagining Future Directions for Service Systems

This area explores the convergence between strategic design and design for services as a way to imagine, in the form of scenarios, new directions for the development of a system or a region. The contributors to this area all have a strong background in strategic design that influences the way they work with services.

In this area design for services contributes with specific tools and competences to larger projects of strategic design that aim at introducing major changes in local patterns, behaviours and systems. The case studies presented here discuss future scenarios rather than specific services, but apply design for services methods and approaches to make these scenarios come into reality.

Strategic design is about the process of defining, with and for social and market organisations, a system of rules, beliefs, values and tools to deal with the ever-changing external environment in order to be able to evolve (and so to survive successfully), maintaining and developing one's own identity, while influencing and changing the external environment itself (Meroni 2008, Zurlo 2010). Scenarios are essential tools of strategic design and work as activators of *strategic dialogues* among different players of a project, whilst exploring potentialities for *social* and *technological innovation*. They are the way a strategic designer transforms visions into plausible hypotheses, sharable visions that translate information and intuitions into perceivable knowledge (Van der Heijden 1996).

Services become part of these scenarios as exemplification of systemic changes at the level of everyday experiences; they help materialise big shifts into tangible lifestyles and business opportunities and, at the same time, easily incorporate new modes of producing and consuming that better answer current societal challenges. The case studies of this area illustrate concrete examples of the potentialities of this convergence:

- Moy and Ryan (Melbourne University) describe how they introduced a strategic perspective into the design of food-service scenarios for Melbourne (Australia); by visualising and sharing possible trajectories for the development of a more sustainable Melbourne, they aimed to influence the expectations for the future (and therefore the behaviours) of both producers and consumers;

- Jégou (Strategic Design Scenarios) reports on a collaborative design process to imagine, with the local government and the community, possible futures for the Cité du Design at Saint-Etienne;

- Meroni (Politecnico di Milano) and Sangiorgi (Lancaster University) use service ideas to support Q-free, a Norwegian company working in the intelligent transport system sector, to imagine business opportunities for the Italian market;

- Meroni et al. (Politecnico di Milano) describe how service design tools have been used to activate social and economic resources of a peri-urban area of Milan (Italy) to support its development and preservation.

These four case studies apply scenario building methods to the design of future services. Key characteristics of this approach are the generation of stories (scenarios) as a way to facilitate convergence of opinions and interests, and the creation and training of skills and competencies (instead of correcting weaknesses) as a way to promote collective well-being. These design projects therefore combine the need to open up alternative futures with the overall aim to facilitate transformational processes (Burns et al. 2006) on a wide territorial scale. As a consequence, the unit of analysis and intervention is no longer the individual but the community, bringing to the fore the concept of *community-centred design* (as opposed or complementary to user-centred design).

We will briefly introduce the key characteristics of the design approach as they relate to the four case studies, to then explore the concept of *community-centred design.*

Generating Scenarios as Stories

Scenarios are stories and narratives that, according to Ogilvy (2002), are based on a 'relational worldview', meaning a worldview that shifts focus from things and materials to relationships and structures. In this sense imagining services help to conceive and build up the structure and relationships that make up a scenario, while redefining the roles, values and capabilities of the different actors. Moy and Ryan, in the VEIL project for Melbourne 2032, use stories and glimpses[1] to shape producers and consumers' expectations for the future; in so doing they produce new worldviews where people, engaging in new service activities, can adopt new roles, values and capabilities and move toward more sustainable lifestyles and economies.

As underlined by several authors (Landry 2000, Manzini et al. 2004, Kahn et al. 2009) scenario building is a key method in engaging multiple and diverse stakeholders and winning over their commitment; this is particularly critical for regional interventions, where the relationship with and support by the public administration is crucial. By systematically engaging the social parties through scenario building activities, governments can buy in and commit to the new visions while sustaining social creativity and innovation.

Creating Convergence

The key objective and strategy of scenario building is to generate convergence among several players over a vision for the future; moreover it is a crucial practice in service co-design processes. Using the words of Kees Van der Heijden (1996), 'scenarios are the

1 A specific solution idea which investigates system changes at a local level.

best available language for the strategic conversation, allowing both differentiation in views, and bringing people together towards a shared understanding of the situation, making decisions' (1996: ix). Here we consider in particular the 'Design-orienting Scenarios' (DOS) methodology (Manzini and Jégou 2000): DOS are a series of motivated and illustrated visions for the future that are displayed through specific solutions, representing the diverse perspectives that the scenario-builder has shared with potential scenario-users.

Services are, in this way, the 'concrete' illustrations and manifestations of the scenarios and the results of a strategic conversation among a diverse set of players. Meroni, Trapani and Simeone adopted a service perspective in a scenario-building exercise to imagine the development of the Agricultural Park in the south of Milan (Italy). The first step of the project was the identification of the existing resources and strengths of the region that needed to be connected and enhanced to bring about the preservation and sustainable development of the park as an agricultural area. In order to achieve this, they then co-designed with the main stakeholders the overall scenario and the specific service solutions that could orient this evolution.

This co-design process has a double benefit: besides the possibility to converge different stakeholders toward the same vision for the future, the design participants can inspire each other in helping social innovation to spread. Mutual inspiration, emulation and support are, in a point of fact, the most effective way for social innovation to diffuse in the current economy (Murray et al. 2008). Rather than scaling up, connecting similar initiatives helps their ideas to become 'contagious' (Gladwell 2002) and their activities to get stronger, as they develop common services and platforms that generate synergy and mutual support.

Supporting Design Thinking

Today, and increasingly in the future, good ideas will come from both amateurs and professionals: new approaches are needed to reverse top-down design processes and shape horizontal frameworks of collaboration. Innovation here is interpreted as a social, cumulative and collaborative activity, where 'ideas flow back up the pipeline from consumers and they share them amongst themselves' (Leadbeater 2008). Today this process is possible and more accessible thanks to the diffusion of cheap and distributed communication and information technologies.

Design thinking represents an approach to idea generation and problem solving that both designers and non-designers can develop and apply: in the early 1990s Buchanan (1992) described design thinking as a capability that, to some degree, can be handled by everybody and mastered by a few experts. Today Brown (2009) underlines the collaborative nature of design thinking. In fact scenario building can bring and apply design thinking principles into collaborative projects to enhance the creativity of communities (Ogilvy 2002). In order to facilitate these collective processes of innovation, designers are developing tools able to orchestrate multiple inputs and idea generations. As an example Jégou facilitated a large collection of 'stories' though which people described their visions of new life systems and eco-behaviours for the new urban site of the *Cité du Design* at St Etienne. He used a blog tool as a way to generate a visual story collection and share it with the wider design team and community. These stories were then turned into a series of short animated video sketches[2] facilitating their dissemination to a broader audience online and through a series of events, aiming to build a collective scenario for the city. With this perspective service designers' role becomes that of a professional agent able to guide this collective process of idea generation and scenario building.

Building Capacity from Within

Enhancing and building capacities in communities and organisations to perceive problems while choosing the right strategies to act is emerging as the very essence of strategic design (Burns et al. 2006, Meroni 2008, Zurlo 2010). Social psychology teaches that the major step in prevention is to systematically build competency and skills instead of correcting weakness (Seligman and Csíkszentmihályi 2000, Seligman 2002). At a societal level, to build 'capacity' is therefore perceived as a way to facilitate collective wellbeing (Von Hippel 2005). In a design perspective, building capacity and supporting people to act in the most appropriate way is, by definition, a matter of service provision, and thus of design for services. At the same time a new service enterprise model is emerging (Parker and Heapy 2006) which is no longer centred on products or services, but on the provision of 'the support' people need to navigate a complex world and to lead their own lives as they wish. Manzini (2007) talks about 'enabling platforms' and 'enabling kits' as ways to *designerly* help people to generate their own solutions.

Today services that aim to enable new behaviours by providing competences and generating motivation, are a fast-growing field (Leadbeater 2008). Meroni and Sangiorgi adopted an enabling approach to design for services by understanding and reinforcing the positive mobility attitudes of city users; in order to reduce the use of private vehicles, service solutions were imagined to build on and reward the good will of people to make affordable, convenient and environmentally friendly mobility choices if adequately informed and supported to do so.

Community-centred Design

As anticipated at the beginning of this introduction, the cases in this area suggest the emergence of a community-centred design approach. They present scenarios where services play a fundamental role in bringing about wider sociotechnical transformations, and require the use of tools of design for services to orchestrate co-design processes.

The dimension of the community is definitely emerging (Ogilvy 2002, Jégou and Manzini 2008) as a new focus for the discipline of design. Concepts such as that of creative communities (Meroni 2007), which exemplifies how users can engage in cooperative problem solving activities, suggest a further step toward what can be defined a community-centred design approach (Meroni 2008). When the aim is to generate systemic and lasting changes, community-centred design is more helpful than a user-centred design approach; the dimension of the community is potentially the dimension of change (Ogilvy 2002), the one that can bring a system to the *tipping point* (Gladwell 2002), meaning the moment when an idea, a trend or a social

2 A video sketch is a quick visualisation (or sketch) of the service, made by using a video camera.

behaviour crosses a threshold and spreads around, not despite but due to the 'law of few' (a few people doing the majority of work to make a certain thing to happen). Having a deep understanding of how a community works, collaborating with it and systematically practising a co-designing attitude makes it possible to start, with a good chance of success, processes of strategic change. One of the reasons why the community, or the dimension of 'some', is the dimension of change, can be explained by studies in the field of social philosophy: here elective communities (defined by interest, geography, profession or other criteria) are seen as sufficiently larger than the individual to impose moral restraints that transcend the individual will, but still small enough to be recognised as representative of individual interests (Ogilvy 2002). Through communities even radical changes are legitimated and implemented by the individual. As a consequence, for a service designer, working with communities doesn't mean only co-designing and making different actors and competences collaborate; it means also being able to imagine how to diffuse or replicate, through service practices, community-based initiatives that 'prototype' innovative ways of doing. The highly motivated and visionary pioneers that usually lead these most outstanding initiatives cannot be scaled up or replicated. Having said this, the work of design for services is to understand the interactions that connect the individuals in a collective pattern, and conceptualise them into evolved service models that translate them into more approachable and accessible systems (Jégou and Manzini, 2008). Adopting the expression of Gladwell (2002), service designers therefore are those who can translate the information produced in a context of experts (pioneers or early adopters) into a comprehensible language for an early majority.

References

Brown, T. 2009. *Change by Design.* New York: HarperCollins.

Buchanan, R. 1992. Wicked problems in design thinking. *Design Issues*, 8(2), Spring, 5–21.

Burns, C., Cottam, H., Vanstone, C. and Winhall, J. 2006. *Transformation Design. RED Paper 02.* London: Design Council. Available at http://www.designcouncil.info/mt/RED/transformationdesign/TransformationDesignFinalDraft.pdf, accessed 31 January 2010.

Gladwell, M. 2002. *The Tipping Point. How Little Things can Make a Big Difference.* New York: Back Bay Books.

Jégou, F. and Manzini, E. 2008. Collaborative organisations and enabling solutions. Social innovation and design for sustainability In F. Jégou and E. Manzini, *Collaborative Service. Social Innovation and Design for Sustainability.* Milan: Edizioni Polidesign, 29–41.

Kahn, L., Ali R., Buonfino, A., Leadbeater, C. and Mulgan, G. 2009. *Breakthrough Cities: How Cities can Mobilise Creativity and Knowledge to Tackle Compelling Social Challenges.* London: British Council and the Young Foundation. Available at http://creativecities.britishcouncil.org/files/data/exploratory/Breakthrough%20cities%20report.pdf, accessed 31 January 2010.

Landry, C. 2000. *The Creative City, A Toolkit for Urban Innovators.* London: Earthscan.

Leadbeater, C. 2008. *We Think: The Power of Mass Creativity.* London: Profile Books Ltd.

Manzini, E. 2007. Design research for sustainable social innovation. In *Design Research Now*, edited by R. Michel. Basel: Birkhäuser, 233–50.

Manzini, E. and Jégou, F. 2000. *The Construction of Design-Orienting-Scenarios. Final Report. SusHouse Project*. Delft: Faculty of Technology Policy and Management, Delft University of Technology.

Manzini, E., Collina, L. and Evans, S. (eds) 2004. *Solution-oriented Partnership: How to Design Industrialised Sustainable Solutions*. Cranfield: Cranfield University.

Meroni A. (ed.) 2007. *Creative Communities: People Inventing Sustainable Ways of Living*. Milan: Edizioni POLI.design.

Meroni, A. 2008. Strategic design: where are we now? Reflection around the foundations of a recent discipline. *Strategic Design Research Journal* 1(1). São Leopoldo: Unisinos (Universidade do Vale do Rio dos Sinos). Available at http://www.unisinos.br/sdrj/, accessed 30 January 2010.

Murray, R., Mulgan, G. and Caulier-Grice, J. 2008. *How to Innovate: The Tools for Social Innovation*. Working paper. London: SIX Social Innovation Exchange.

Ogilvy, J. 2002. *Creating Better Futures: Scenario Planning As a Tool for a Better Tomorrow*. New York: Oxford University Press.

Parker, S. and Heapy, J. 2006. *The Journey to the Interface. How Public Service Design can Connect Users to Reform*. London: Demos. Available at http://www.service-design-network.org/sites/default/files/13_Parker_The%20Journey_0.pdf, accessed 31 January 2010.

Seligman, M. 2002. *Authentic Happiness*. New York: Free Press.

Seligman, M.E.P. and Csíkszentmihályi, M. 2000. Positive psychology: an introduction. *American Psychologist*, (55), 5–14. Available at http://www.ppc.sas.upenn.edu/apintro.htm, accessed 31 January 2010.

Van der Heijden K. 1996. *Scenarios: The Art of Strategic Conversation*. Chichester and New York: John Wiley & Sons.

Von Hippel, E. 2005. *Democratising Innovation*. Cambridge, MA and London: MIT Press. Available at http://web.mit.edu/ evhippel/www, accessed 23 December 2010.

Zurlo, F. 2010. Design Strategico. In various authors, *Gli spazi e le arti. Volume IV: XXI Secolo*. Roma: Enciclopedia Treccani.

DIANNE MOY AND CHRIS RYAN

CASE STUDY 14 USING SCENARIOS TO EXPLORE SYSTEM CHANGE: VEIL, LOCAL FOOD DEPOT

This case study describes how a strategic perspective into the design of food service scenarios for Melbourne city (Australia) was introduced; by visualising and sharing possible trajectories for the development of a more sustainable Melbourne, the project aimed to influence the expectations for the future (and therefore the behaviours) of both producers and consumers.

Scenarios are valuable design tools that assist designers to visualise, communicate and explore intangible design ideas. Scenarios are particularly useful for service design as they offer designers a way to prototype and communicate service opportunities and improvements that could result from design intervention. The Victorian Eco-Innovation Lab, an Australian university-based design-led project, uses scenarios to bring a sustainable world into vision, creating mechanisms that open up the space for innovative thinking and expanding the market for eco-innovation. Scenarios are used within the project to prototype, probe and communicate possible alternative sustainable futures.

Funded by the Victorian government, Victorian Eco-Innovation Lab (VEIL) brings design and architecture staff from four of Victoria's leading universities into scenario-based think tanks. The think tanks (hubs) develop scenarios based in the year 2032 (twenty-five years from the commencement of the VEIL project). The scenarios are then turned into design briefs, which are further explored through design studios for later year students in architecture, landscape architecture, industrial design, visual communications and systems, and service design. The students test and develop the scenarios, carefully considering potential actors and their motivations whilst they explore design opportunities that will potentially shape their future.

Australia (and Victoria in particular) is already experiencing the very real effects of climate change. The last decade has seen an unprecedented reduction of rainfall and an increase in high temperatures across much of Australia. Recently we have experienced heatwaves, fires unusually severe cyclones and floods, all events that have damaged critical production systems across the country, some of which will take years to recover. The need for Australia to address the effects of climate change and to rethink our current systems has never been more pressing. It is apparent that we need to develop new systems that are sustainable and resilient to the effects of climate change (Ryan 2001, 2007, 2008, 2009 and Biggs et al. 2010).

VEIL aims to reshape producer and consumer expectations of the future and identify possible trajectories of change that can lead to lifestyles and economies high in well-being and low in environmental impacts. In one of our investigations, we identified that Australia's food systems are under pressure from: the rising cost of oil, the scarcity and cost of water and the flux of unpredictable climatic events. The current linear model of agriculture with its long distribution chains, its large-scale monoculture production and poor soils along with encroaching urban development has resulted in a carbon-intensive food system.[3] Our food system is not only vulnerable, it is also becoming more expensive.

VEIL embarked on investigations to envision systems of food production, consumption and distribution within urban Melbourne (Larsen et al. 2008). A renewed interest in the re-localisation of food (niche local brands and backyard/community production) seemed to point to new possibilities and support for a more distributed system of food production. Using our scenario technique, we concluded that in 2032 a significant proportion of food production has moved back into the urban environment.

VEIL scenarios have become powerful tools that enable collaborative conversations with industry, policy makers, and the wider public audience. The creation of VEIL scenarios are approached through service design thinking; we investigate opportunities for system change by exploring new relationships (producer/consumer), behaviours (peer-to-peer, user-producer), enabling technologies (web.2, wireless) and services (collaborative entrepreneurial), all based on paradigm shift in systems organisation to a networked, distributed framework. VEIL also uses service design techniques to frame the design activity within the project; facilitating collaborative design processes, probing and identifying problem/solutions territories, and developing specific solution ideas (actors, models and motivations).

There are two different types of VEIL scenarios: meta-scenarios and glimpses. The meta-scenarios are broad-scale speculations about how a particular system has changed in 2032. VEIL's metanarratives are created through a workshop process involving designers, academic researchers, key stakeholders such as policy makers, local council officers and representatives from community and non-government agencies.[4] These participants represent clients of the future, agencies that will be delivering or supporting the public services and social innovations of the future. In our food investigations the 'New Food Solutions 2032' meta-scenario projects that 40 per cent of fresh food eaten by people in the city is sourced from within its metropolitan boundaries. Questions immediately identified a range of new system and service territories; where, how and who is growing the food, how is food distributed locally and what happens with seasonal excess?

In order to understand the design and innovation territories within the scenario we investigated potential actors and motivations that could alter the current trajectory, delivering such large-scale system change. In New Food Solutions the following actors were identified:

3 What was once valuable farming land has been lost to urban sprawl. Today's farms are now located far from the city centres. Food is 'shipped' back to the cities. Dependent upon oil-based transport systems for distribution over large distances, often using refrigerated vehicles, our food systems have become highly carbon intensive.

4 The process described in this article was joined by special guest François Jégou who led the New Food Solution stakeholder and design hub workshops.

1. concerned/active individuals;
2. community groups and organisations;
3. local government and local councils;
4. commercial business and entrepreneurs.

The meta-scenarios and trajectories then inform research into social innovations within the existing system. In a process similar to the EMUDE project (Manzini 2007, Meroni 2007) the scenarios are used as a lens to reveal innovations and initiatives currently taking place from the 'bottom up'. These initiatives are grass roots social innovations aligned to the visions and represent what might be a possible trajectory of change. The social innovations identified as a part of the New Food Solutions investigations are all located within the Melbourne metropolitan area.[5] Using local cases not only speeds up the scenario creation process but also strengthens innovation and diffusion opportunities by embedding the scenarios into a local Victorian and Australian cultural context (Figure 2.4.1).

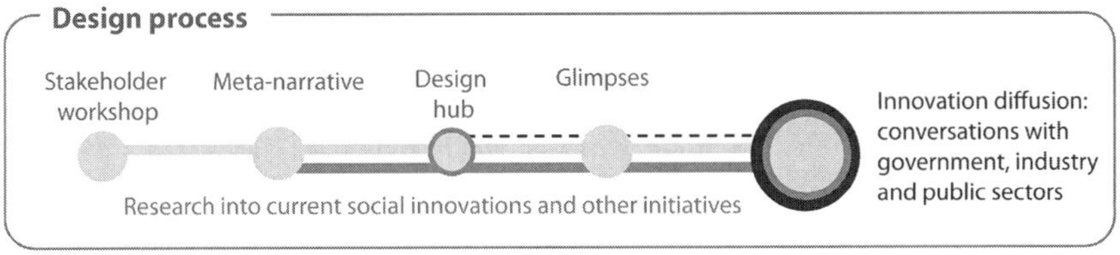

Figure 2.4.1 VEIL scenario design and research process
Source: VEIL.

Incorporating current social innovations into collaborative conversations communicates the initiatives to a broader audience and sustains the idea of a trajectory of change. In this sense design is used to add value to current initiatives, placing them into an innovation path exposed to large well-resourced networks where they may be enabled or promoted. Along with revealing bottom-up trajectories of change the scenarios allow us to have conversations with policy makers about new production and consumption arrangements, and the policy implications resulting from large-scale system change. These are important conversations as they reveal potential barriers and areas in need of further research and design rethinking.

Design explorations continue alongside the research into current innovations and produce more detailed scenarios. These scenarios are what we call 'glimpses', specific solution ideas that respond to the metanarrative. Glimpses describe future social innovations, entrepreneurial services and slices of life (everyday activities and interactions). They have become important tools and allow us to describe to

5 All cases are discussed in more detail in a briefing paper on Melbourne's urban food movements, along with the VEIL Food Map which maps the location of urban agricultural activity. Both are available from www.ecoinnovationlab.com, accessed: 30 January 2010.

stakeholders and students specific elements of a changed systems, demonstrating how the meta-scenario has been realised. Glimpses are created by viewing the meta-scenario through actors and motivations; this allows new service models to be probed and identified. In New Food Solutions this led to proposing the following glimpses:

- *Jim's Urban Food*: a franchised service model whereby a food gardener rents adjoining backyard land to create a distributed market garden;
- *Quarter Schools*: a food programme that runs in an extended schools system, where the school is distributed in 'quarters' within the suburb. Each quarter-school has a kitchen garden for students, which outgrows the available space, 'wandering' onto council land and into houses of parents of schoolchildren and teachers, propagating a food culture around the school and extending the school territory;
- *Local Food Depot*: the local provider of food services and urban food production information.

Glimpse scenarios are devised quickly and initially described using image collages and stories as communication tools. In a way these act like traditional design sketches, outlining key elements of the solutions but not locking in explicit details (Figure 2.4.2). We shall explain this methodology further through discussing the Local Food Depot glimpse.

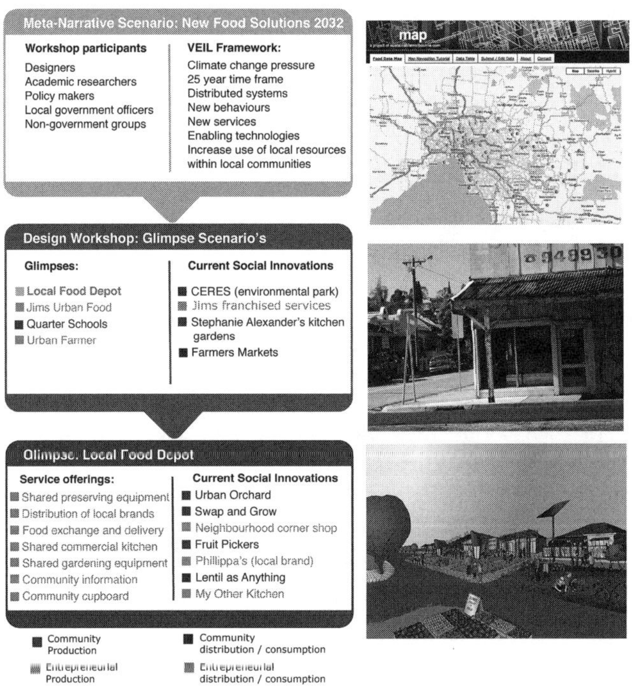

Figure 2.4.2 Design process for the Food Depot
Source: VEIL.

The Local Food Depot: Social Innovation and Entrepreneurial Business

In many ways the local food depot revitalises the role of the corner shop, a small neighbourhood shop that once serviced its immediate local urban community with daily food needs. The corner shop was an example of a localised distribution system; rather than travelling to larger supermarkets local residents could walk to the corner shop and purchase perishable goods such as bread, milk, deli goods and the daily newspaper. It was also an important part of the local community; a place where people met and where local information was exchanged. The corner shop has disappeared over the years, priced out of the market by large supermarkets, one-stop shopping centres and the escalating value of land.

The Food Depot is a way of rethinking how entities such as the corner shop might be revitalised with emerging economies of food (with increases in price due to oil and water scarcity and the introduction of carbon pricing), regaining its information exchange role to disseminate and encourage sustainable practices within local communities.

The scenarios are visions from the future (2032):

> *For years, there was a rise in food grown by individuals within their home environments. These localised activities encouraged a number of businesses to centre on local food systems. Initially these systems were focused on supporting food production (assisting residents with information, services and supplies). Backyard producers were so successful that soon residents were seeking new distribution systems for their excess produce. Initially individual growers traded surplus amongst themselves, soon local shops offered to take surplus for sale, or free to regular customers.*
>
> *The increase in backyard production and localised food cultures led to a rise of (often home-based) food production and manufacturing businesses. These businesses approached local shops to sell their produce, soon local shops and cafés became centres of local food systems – places where information and supplies could be purchased, and local food produce distributed. Some of these evolved into Local Food Depots redistributing excess supply and providing services for safe and effective food preservation. Several became 'locally branded production facilities' distributing food derived from local and regional areas.*
>
> *Local Food Depots often appeared in dense urbanised settings, connecting with urban agricultural systems and expanding to include associated services such as the collection of organic waste, the provision of shared preserving equipment, shared commercial kitchens, cultural activities such as cooking classes, sustainable education, and food risk/certification services.*

The concept of the Local Food Depot is rich in social capital, strengthening community connections. It also incorporates changes of practice with regards to food growing, distribution, consumption, water-use, composting and transport, suggesting new directions for local business as well as food and agriculture policy (Figure 2.4.3). Each of these areas are rich territories for commercial and collaborative services, and therefore service design opportunities.

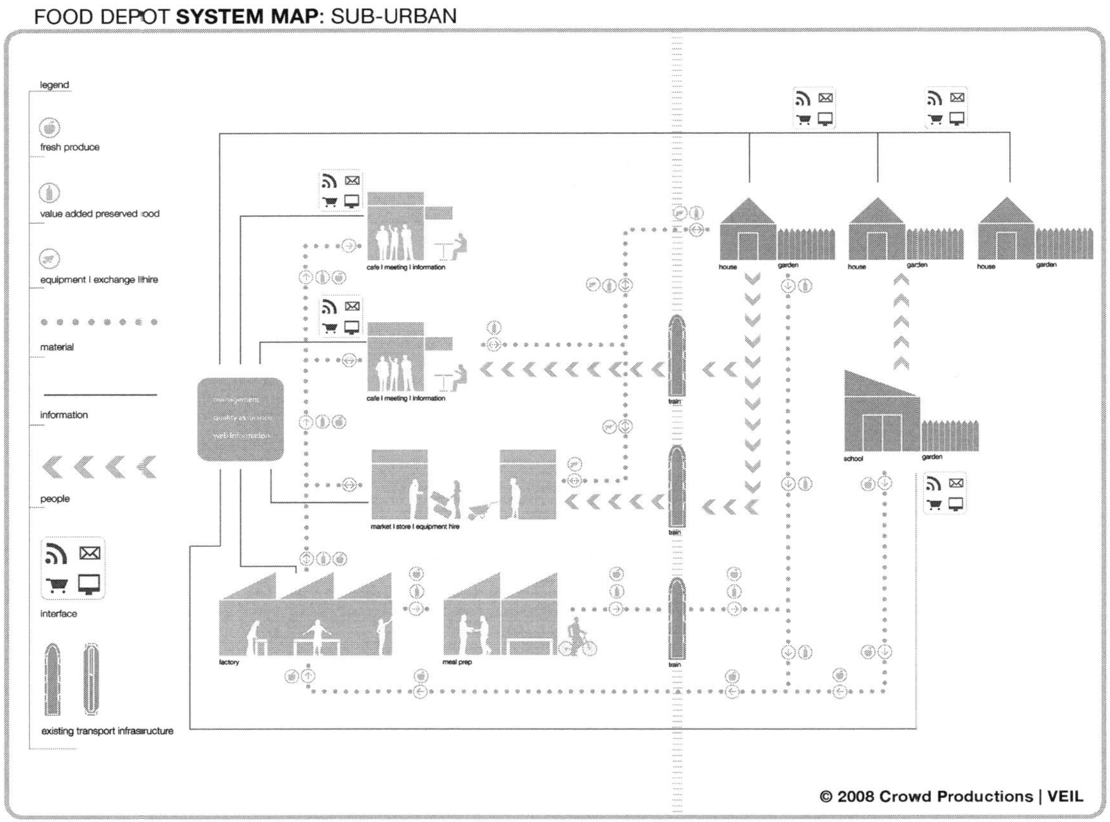

Figure 2.4.3 Local Food Depot: suburban system map
Source: VEIL.

The Food Depot has not been conventionally prototyped or piloted. Instead we have created 'prototype visualisations' (images and storyboards) that allow for the idea to be explored and tested in different locations across Melbourne. The prototype visualisations were produced in a joint investigation with Crowd Productions, a Melbourne-based interdisciplinary design studio. Responding to neighbourhood conditions the Food Depot in these visions is a flexible idea, a collection system for different localised food activities that are responsive to local resources and conditions. Possible Food Depot components include:

- shared commercial kitchen (classes, domestic, small businesses);
- hire/access of food preserving cooking equipment (e.g. solar dryers, smokers, bottling equipment, mobile kitchens);
- marketing services for community brand (packaging, labelling);
- retailing and storage of surplus (community cupboard);
- food exchange programmes;
- access to sophisticated gardening equipment;
- food delivery schemes (veggie boxes, precooked meals, for example Meals on Wheels);
- information – diffusion of best practices, information from local authorities, local community information;
- gardening supplies (e.g. seeds, seedlings, mulch, compost, worms);
- food waste services (e.g. community composting);
- community space (events, meetings, specialist groups);
- depot distributor (connection to larger food network, for example distributing goods to and from the local area);
- café;
- quality control (liaising with licensing and other authorities, for example organic certification, pest management);
- management of booking systems (IT) for depot functions.

The flexibility of the system is demonstrated in the following visualisations (Figures 2.4.4, 2.4.5, 2.4.6 and 2.4.7), presenting the Food Depot in a suburban and a denser inner-urban environment context. Both settings involve a number of different actors who may be involved in Depot activities.

Louise is visiting her Food Depot Café, her local corner store. She is a pensioner and has a grove of fruit bearing olive trees in her backyard. She has heard that the Food Depot can arrange for her crop to be cultivated and she will be reimbursed with food and utility vouchers freeing up her funds for a holiday she has been hoping to afford. The Food Depot is always a great place to catch up on the latest local developments and to meet people. It also has great coffee and a fantastic range of fresh food and delicatessen produce. Much of it is locally produced and of a very high quality. She is hoping that her suburb will be in the running to win a producer award at the Melbourne International Food Fair show this year.

Figure 2.4.4 System Story Suburban 1
Source: VEIL.

On Wednesday the Food Depot cropping crew arrive. They are some students and a teacher from the local high school. They are doing a food nutrition and technology subject and learning about distributed systems of production and sustainability logistics. Their physical involvement in the network's operation greatly enhances and speeds up their learning and provides them with valuable life skills as an added bonus. The Food Depot can offer Louise a garden maintenance package if she likes and she will receive credits for cut flowers and fruit harvested from her garden as part of the deal.

Figure 2.4.5 System Story Suburban 2
Source: VEIL.

Darrin, a part-time food transport officer working for the Food Depot network, starts his daily collection with a trip to the rooftop garden at the apartment building on the corner of Spring and Collins Street. He meets Jeff, the garden co-ordinator, who has organised the harvest for today. Rather than pick all of the fruit and vegetables at once the Food Depot network tracks and logs daily demand against optimal availability and picks, transports and processes only what is required allowing more fruit to naturally ripen and keep storage volume and times to a minimum. Many of the city rooftop gardens have sensing systems to record plant and soil health and crop maturity, information that is fed into the distribution scheduling.

Figure 2.4.6 System Story Urban 1
Source: VEIL.

It is only a short journey to the tram station as all of the Food Depot physical infrastrcture has been sited close to major public transport networks. In fact the Food Depot market and equipment hire is adjacent to the station. After dropping off his packages Darrin stops by the Food Depot equipment hire to pick up a compact automated solar powered watering system to deliver to the Food Depot supply nursery. The unit can be run as part of a cellular network for large plantings or individually for small domestic scale gardening. Darrin uses one at home for his own small balcony garden. The equipment hire has a fantastic array of food preparation and gardening equipment, much of it designed to integrate into remotely controlled networks which is an ideal way to economically manage the delicate biological systems in farming with a smaller labour force. He will come back after he rosters off tonight to check out some of the new tools.

Figure 2.4.7 System Story Urban 2
Source: VEIL.

Service Prototyping through Visualisations

The prototype visualisations have been presented in model form rather than as a completed scenario. These evocative but schematic ideas of the Food Depot can then be interpreted, or contextualised, in a number of different ways. The activities might represent the revitalisation of the neighbourhood 'corner shop' or a new extended role for a school, new services for local councils, the extension of a local café, or a community cooperative. Thinking about the Food Depot with different contextual interests, and different actors, reveals that the Depot is not necessarily a shop, a café, a coop or a school, rather the Food Depot is a portfolio of community-based initiatives that support a more diffuse and localised system of food production, distribution and consumption. It is a platform in which social innovation and local community entrepreneurial activity and services can be enabled. The shape and form that the Depot assumes is entirely dependent on the actors and activities (functions) involved. Viewers can write and create their own story, mixing and matching appropriate service elements. The lack of contextual specificity encourages people to explore the possibilities in more detail, to test the ideas and to design new service systems and solutions that relate to different, specific contexts.

Such schematic interpretations of scenarios are a way to prototype services and system change. The depictions of the Food Depot do not represent 'the future', what they represent is an idea of change. Visualising and communicating large-scale system change is often difficult as people make immediate judgements on whether they like or dislike what is projected. These schematic models are sufficiently open that they invite interrogation and require a level of engagement to interpret specific elements of change, to relate them to familiar contexts and locations. They invite co-creation and co-design by providing an alternative system framework able to open up the conceptual space for the design of future possibilities. The value of this approach is often seen in the shift of design domains evident when student classes work on such projects. Students are drawn out of their specific design domains: instead of designing buildings, architecture students explore the design of food, mobility and exchange systems in local contexts; industrial design students investigate the design of exchange systems, social enterprises or local food brands.

As a part of VEIL ongoing research and innovation activity, ideas such as the Food Depot and the corresponding student interpretations are seeded within community groups, local councils, government departments and expert groups. VEIL specifically uses the Food Depot as a tool to promote the concept of 'Food-Sensitive Urban Design', a process that integrates urban design and planning with the production, distribution, and access to healthly and sustainable food. The use of service design in the vision allows elements of the Depot (tools, actors, stages) to be recognised and considered, and pathways for implementation designed. In this context VEIL uses service design to create visions that can be easily understood, reinterpreted and used by public sectors to stimulate and drive new social innovations opportunities that lead to more sustainable lifestyles.

References

Biggs, C., Ryan C. and Wiseman J. 2010. *Distributed Systems – a design model for sustainable and resilient infrastructure*. VEIL Briefing Paper No. 3. University of Melbourne.

Larsen, K., Ryan C. and Abraham, A. 2008. *Sustainable and Secure Food Systems for Victoria*. VEIL Research Paper No. 1. University of Melbourne.
Manzini, E. 2007. A laboratory of ideas. Diffuse creativity and new ways of doing. In *Creative Communities. People Inventing New Ways of Living*, edited by A. Meroni. Milan: Edizioni Polidesign.
Meroni, A. (ed.) 2007. *Creative Communities. People Inventing New Ways of Living*. Milan: Edizioni Polidesign.
Ryan, C. 2001. EcoLab, part I: a jump toward sustainability. *Journal of Industrial Ecology*, 5(3), 9–12.
Ryan, C. 2007. *Melbourne 2032: Looking Back at the Last 25 Years*. Available at http://www.ecoinnovationlab.com/glimpses/91-melbourne-2032, accessed 30 January 2010.
Ryan, C. 2008. Climate change and eco-design part 1: the focus shifts to systems. *Journal of Industrial Ecology*, 12(2), 140–3.
Ryan, C. 2009. Climate change and eco-design part 2: exploring distributed systems. *Journal of Industrial Ecology*, 13(3), 350–53.

FRANÇOIS JÉGOU

CASE STUDY 15 DESIGNING A COLLABORATIVE PROJECTION OF THE 'CITÉ DU DESIGN'

This case study reports on a collaborative design process to imagine, with the local government and the community, possible futures for the Cité du Design in Saint-Etienne.

Saint-Etienne, a medium-sized town in the Rhones-Alpes region, plays host to the Biennale Internationale du Design, a fair that has established itself, over the last ten years, as one of the major design events in France. The city decides to follow this trend and create a permanent institution, called la Cité du Design, including research facilities, an art and design school and exhibition halls, in order to boost the local social and economical fabric in difficulties and promote Saint-Etienne as major capital of design.

This chapter presents the co-design process of a macro-service at the local, regional and international levels, aiming at defining the various modes of operation of the new Cité du Design. More specifically, we will attempt to demonstrate how a 'collective projection' process can, over a year, reveal the vocational nature of this public institution to become an activator of the sustainable development of the region.

We will discuss the mechanisms and tools of storytelling and video sketching that were used, so that all actors could converge around a shared vision about the range of services that the Cité du Design provides, and of its specific mission to put Saint-Etienne metropolitan area on the path of sustainable growth.

A Participative Approach to Build 'Life Systems'

How will la Cité du Design accommodate the various audiences it is reaching out to? How will it fit in to its surroundings in the Carnot area? How will it invigorate the local economy and encourage research in France and beyond? How will it organise its internal operations to reduce its impact on the environment, regenerate the fabric of society and accelerate Saint-Etienne's reconversion into a city that offers both high and sustainable living standards?

In early 2007, Saint-Etienne and la Cité du Design commissioned our company, Strategic Design Scenarios, to define the 'life systems' of la Cité du Design in order to encourage a debate, and find answers to these questions.

More than a 'study', the objective here was to trigger a 'social conversation' amongst all actors inside and outside la Cité: to consult, involve, and take stock of individual expectations and constraints in order to build collectively the Cité du Design service as a whole.

Very much in the limelight, la Cité du Design is use to be a popular topic of conversation among the inhabitants of Saint-Etienne. People were keen to find out how the newcomer would have settled in; the attention was further enhanced by the Biennale Internationale du Design, a major international event. How could, this hotbed of ideas, intentions and projects, vulnerable to criticism, be streamlined into a constructive process of social conversation, with a view to defining the practices, services and projects of the young institution?

The methodology we suggest uses the *participative* scenario building approach. This approach was chosen essentially because it is a classic design approach, with a view to defining a macro-service taking into account a particular context of use.

La Cité du Design is certainly a complex institution, combining multiple functionalities and user typologies. Scenario building is the most appropriate design tool to trigger social conversation in such a complex, interdependent and evolving environment. This construct cannot be elaborated by the service designers alone: they should hear all the actors involved in the project (however remotely) and interact with them in a collaborative process, where vision and consultation balance out.

We will now look at this approach in more detail.

Building a Collective Projection through Storytelling

As discussed before, high expectations surround the 'life systems' initiative. After several years of incubation and three years ahead of inauguration, la Cité du Design is becoming a project of some proportion and an event for the people of Saint-Etienne.

> *After the city's major public works, this is the other important project for Saint-Etienne in the last 5 years.*

It is on people's minds and in public declarations. There is a strong aspiration for la Cité, which people hope will:

> *Reveal Saint-Etienne to the world, create employment and economic development in the region.*

However, the town authorities are still quite vague when it comes to the kind of applications and uses la Cité will have:

> *There is a lot of talk about la Cité, but no one seems to know what it will actually be there for.*

Its features seem to distract from its purpose:

> *the library of materials, the exhibition volumes, the restaurant; the only centre in the world that can offer research, education and dissemination under one roof.*

But any attempt to describe its purpose is glossed over with generic ideas:

> *'a resource centre for communal purposes', 'a living space of interaction', 'an experimental social laboratory and a place for discovery', 'a force for change', 'a place for inspiration and creativity'.*

We introduced a storytelling approach to give shape and form to all this creative energy. Participants were asked, quite literally, to tell a story so that the diffused vision that exists within this complex system could settle and materialise into a series of small and characteristic narratives (Figure 2.4.8). These stories explain what la Cité du Design is from the point of view of a local company executive, a student in Saint-Etienne or a retired person who lives on place Carnot.

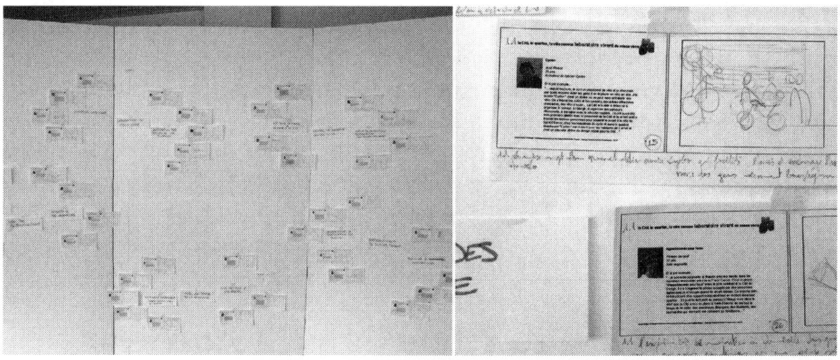

Figure 2.4.8 A collective writing process involving all actors of la Cité du Design gives form to a collective projection around five macro-themes of the institution's future
Source: François Jégou.

Of all the scenario building techniques, storytelling is probably the most appropriate means of participatory projection for a wider audience, in this case essentially it asks the subject to describe the perceived advantage of a particular product or service provided by la Cité, without having to care for how it could be provided.

Nevertheless we have, as a result of this process, achieved the first step of macro-service design by identifying some consistent elements of both a desirable vision (at least for a participating sample: 'it would be nice to do this, this would be reasonable'), and a feasible vision (formulated through realistic narrations: 'I could be a part of this, I could make the effort').

As a result of this process, a collection of more than 100 stories reflects the collective projections of the subjects in the audience.

A Co-elaboration on Several Levels Involving Internal and External Actors in an Iterative Approach

A progressive and multifaceted approach is required in order to achieve a collective projection based on a collection of intricate stories, and this does not happen overnight.

Many actors play a part in la Cité du Design: industrialists, local designers, students and professors, local inhabitants, tourists of Saint-Etienne, cultural organisations, Saint-Etienne's institutional entities.

Their involvement in the social conversation process happened on two levels. It was agreed with la Cité that a restricted group of people were selected as representing the core actors who had a role in the institution. They were chosen on the basis of availability and direct involvement to be part of a pilot committee that was consulted on a regular basis. A second and wider group was also created, more diverse and more representative of all the actors involved. This group was mainly solicited in the writing process, so that more opinions and points of view could be collected.

The actors in la Cité are numerous and diverse. The tools of dialogue used in the process of social conversation had to be flexible enough to accommodate everyone. The social conversation was also implemented online (Figure 2.4.9), so that storytelling process could be published in real-time and read by all actors as they gradually became more involved in the discussion. Saint-Etienne's School of Arts and Design took part actively in the process through creative workshops and internship with stakeholders. Remote micro-interviews and discussion groups were set up to channel the dialogue to involve remote actors in the conversation.

The dialogue process was applied in an iterative fashion, collecting and confronting stories, and progressively modifying them until the different categories of actors converged. But unlike a typical participative mediation process, the idea here is to explore most of the possibilities. If we reverse Watzlawick's metaphor, the captain who sails in heavy fog should not only find the route that is obstacle-free; he should pinpoint the obstacles so that he can picture all possible routes (Watzlawick 1988). A large range of possible roads emerges from the co-elaboration of a collective projection, reflecting the clear and compatible visions of all actors.

Figure 2.4.9 The blog progressively collecting the various stories proposed by the stakeholders involved in the social conversation around an articulated vision of the future Cité

Source: François Jégou.

A Shared Definition of a Feasible Vision

Clustering the stories, stimulating the generation of new ones and combining more loops of deductive and inductive reasoning brought us to a point where the collected stories settled to reflect a sufficiently representative and stabilised collective projection (Figure 2.4.10). The specifications for the Cité du Design macro-service were then extrapolated: from any given story, one can infer the necessary characteristics that are required to reproduce what is told and from the collective projection one can infer a briefing specification about the functionalities, the atmosphere and spirit to be given to the macro-service Cité. Five different visions potentially driving the design of the services came out of the story collection:

Figure 2.4.10 An illustrated collection of approximately 40 stories about the future of the Cité: made available online but also in a micro-booklet which was printed and circulated
Source: François Jégou.

1. Stimulating the local economy: *'La Cité as a hub, connecting industrialists, designers and citizens'*, allowing various local and international actors to network and discuss shared requirements and other issues.

2. Appealing to the people of Saint-Etienne: *'La Cité as a dynamic cultural centre'* with scheduled events on weekdays and weekends to entertain a local audience but also international visitors.

3. Part of the local fabric of society: *'La Cité, the local neighbourhood and the city itself as a laboratory for a better life'* where citizens and la Cité collaborate, experiment and build models of sustainable development together.

4. Creating an international research centre for design: *'La Cité as engine of prospective research programmes'*, creating synergies with the Biennale, the school, the in-house researchers, the conference and exhibition programmes, the network for projects on a local or global scale.

5. Exploring the full potential of la Cité: *'La Cité as a resource centre'*, including a public media library, a library of materials, conference rooms, studios and laboratories, a dynamic and creative infrastructure.

The participative approach therefore contains two complementary and iterative processes, a deductive one, based on story collection, extraction and specifications, and an inductive one which projects a number of visions and positions (Jégou et al. 2006). This approach, referred to in innovation management as design-driven, characterises la Cité as a place that can be seen as a design-driven institution that grows creatively through a permanent dialogue with its surroundings.

Enlarging Social Conversation towards Public Engagement

Parallel to the specification of the service, the collective projection through storytelling is a very supportive tool to foster public engagement. The synthetic final corpus of

40 stories has been turned into a series of short animated video sketches in order to facilitate their dissemination to a broader audience online and through a series of events. The video sketches (Figure 2.4.11) show a mixed reality, which is realistic enough to induce the projection of subject watching them, but still rough and fuzzy to be still open to further interpretation and adaptation. In the taxonomy of design visualisation tools, they belong to the sketch rather than to the rendering. They are 'open visualisations' (Jégou 2009) designed to engage in collaborative processes.

The follow-up engagement process uses the video sketches to stimulate and start implementation (Figure 2.4.12). Two examples could be given along one of the five main visions: 'La Cité, the local neighbourhood and the city itself as a laboratory for a better life' where citizens and la Cité collaborate, experiment and build models of sustainable development together.

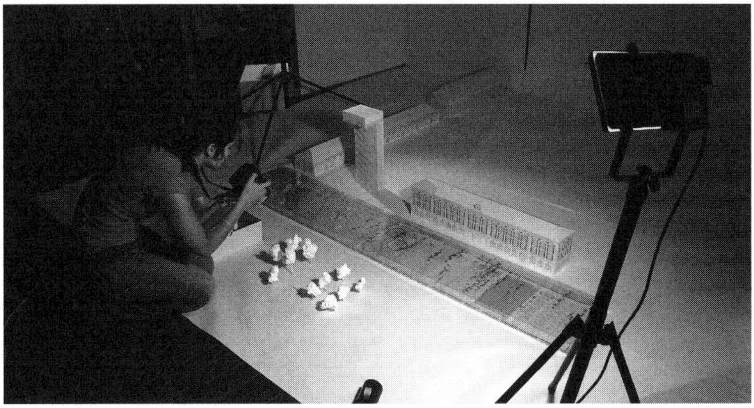

Figure 2.4.11 The making of the visualisations: pictures of realistic models enhanced with additional sketches for a more vivid and compelling result, allowing the viewer to imagine the experience of the services

Source: François Jégou.

Figure 2.4.12 Forty bits of 20-second video excerpts. Video sketches were made for sharing the visions of the Cité with a large public

Source: François Jégou.

On a local scale, La Cité's geographical location in the popular Carnot neighbourhood holds a potential challenge for the future: the prestigious institution must win over local inhabitants if it is to engage with them to face the challenges that lie ahead in the transition of Saint-Étienne to sustainable development. La Cité du Design is immersed in a very dynamic social fabric willing to overcome the difficult past decades and benefits from both top-down initiatives in line with creative cities ideas (Landry 2000) and bottom-up initiatives from vivid creative communities (Meroni 2007, Jégou and Manzini 2008) and it is linked to and enhanced by the rich associative heritage from the industrial past of the city.

The Biennale International Design 2008 built on these scenarios and ideas in all possible ways, showing both local and non-local initiative, from regional development to eco-design. The core idea – and core exhibition of the Biennale – is to promote the event as a City-Eco-Lab (Figures 2.4.13 and 2.4.14) exploring ongoing social initiatives

Figure 2.4.13 All the scenarios were on display at the Biennale Internationale Design 2008 in order to fully engage all actors ahead of the official inauguration in 2010
Source: François Jégou.

Figure 2.4.14 The Biennale 2008, and especially its core exhibition City-Eco-Lab, developed one of the service visions to show how local social innovation may inspire new and more sustainable lifestyles
Source: François Jégou.

that have the potential for a transition towards more sustainable ways of living and applying design skills to give them more visibility and strength in an international context.

On a global scale, Saint-Etienne wishes to have the particular status of the 'new capital of design' (Lacroix 2005). The city is dynamic and its commitment to innovation is widely acknowledged even though it does not enjoy the traffic and influx that major international capitals have. Therefore, the city must carefully address its involvement on both the local and the international stage through an idea of 'multi-locality' (Manzini and Jégou 2003) whereby it must be firmly rooted in the local surroundings and connected with the world from a global perspective. This issue brought about the idea of an original online presence of la Cité: beyond the classical web facilities and remote access services, a Cité Virtuelle is currently under development. This 'virtual city', playing in French with the word 'cité' meaning both the new institution and the city itself, will embody the vision of Saint-Etienne as a Cité du Design: a City of Design (promoting it) and by design (transformed by it).

The complete process reported here shows an approach to the design for services – and in particular macro-public services – with a strong level of stakeholder participation using a simple storytelling process to stimulate people creativity and engagement from the very beginning until their progressive implementations in the territory. In addition to being a powerful tool to facilitate conversation within a large arena of different players, the collectively generated stories are used for two main reasons: to shape the macro-service and reach a consensus on its specifications and to provide a useful and attractive support to promote dissemination and public engagement in the implementation of the service vision.

References

Jégou, F. 2009. Co-design approaches for early phases of augmented environments. In *Designing User Friendly Augmented Work Environments. From Meeting Rooms to Digital Collaborative Spaces*, edited by S. Lahlou. London: Springer Verlag, 159–89.

Jégou, F. and Manzini, E. 2008. *Collaborative Services: Social Innovation and Design for Sustainability*. Milan: Edizioni Polidesign.

Jégou, F., Verganti R., Marchesi, A., Simonelli, G. and D'ell Era, C. 2006. *Design-driven Toolbox: A Handbook to Support Companies in Radical Product Innovation*. Cantù: Clac.

Lacroix, M. J. 2005. *Les nouvelles villes de design*. Montréal: Infopresse.

Landry, C. 2000. *The Creative City, A Toolkit for Urban Innovators*. London: Earthscan.

Manzini, E. and Jégou, F. 2003. *Sustainable Everyday, Scenarios of Urban Life*. Milan: Edizioni Ambiente.

Meroni, A. (ed.) 2007. *Creative Communities: People Inventing Sustainable Ways of Living*. Milan: Edizioni Polidesign.

Watzlawick, P. 1988. *L'invention de la réalité*. Paris: Seuil.

ANNA MERONI AND DANIELA SANGIORGI[6]

CASE STUDY 16 ENABLING SUSTAINABLE BEHAVIOURS IN MOBILITY THROUGH SERVICE DESIGN

This case study uses service ideas to support Q-free, a Norwegian company working in the intelligent transport system sector, to imagine business opportunities for the Italian market.

This case study presents a service design project aiming to widen up the scope and business of a technology-driven company, exploring through a user-centred approach the possible service spin-offs of a complex technological system.

The project has been commissioned by the Norwegian company Q-Free, which produces an electronic toll collection technology currently used to collect tolls from motorways, parking and urban traffic. It is based on onboard units endowed with a smart card that can communicate via microwaves with antennas placed at specific points of transit. The smart card could be used also separately from the vehicle as personal card to access various kinds of services such as public transportation, touristic services or access to various facilities.

Within the framework of the so-called Intelligent Transport System (ITS) sector, the features of this system enable the introduction of a new approach to urban mobility management that opens the way to a new generation of services.

New Applications for an Intelligent Transport System Technology

A service design research team of Polidesign, Consortium of Politecnico di Milano, was requested to develop sustainable service scenarios for the introduction of the Q-free electronic toll collection technology in the Italian mobility market.

6 This project is the result of a collective work, but for the purpose of this publication Anna Meroni has written the sections 'Work methodology' and 'Scenarios and service concepts', and Daniela Sangiorgi the sections 'New applications for an intelligent transport system technology', 'The mobility issue' and 'What's new for the service design discipline'.

The project applied a solution-oriented approach (Meroni 2004) to explore alternative applications and possible developments of the technology and to facilitate new collaborations between various kinds of stakeholders that could generate radical changes in the existing mobility system.

Focusing on imagining new service solutions, the design team helped the company to identify areas of opportunity for the technology to be exploited and further developed; this suggested potential new markets in which to reposition their business. Service design supported them to move away from a simply tolling and controlling logic, detached from the mobility system and not providing alternatives to users, to a service one, where users are enabled to access different means of transportation and related services, that foster more sustainable behaviours.

In order to achieve this, electronic toll collection technology has been interpreted as a platform to integrate and improve both efficiency and personalisation of the mobility service system; our hypotheses were that more aware mobility behaviours could emerge if users could have a wider choice, access and transparency to mobility services and if they could be rewarded in case of more sustainable choices, instead of punished for biased (or incorrect) behaviours.

Service design managed to open up the scope of electronic toll collection technology, bringing in a user-centred approach that aimed at balancing the technological and social dimensions of mobility innovation. The project highlighted the necessity to work on motivations, rewards and values to stimulate relevant changes in people lifestyle and to use technology as a potential enabler of this behavioural shift (Meroni 2007).

The Mobility Issue

In the last decades people mobility has increased and become less standardised; traditional collective transportation services are unable to answer to these new patterns, while individual car-based mobility is no longer sustainable. Therefore, integrated flexible and hybrid mobility services able to give a wider choice opportunity to users while orienting toward more sustainable behaviours are today an urgent need (Dennis and Urry 2007).

Q-Free is a global supplier of solutions and products for road user charging and traffic surveillance, its applications are mainly within electronic toll collection for road charging, truck-tolling, law enforcement and parking control. In 2006 Q-Free provided an integrated transport solution for the Olympic Winter Games in Turin in collaboration with the Italian highway operator Sitaf, GTT (Turin's public transport company) and its partner Ativa: a system called Si.Pass, Europe's first integrated public and private transport system payable via one tolling method. Road users were enabled to pay automatically a queue-free toll, and also buy services such as access to public transport, parking, or ski-passes, all using the same device. It consists of two components: the OBU (on board unit) and the smart card, which combines three interfaces (contact, contactless and magnetic stripe), and is Calypso standard compliant. When the smart card is inserted into the OBU, it allows for automatic payments on motorways without having to stop. Used independently, it can provide access to other services.

The success of this pilot experience motivated Q-Free to further explore the concept of an integrated public and private transport system in the extremely varied context of the Italian market. Polidesign was then commissioned to explore innovative scenarios, where the application of the Si.Pass technology could be extended to new areas and become the mean for new mobility-related services. The scenarios could then be used to promote Q-Free electronic toll collection to municipalities and other potential stakeholders as a key element for the development of new mobility solutions.

Italy has been selected as context of research because of the peculiarities of its geo-socio conditions: historical cities, small metropolis, tourist natural territories, mountains and sea. Six *meta contexts*, that's to say typologies of emblematic urban or extra-urban settlements with recurring features, have been identified as characterising the Italian peninsula from a mobility perspective. Each of them has been investigated via a real example: the Italian metropolis, Milan; the hinterland with a trade fair site, Rho Fiera; the historic/productive town, Como; the motorway system; the skiing area, Alta Val Badia; the seaside inhabited natural park, Parco Nazionale delle 5 Terre.

Work Methodology

The research group was established at the onset with the aim of being multidisciplinary: strategic designers, service designers, mobility and managerial engineers.

To handle the complexity of mobility scenarios, the research team has worked on three main interrelated levels – context, technology and users – and have moved backwards and forwards from the analysis and design within real contexts to the visualisation and design of abstract scenarios (Figure 2.4.15).

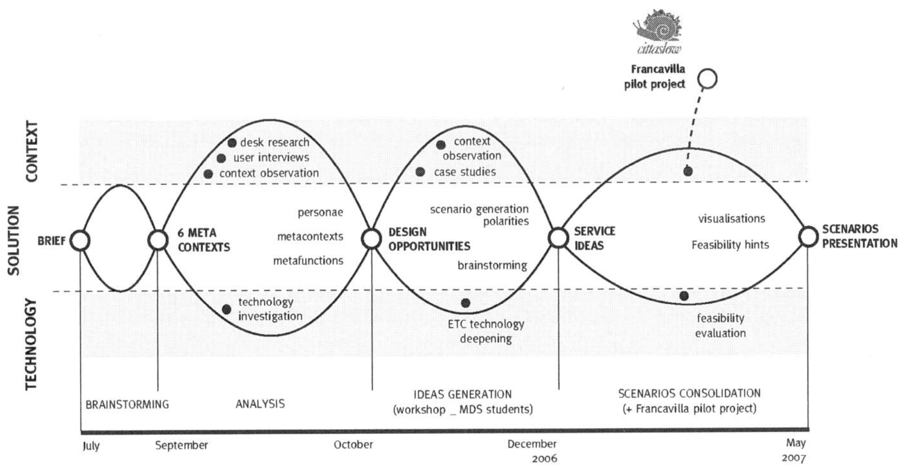

Figure 2.4.15 The design process
Source: Politecnico di Milano.

WORK PHASES
The project has been organised in four main phases of work.

1. Initial brainstorming: it generated a counter-brief (Zurlo 2004) amplifying the range of possible contexts of application. This phase ended with the definition and identification of six *metacontexts* to investigate;

2. Analysis: the design team explored the mobility contexts by direct observation, user interviews, desk research and case studies, while the engineering team investigated the potential of the technology. This knowledge was then visualised and abstracted to highlight design innovation opportunities: real contexts have been abstracted in *meta context*, real persons behaviours have been condensed into personae (typical users), technological mobility related function (paying, access, tracing and tracking) have been simplified in *meta functions* (recurring activities that constitute functional typologies);

3. Ideas generation: a creative workshop has been organised involving a group of international students of the Master in Strategic Design (MDS, by Polidesign). Fuelled by materials collected and generated in the previous phase, the workshop took a fresh look at the mobility project, creating a set of service ideas;

4. Scenarios consolidation: the services ideas have been discussed (within the research team and with the client) and refined, focusing on their main concepts. Finally, technology has been used to suggest and support specific behaviours that could favour more sustainable and practicable routines in everyday commuting. A first feasibility evaluation was then conducted that led to a pilot project study in city of Francavilla (Abruzzo).

The design process has been managed as a 'strategic conversation' (Nardone and Salvini 2004) among different actors, aiming to define service scenarios as a collective contribution. A strategic conversation, led by design and a problem-solving approach, can be defined as a process by which inputs and opinions, coming from various competences, are paraphrased (and therefore re-elaborated) and discussed until they are fully shared and agreed upon.

Scenarios and Service Concepts

As a result of the research work, Polidesign developed six scenarios (Figure 2.4.16) of possible service solutions:

- Milano: multimodal possibilities to integrate public and private transportation;

- Rho-Fiera: access to organised mobility and fair services for exhibitors;

- Como: multimodal mobility system based on the use of green vehicles to access an historic city downtown;

- Alta Val Badia: integration of skiing services integration through the electronic toll collection system and built-in additional technologies;
- Parco Nazionale delle 5 Terre: integrated harbour service system;
- Motorways: introduction of the electronic toll collection system in the motorways adopting a mobility credits model.

Figure 2.4.16 Scenarios: advertising posters synthetically presenting the six scenarios
Source: Politecnico di Milano.

All the mobility scenarios are based on four key concepts (Figures 2.4.17 and 2.4.18):

1. *The creation of an integrated mobility system supported by a mobility-credit concept.* The complexity of contemporary mobility behaviours asks for a service design approach that doesn't move from regulation and prohibitions, but from motivations, rewards and values to stimulate relevant changes in people's everyday lifestyle. Service design is in fact increasingly about designing for behaviours rather than defining rules, and can use technological platforms as significant drivers for change (Sangiorgi and Villari 2006, Manzini and Meroni 2007). The point is creating solutions that not only satisfy a function or solve a problem, but that are also desirable, aspirational, compelling and delightful (Burns et al. 2006); in order to achieve this we adopted a user-centred approach, where technology has been rethought in the light of the user experience viewpoint. The electronic toll collection (ETC) technology can therefore contribute to develop a win–win strategy where the users, being recognised and tracked by the technology, can be encouraged and awarded for the good and sustainable behaviours (such as using public transportation, sharing cars or using green vehicles). This system is enabled by the introduction of the concept of *mobility credits* (Kalmanje and Kockelman 2004, Fondazione Italiana Accenture 2006), where users can buy, spend and gain credits according to their behaviours, in a multimodal mobility scenario. This concept is transferred from the one of *local currencies*, local systems of value based

on non-market parameters but on local, real value parameters. A credit is a unit which can be used to access operations inside a given system: ETC technology enables credits to be collected and stored automatically in the smart card, which becomes the main means of activating the services and enabling a set of interlinked and sequential actions.

2. *The adoption of a positive perspective that encourages and awards more sustainable behaviours.* The project adopted, as guidance, the positive psychology approach (Csíkszentmihályi 1990, Seligman 2002, Inghilleri 2003). The main idea behind the project was therefore to design services that, instead of frustrating the user with prohibitions, would reward them with credits for their positive behaviour providing access to valuable mobility alternatives. Understanding the alternatives and being able to choose the best solution for their needs can help people to better navigate today's multimodal mobility systems. From this perspective, a mobility credits system, based on the ETC technology, could: 1) provide an orienting digital map of the system (info-mobility and advanced navigation systems), 2) help fluidise transitions between different transportation means with real time information, 3) recognise and reward sustainable behaviour and choices (Meroni et al. 2008).

3. *Use of a set of key service concepts.* These concepts result from abstracting the scenarios to identify transferable service ideas, such as: mobility credits, user profile personalisation, privileged access, multimodality in interchange nodes, shared mobility access, info-mobility, all-inclusive personalisation, pay per use, integrated mobility in a bounded space, integrated private and public transportation. Conceived as parts in a modular architecture, different combinations of the key concepts can generate different solutions;

Figure 2.4.17 Key service concepts adopted to give structure to the multimodal scenario of mobility
Source: Politecnico di Milano.

4. *Service contextualisation and personalisation.* Users, provided with a smart card that can be customised to their needs, can select the services and the mobility modes they prefer. They can activate a personalised access to different kinds of services and information systems as offered in a given context. As an example, a user can decide to maximise freedom of movement, using all the means available, from private cars, to shared vehicles and the public transport system, with the maximum of flexibility and reliability.

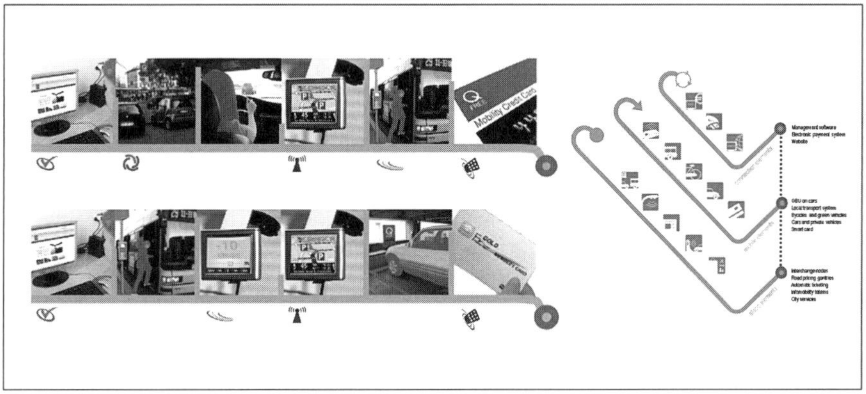

Figure 2.4.18 Two storyboards presenting the service for the context of Milan and a visualisation of the different service elements constituting the system service break down

Source: Politecnico di Milano.

What's New for the Design for Services' as a Discipline

This research project has developed a service design approach that could be transferred to similar assignments working on large and complex service systems. As a conclusion we can highlight in particular that:

1. The adoption of a service-oriented design can lead to a shift in perspective (user-centred), scale (system design) and approach (behavioural changes):

   - The project started from mobility profiles and context needs instead of technical solutions or single mobility paths, helping to move away from technical and tolling solutions toward service and enabling ones;
   - The team worked at a systemic level (multi-service) to solve highly complex issues such as mobility and sustainability;
   - The service ideas conceived to facilitate behavioural change, adopting a positive psychology perspective, and using technology as an enabler to provide a platform for change.

2. The transfer of concepts and service ideas from other fields:

   - The idea of mobility credits was developed from the one of local currency;
   - The pay per use concept was developed from the telecommunication context (pay per view).

3. The development of an overall vision with scalable solutions; the multiple possible combinations of the key service concepts within the wider scenarios can help a company to introduce a technological system to potential stakeholders, helping them to visualise service solutions for different contexts and needs.

4. The elaboration of visualisation tools to support the description of the service scenarios according to a solution-oriented partnership strategy (Manzini et al. 2004): service elements are listed and service experiences are described through story boards allowing the company to better communicate the potentialities and flexibility of their technological platform to a varied set of potential partners.

References

Burns, C., Cottam, H., Vanstone, C. and Winhall, J. 2006. *Transformation Design. RED Paper 02*. London: Design Council.

Csíkszentmihályi, M. 1990. *Flow: The Psychology of Optimal Experience*. New York: Harper and Row.

Fondazione Italiana Accenture. 2006. *Progetto crediti di mobilità, città di Genova*. Available at http://www.fondazioneaccenture.it/mobilita.html, accessed 30 January 2010.

Dennis, K. and Urry, J. 2007. *The Digital Nexus of Post-Automobility*. Lancaster: Department of Sociology, Lancaster University.

Kalmanje, S. and Kockelman, K.M. 2004. Credit-based congestion pricing: travel, land value, and welfare impacts. Paper presented to the Conference Transportation Research Board Annual Meeting, Washington, DC, 11–15 January. Available at www.ce.utexas.edu/prof/kockelman/public_html/TRB04CBCPApplic.pdf, accessed 30 January 2010.

Inghilleri, P. 2003. *La 'buona vita': Per l'uso creativo degli oggetti nella società dell'abbondanza*. Milan: Guerini e Associati.

Manzini, E., Collina, L. and Evans, S. (eds) 2004. *Solution-oriented Partnership: How to Design Industrialised Sustainable Solutions*. Cranfield: Cranfield University.

Manzini, E. and Meroni, A, 2007. Emerging user demands for sustainable solutions: EMUDE. In *Design Research Now: Essays and Selected Projects*, edited by R. Michel. Basel: Birkhäuser, 157–79.

Meroni, A., Sangiorgi, D., Simeone, G. and Villari, B. 2008. Service design to foster premium prize and sustainable mobility in urban contexts. Paper presented to the conference Changing the Change. Visions, Proposals and Tools, Turin, 10–12 July 2008. Available at http://www.allemandi.com/cp/ctc/, accessed 30 January 2010.

Meroni, A. (ed). 2007. *Creative Communities. People Inventing Sustainable Ways of Living*. Milan: Edizioni Polidesign.

Meroni, A. 2004. Solution-oriented partnership methodology. In *Solution-Oriented Partnership: How to Design Industrialised Sustainable Solutions,* edited by E. Manzini, L. Collina and S. Evan. Cranfield: Cranfield University, 87–96.
Nardone, G. and Salvini, A. 2004. *Il dialogo strategico.* Milan: Ponte alle Grazie.
Sangiorgi, D. and Villari, B. 2006. Community-based services for elderly people. Designing platforms for action and socialisation. Paper presented to the International Congress on Gerontology: Live Forever, Lisbon, 23–25 October.
Seligman, M. 2002. *Authentic Happiness.* New York: Free Press.
Zurlo, F. 2004. Il Design del sistema prodotto In *Design multi verso,* edited by P. Bertola and E. Manzini. Milan: Edizioni Polidesign, 129–37.

ANNA MERONI, GIULIA SIMEONE AND PAOLA TRAPANI[7]

CASE STUDY 17 SUPPORTING SOCIAL INNOVATION IN FOOD NETWORKS

This case study describes how service design tools have been used to activate the social and economic resources of a peri-urban area of Milan (Italy) to support its development and preservation.

This case illustrates the contribution of service design to the creation of a network of food-related services as a way to support the sustainable development of agricultural peri-urban areas which are critical areas lying between towns and rural surroundings (Donadieu 1998, Fleury 2005).

In this project service design has complemented regional and urban planning disciplines and methods providing a specific perspective on food system relations and interactions; the work has been directed by a new concept of agricultural multifunctionality based on de-mediated distribution systems, and on short food chains between the productive countryside and the city (Petrini 2005, Meroni 2006).

The project illustrates the relevance of adopting a service-driven approach to:

- understand and develop the potential of a territory and its resources by detecting existing social innovation phenomena;
- envision and give structure to the network of economical and social relations that constitute the basis of a local, self-sustainable and distributed system.

The Agricultural Park South of Milano

The project is an action research conducted by a multidisciplinary team in 2006–2008, under the auspices of the Italian University and Research Ministry, aiming to lay a theoretical and instrumental foundation to a new way of planning Agricultural Parks, special areas protected and devoted by law to agricultural production (Ferraresi 2009).

7 This project is the result of a collective work, but for the purposes of this publication Anna Meroni has written the sections 'Network structure' and 'Conclusions', Giulia Simeone the section 'A network of services', and Paola Trapani the section 'The Agricultural Park South of Milano'.

A service design team belonging to the Design Department (INDACO) of the Politecnico di Milano has joined a multidisciplinary research group[8] working together for the Agricultural Park South of Milano. This Park is an emblematic example of the so-called peri-urban areas that has analogous characteristics all around the world. The project generated a scenario of interconnected services, aiming to become the conceptual basis to develop the regional plan and the related system of infrastructures (Meroni et al. 2008, 2009).

The main problem in defining an identity, and therefore a strategy, for peri-urban areas is the apparent lack of profitable and practicable alternatives to production sites (housing, offices or commercial). However, increasingly supported by virtuous examples, designers have assumed as feasible and economically viable, the development of existing small agricultural concerns in a local network that uses resources and opportunities offered by the place (Magnaghi 2000, Latouche 2004).

As a consequence the role of service design is to activate and develop collaborative local enterprises[9] (Manzini and Meroni 2007) creating a network of interconnected and complementary *service models* developing a different partnership between town and the countryside (Ferraresi 2007). Using the tools and the language of the design discipline, this partnership has been redefined in a *scenario framework* (Ogilvy 2002) that challenges the overflow of urbanisation by presenting sustainable alternatives; a scenario that describes peri-urban areas as places where the *network economy* answers the need of the *collaborative services* (Jégou and Manzini 2008), giving rise to a *multifunctional urban countryside.*

The Agricultural Park South (managed and overseen by the local authority) is made up of different kinds of fields, partially rented out to farmers and partially owned. It is currently in decline as small farmers abandon the territory and the soil is overexploited by agro-industrial production. It is also subject to aggressive building programmes and, as their contracts expire, leaseholders fail to invest in new infrastructures and services. Money investments in the agricultural business are not promoted by small producers, as they are no longer profitable in a mass distribution scenario.

Despite this situation, a vanguard of social innovation, going under the definition of *creative communities* – people who challenge the traditional way of doing things and introduce a set of new, more sustainable ones (Meroni 2007) – has emerged. Partially referable to a concept of economic solidarity, they practice different promising initiatives that appear to open the way to a sustainable development, but ask for a proper support to flourish (Nuovo Stili di Vita 2007).

The project has taken these virtuous situations as a starting point to develop a coherent system of interconnected services and actors mutually reinforcing and producing business and society. Considered as best practices of social innovation (Manzini 2007), these initiatives have inspired the outlining of some *service models* (resulted both from modelling the existent typologies and inventing new ones) combined in networks and used to generate the *scenario framework* for the project. Detected and collected during the field research, these cases are a mix of three kinds of activity: 1) production, exchange and consumption of food, 2) leisure, 3) innovative housing and hospitality systems.

8 PRIN, Miur, 2006. A group consisting of urban planners, architects, agronomists, geographers and service designers. Four main Italian universities were involved: Università degli Studi di Firenze; Politecnico di Milano – Departments DIAP e INDACO; Università degli Studi di Genova; Università degli Studi di Palermo.

9 Emerging user demands for sustainable solutions. VI FP, 2004–2006, research coordinated by the INDACO Department of the Politecnico di Milano and involving nine European partners plus eight design schools.

The local cases of social innovation have become the basis of a method of work structured as follows:

- field observation and collection of best practices of social innovation;
- derivation of inputs and stimuli for the project;
- outlining of these stimuli in new service models;
- building of the scenario framework;
- development of the scenario by structuring a network of specific services.

A Network of Services

Eight service models emerged as constitutive elements of the network that have been visualised through micropanoramics, system maps, and condensed story-boards (Jégou, Manzini and Meroni 2004). These models outline a scenario where agricultural activities, and particularly food production and exchange on a local scale, become the means for the sustainable development of peri-urban areas.

They rely on collaborative patterns giving rise to economies of purpose and scale, by sharing infrastructures and mixing activities in a multifunctional fashion.

In short, these service models are:

THE FARMERS' MARKET: THE MARKET FOR THE PRODUCE AND SERVICES OF THE PARK
Connected to the well-rooted street markets of Milano and following a weekly rota, the initiative is organised by a consortium of local producers, and supports the de-mediation of both product and services, encouraging practical and conceptual access to the park from the city (Figure 2.4.19).

THE PUBLIC GREEN PROCUREMENTS: GREEN PURCHASING
The service creates touchpoints between virtuous producers and critical consumers through the realisation of critical mass and the organisation of shared platforms for goods exchange based on the model of group purchasing organisations (Figure 2.4.20).

THE FOOD BOX SUBSCRIPTION
The service is a periodical delivery of fresh produce from the Park: it is conceived to be accessible in terms of costs, because of the short chain, and in terms of convenience, because of the regular home or near-home delivery (Figure 2.4.21).

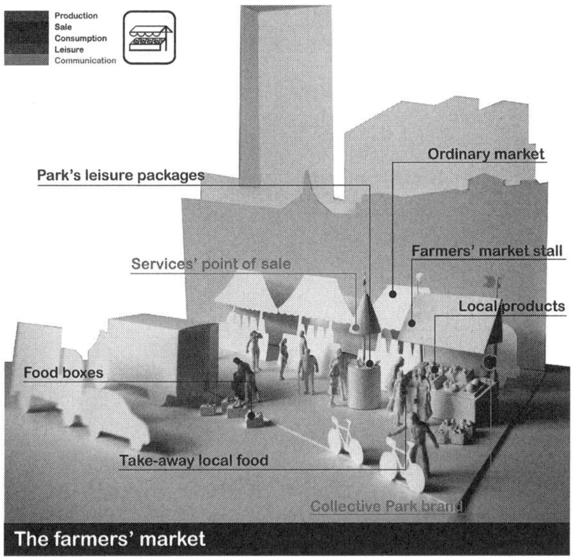

Figure 2.4.19 The farmers' market
Source: Politecnico di Milano.

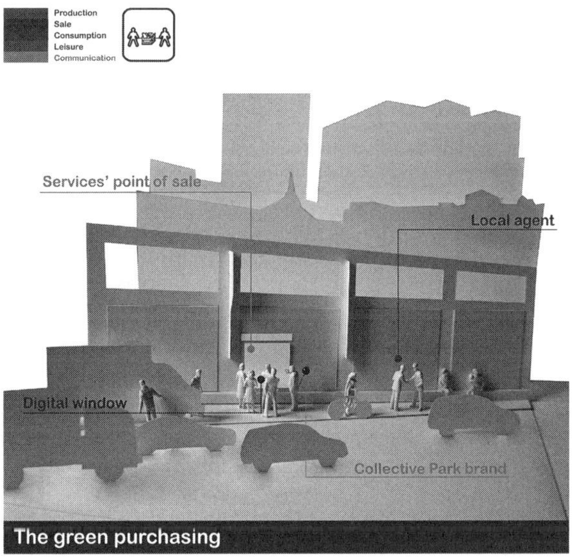

Figure 2.4.20 The green purchasing
Source: Politecnico di Milano.

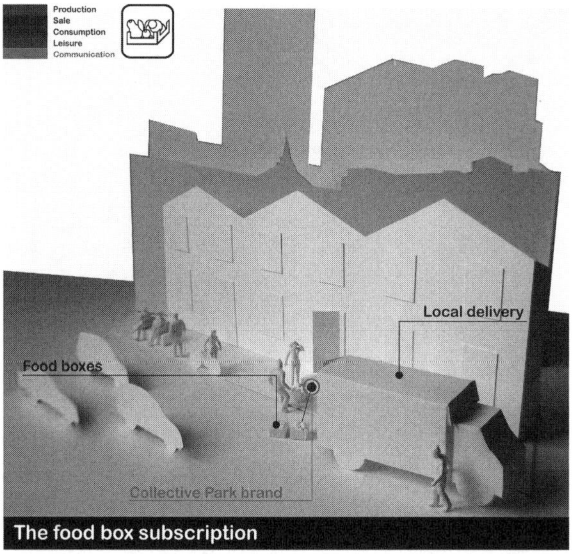

Figure 2.4.21 The food box subscription
Source: Politecnico di Milano.

VISITORS' CENTRE: THE PARK POINTS

The Park Points are welcoming places, located at strategic points in the Park, combining physical access to the territory with access to its knowledge and produce. They offer both information and local produce on sale, agritourism and hospitality (Figure 2.4.22).

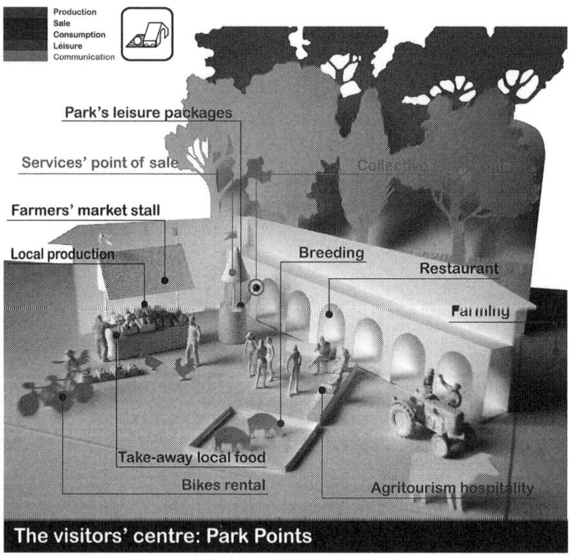

Figure 2.4.22 The visitors' centre
Source: Politecnico di Milano.

THE RURAL CULTURAL CENTRE (AT AN HISTORICAL BUILDING)

The idea of a Cultural Centre is to enhance the value of local biodiversity through activities carried out by scientific researchers (from universities) and experienced local farmers (Figure 2.4.23).

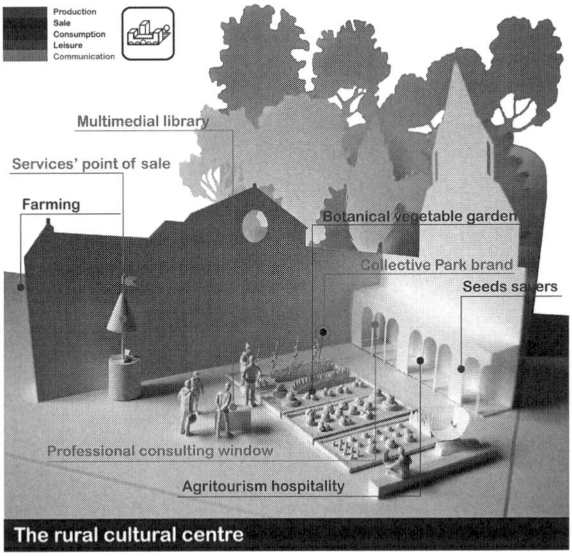

Figure 2.4.23 The rural cultural centre
Source: Politecnico di Milano.

HORTICULTURE

The service transforms available fields of the farms into allotments to be rented and cultivated by amateurs, as small vegetable gardens. The garden is a hybrid space where individual and collaborative activities are connected as for a time bank, where participants can rely on an internal exchange of favours and products, managed on a credit system (Figure 2.4.24).

URBAN INDOOR/OUTDOOR AGRICULTURE

Advanced building and gardening technologies can help urban farming: the service supports citizens to cultivate their own food, in metropolises as in smaller towns, where several solutions like green walls and green roofs, or simplified hydroponic and aeroponic systems, are gaining a footing (Figure 2.4.25).

THE COLLECTIVE PARK BRAND

The brand connoting the short chain initiatives and activities and that are the result of networked collaboration between different actors.

These services become profitable when able to use the local resources at their best: the availability of such resources and the possibility of having direct control over them, as far as quality and quantity are concerned, is actually the key factor that makes the difference in the market. In this way small enterprises can mature distinctive features attracting the critical consumers, and activate a quality market beside the mass one.

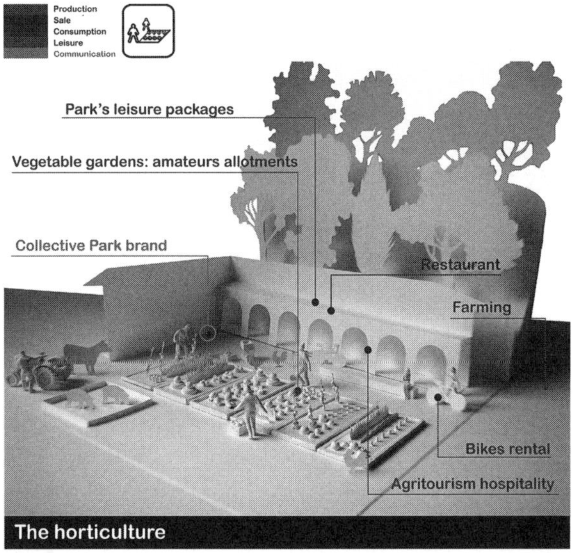

Figure 2.4.24 The horticulture
Source: Politecnico di Milano.

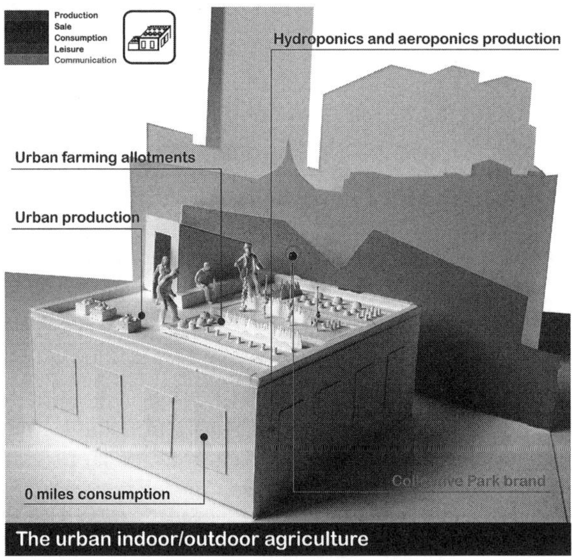

Figure 2.4.25 The urban indoor/outdoor agriculture
Source: Politecnico di Milano.

Nevertheless, without a network strategy to share and complement assets and resources, such initiatives are unlikely to have sufficient power to influence the way the area takes shape: only when these services become self-sustaining can they create a social and economic background countering the building speculation.

One of the challenges of design to support the diffusion of these services is to make them more accessible and affordable for a larger number of users and, at the same time, more practicable for a larger group of producers (Jégou and Manzini 2008); all this happens due to the nature and the quality of the interaction.

The functional basis for building the network is the need to share or complement the main elements that constitute the services. The social and relational basis is to enhance the actors' perception of a coherent community, where everybody contributes to the collective success.

Network Structure

An analytic exercise has been done to shape the network: having formulated the structure of these eight service models so as to be quite consistent with each other, a deeper analysis has been carried out to understand how they could overlap, integrate and share resources, creating a symbiotic network (Mirata and Ristola 2007). An analytical framework has been used (Jégou, Manzini and Meroni 2004) breaking the services down into *assessable elements* (the minimum material or immaterial self-coherent constituent needed to deliver the service); these have then been clustered under the following categories: logistics and infrastructures, material goods, immaterial goods, human resources and communication.

By repeating this analysis over and over again for all services, we ended up developing a conceptual map that showed how services could complement with each other and that illustrated various kinds of possible synergies:

- overlapping elements: where there are potential economies of scale and convenience in joining the services, because of the similarity of elements and activities;
- complementary and compatible elements: where there are potential economies of scope and convenience in linking the services, because of the subsidiary or integrated nature of the elements.

This approach enables to design a concept of agricultural *multifunctionality* (Viljoen 2005), where multiple, but synergic, activities become conveniently manageable by a mix of actors, without wasting working capacity, but rather increasing it.. A self-help group of amateur farmers can, for instance, cultivate a field on the farmer's property with a relatively autonomous attitude, using equipment in exchange for labour. A group of professional farmers can run direct sales more easily by managing turnovers and sharing logistics.

The emerging network (an articulated model of community-supported agriculture), takes the shape of a web of services, which operatively tends to concentrate around crucial points where, for the convenience of the enterprise, several service models can co-exist. These points can be called *service hubs*, because of their crucial role in making the whole system work. They result from the sum of different overlapping and complementary opportunities, where food production, exchange, hospitality, leisure, cultural and social activities create a unique mix of functions that add value to the territory.

A hub manages considerable flows of goods, resources and persons, gathering together several smaller activities. Because of the availability of adequate resources and infrastructures and its strategic location, it plays the role of operational support for businesses gravitating around it, thanks to a win–win alliance with smaller businesses in geographic proximity.

The possibility of activating synergies or sharing resources with other businesses in close proximity is, moreover, a way to create virtuous circles that valorise also the offer of leasehold farmers unable to benefit from huge investments in adequate standards of service. This dynamic can activate an *economy of reciprocity* where services and goods are exchanged outside traditional market rules, creating a flexible local system.

For all these reasons hubs are the means by which *soft policies* (bottom-up rules and behaviours self-imposed by local communities in order to increase quality) could be implemented in the territory; also, they represent crucial entities that institutional policies and local authorities could effectively support to promote a sustainable local development.

Conclusions

The network of services ideated by this project aims to create a relational pattern at the basis of the development of the region, and to become an input for urban planners to design infrastructures. Actually, many disciplines dealing with regional planning (architecture, urban planning, economics) increasingly look at the territorial relationships and vocational identities as key starting points of any designing activity. They tend, eventually, to adopt what we can define as a service design approach, whereas scenarios become synthetic and effective tools (Manzini and Jégou 2003) to discuss and share a vision with several different subjects involved in regional projects.

The framework scenario for peri-urban agriculture has been derived from the identification of cases of social innovation, their conceptualisation into service models, and the consequent generation of new service ideas. This kind of scenario helps capitalising on vanguard initiatives by imagining distributed changes for the region that hold a reasonable chance of success. From a methodological perspective, this way of designing scenarios shifts the emphasis from the individual 'user' to the 'community', adopting a community-centred design approach (Meroni 2008); here the community seems to play the role that was previously reserved to the 'user' in helping the designer to decode and interpret emerging design demands. It is a challenging opportunity for design for services to enter this transformation and the consequent demand for innovation that calls for collaborative design practices and distributed creativity.

The research described here laid the foundations for an implementation project, started in 2009, with the aim of creating a model of sustainable food shed in the region of Milano.

References

Donadieu, P. 1998. *Campagnes urbaines*. Versailles: Ecole nationale superieure du paysage.

Ferraresi, G. 2007. Neoagricoltura e nuovi stili di vita: scenari di ricostruzione territoriale. *Urbanistica*, (132), 54–63.

Ferraresi, G. (ed.) 2009. *Produrre e scambiare valore territoriale. Dalla città diffusa allo scenario di forma urbis et agri*. Firenze: Alinea Editrice.

Fleury, A. (ed.) 2005. *Multifonctionnalité de l'agriculture périurbaine. Vers una agriculture du projet urbain, Les Cahiers de la multifonctionnalité, (8)*. INRA, CEMAGREF, CIRAD.

Jégou, F., Manzini, E. and Meroni, A. 2004. Design Plan, a toolbox to facilitate solution-oriented partnerships. In *Solution-oriented Partnership. How to Design Industrialised Sustainable Solutions*, edited by E. Manzini, L. Collina and S. Evans. Cranfield: Cranfield University, 108–19.

Jégou, F. and Manzini, E. 2008. *Collaborative Services: Social Innovation and Design for Sustainability*. Milan: Edizioni Polidesign.

Latouche, S. 2004. *Survivre au dèveloppement*. Paris: Mille et un nuits.

Magnaghi, A. 2000. *Il progetto locale*. Torino: Bollati Boringhieri.

Manzini, E., Collina, L. and Evans, S. (eds) 2004. *Solution-oriented Partnership: How to Design Industrialised Sustainable Solutions*. Cranfield: Cranfield University.

Manzini, E. and Jégou, F. 2003. *Sustainable Everyday. Scenarios of Urban Life*. Milan: Edizioni Ambiente.

Manzini, E. and Meroni, A. 2007. Emerging user demands for sustainable solutions: EMUDE. In *Design Research Now: Essays and Selected Projects*, edited by R. Michel. Basel: Birkhäuser, 157–79.

Meroni, A. 2006. Food de-intermediation. Strategic design for the creation of transparent food networks. *Cumulus Working Papers. Nantes,* edited by E. Salmi and L. Anusionwu. Helsinki: University of Art and Design, 50–58.

Meroni, A. (ed.) 2007. *Creative Communities. People Inventing Sustainable Ways of Living*. Milan: Edizioni Polidesign.

Meroni, A. 2008. Strategic design: where are we now? Reflection around the foundations of a recent discipline. *Strategic Design Research Journal* [Online], 1(1). São Leopoldo: Unisinos (Universidade do Vale do Rio dos Sinos) Available at http://www.unisinos.br/sdrj/, [accessed: 30 January 2010].

Meroni, A., Simeone, G. and Trapani, P. 2008. A vision of an urban countryside. Service design as a contribution to the rururban planning. Paper presented to the conference: Changing the Change. Visions, Proposals and Tools, Turin, 10–12 July 2008. Available at http://www.allemandi.com/cp/ctc/, [accessed: 30 January 2010].

Meroni, A., Simeone, G. and Trapani, P. 2009. Servizi per le reti agroalimentari. Il Design dei Servizi come contributo alla progettazione delle aree agricole periurbane. In Ferraresi, G. (ed.). *Produrre e scambiare valore territoriale. Dalla città diffusa allo scenario di forma urbis et agri*, edited by G. Ferraresi. Firenze: Alinea Editrice, 161–200.

Mirata, M. and Ristola, P. 2007. Industrial symbiosis for more sustainable, localized industrial systems. *Progress in Industrial Ecology, An International Journal (PIE)*, 4(3/4),184–204.

Nuovi Stili di Vita. 2007. EQUAL research's final report.

Ogilvy, J. 2002. *Creating Better Futures: Scenario Planning As a Tool for a Better Tomorrow*. New York: Oxford University Press.

Petrini, C. 2005. *Buono, pulito e giusto*. Torino: Einaudi.
Viljoen, A. (ed.) 2005. *Continuous Productive Urban Landscapes: Designing Urban Agriculture for Sustainable Cities*. Oxford: Elsevier.

2.5 A Map of Design for Services

The collection of case studies presented in this publication illustrates design projects in a variety of sectors such as education, transport, communication, healthcare, food provision, entertainment, security and community services. These kinds of services differ immensely from each other depending for example on their complexity, heterogeneity, service provision (product- or human-based) or area of application (for example if they are applied to people, information or objects).

Moreover, each research or design project has been approached from a variety of perspectives, focusing on service experiences, touchpoints, service model or system configuration; and considering different mix of variables such as usability, feasibility, sustainability, service modularity, or experiential quality.

Notwithstanding this variety, some commonalities and key considerations emerged out of the analysis of the case studies, helping us to make sense and map out design for services. We identified a strong common denominator, a human-centred design approach to services, and specific design contributions that we grouped into four main areas of application, as summarised in Table 2.5.1. This detailed analysis of cases studies has allowed us to gradually build up a map of the discipline – the design for services map (see Figure 2.6.1) – that we used as a compass to reflect on service designers' profiles and on their relationship with other service-related disciplines. The map is not necessarily comprehensive or willing to set up limitations to the evolution of the field, it is rather a useful tool that provides a foundation to ongoing conversations, research and education projects on design for services. It has helped us to better understand where design for services comes from, how it is currently working and the possible directions for future research and practice.

In this chapter, we will use the map to describe our current understanding of design for services. Based on this description we will reflect on the competences and skills designers working on services need to acquire and develop; we will do so also by identifying what other disciplines and research fields are useful to further shape design for services as a discipline.

Table 2.5.1 Analysis of case studies

Areas of interventions	Summary of case studies	Design contributions	Key concepts	Emerging tools
Designing interactions, relations and experiences	This area explores the links between design for services and human experience as it unfolds during service interactions and via the mediation of the service interface. It suggests that understanding experience is crucial for design for services, as experiences are connected to and affected by all the elements that shape the nature and the quality of a service. The case studies in this area describe several approaches to understand and interpret experiences in order to design better services.	• *Designing for co-creation*: facilitating creative collaborations and participation • *Designing for co-experience*: understanding people's behaviours, experiences and practices • *Designing interactions*: supporting empathic interactions	Co-experience Co-creation Empathic design	Design documentary Video blog Storytelling and directed storytelling Emotional map Film diary User diary Customer journey map
Designing interactions to shape systems and organisations	This area explores how service designers often start (re)designing service interactions to then enter into wider organisational dynamics and issues such as organisational culture, stakeholders' collaborations and configurations, work practices and business models. The case studies in this area have in common an interest and a focus on evaluating and/or (re)designing interfaces and interactions as a starting point for their design interventions.	• *Designing interactions*: evaluating and improving service interactions and interfaces • *Shaping service systems*: promoting new value configurations • *Fostering organisational change*: promoting a human-centred service culture	Design of interactions between: • User and service interface • Service staff and service system/ organisation • Service systems	Interaction design guidelines Visual service scripts Idea sketches Service blueprint Expressive service blueprint Desirability, viability, feasibility
Exploring new collaborative service models	This area explores the role of design for services to imagine collaborative service models as a way to redesign public and community services. Case studies show how service designers work with and within public organisations and user communities to develop platforms and skills to: • enable a culture of change • explore new radical service models and • explore innovative usages of social technologies.	• *Fostering organisational change*: applying transformational and experimental approaches • *Designing collaborative solutions*: engaging and connecting people • *Proposing new behaviours*: prototyping new service models	Emphasis on co-creation Transformational and experimental approaches New service system configurations New media as enabling platforms	Self-report techniques (Myspace) Experience prototype Living Labs FASPE – fast service prototyping and simulation for evaluation
Imagining future directions for service systems	This area explores the convergence between strategic design and design for services as a way to imagine, in the form of scenarios, new directions for the development of a system or a region. Services are here considered as manifestations of these scenarios; they exemplify systemic changes at the level of everyday experiences, concretising big shifts into tangible lifestyles and business opportunities. The case studies combine the need to open up alternative futures with the overall aim to facilitate transformational and evolutionary processes on a wide regional scale.	• *Proposing new behaviours*: manifesting future scenarios • *Generating future scenarios*: building and sharing visions of the future • *Designing for co-creation*: community-centred design approach	Generate scenarios as stories Facilitate convergence Collective design thinking Building capacities Towards a community-centred design	Glimpses Story collection Video sketch Story board Service moodboard Micropanoramic System map Service breakdown

2.6
What is Design for Services?

Design for services, as it has emerged from the analysis of 17 case studies, is a wide and varied area of application. Services can in fact differ significantly from each other and designers can approach services in diverse ways; the case studies show designers working at different levels (from an operational to a more strategic level), with different methods (adapting methods and tools from different fields), and with different aims (for example aiming to improve existing services or to initiate wider transformations). Designers can work on parts and segments of services, redesigning interactions and experiences, or can foster wider service reconfigurations, suggesting new business models and value networks; moreover they can use services as vehicles for societal change, generating the conditions for a more sustainable society and economy to come.

Observing all these practices a common feature emerges; this is the application of a human-centred approach, meaning that designers consider a deep understanding and respect for human behaviours, attitudes, dreams and capacities the essential premise for any design action having as its main aim to support and advance the human dignity (Buchanan 2001). This focus on people (being users, service staff, communities or humanity in a wider sense) and on providing them with the tools to effectively engage with their environment is central to design in general, and particularly strong in the rhetoric and practice of designing for services.

A human-centred design approach to services manifests in the capacity and methods to investigate and understand people's experiences, interactions and practices as a main source of inspiration for redesigning or imagining new services. These investigations can look at experiences and interactions at different levels, as already anticipated. Designers can observe and evaluate people's experiences (or better co-experiences) in their interactions with the service, but also at wider scale within their communities or organisations; they can look at service interactions among users and staff, but also between staff and their organisations and between different service systems.

On another level a human-centred design approach to services manifests itself in the capacity and methods to engage people in the design and transformation processes. This can vary from adopting participatory design methods, including users in the redesign of their services, to considering services as co-created solutions where users are not only the co-designers but also conscious participants in the delivery and development of the solutions. In practice, this means developing capacities for people to participate in design processes, creating 'service prototypes' for people to experiment in advance future possibilities and designing the platforms to enable service collaborations.

Drawing a representation of design for services, a human-centred design approach becomes the core and the driver of the discipline. It is positioned at the centre of the map and influences all areas of applications (Figures 2.6.1 and 2.6.2).

AREAS OF APPLICATIONS

Based on and driven by a human-centred design approach, design for services then works on four main areas related to service experiences, service systems, service models and future scenarios (see Figure 2.6.1). These areas of application, which we will describe in more detail below, represent specific focuses and aims of design projects, and help us to better describe how designers can qualify and position themselves when working within interdisciplinary design teams. Within these areas, designers draw on competences and tools coming from relevant design and service-related disciplines as a way to inform their practice (see Figure 2.7.1).

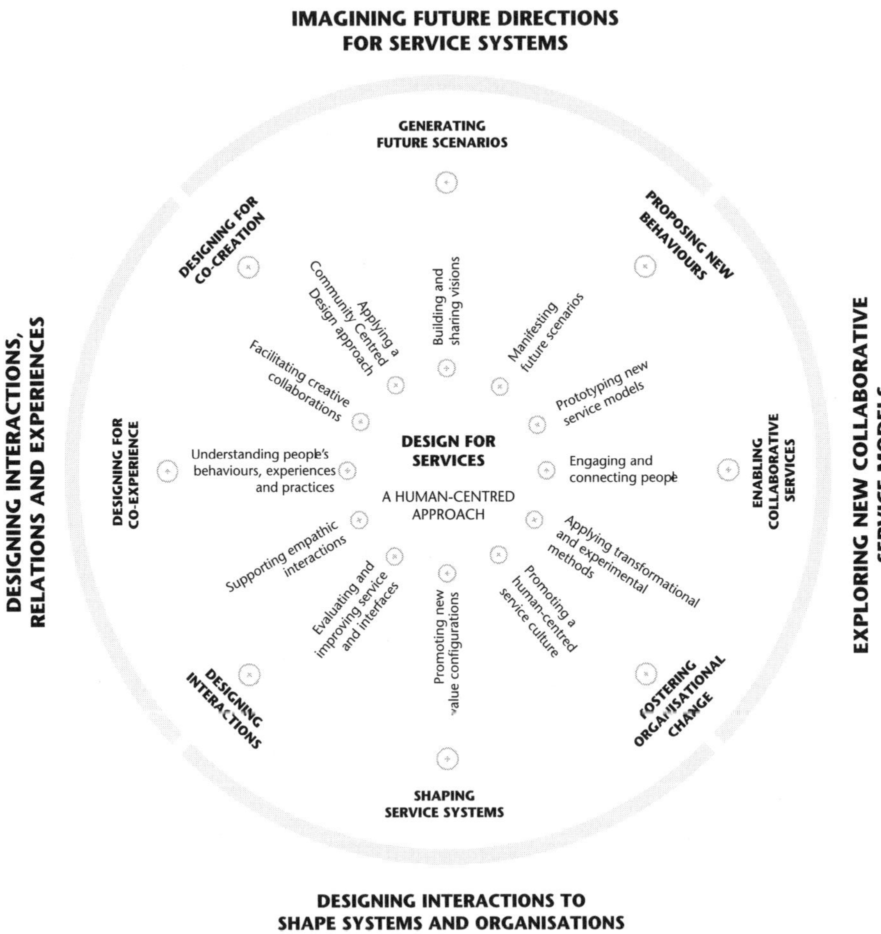

Figure 2.6.1 Map of design for services

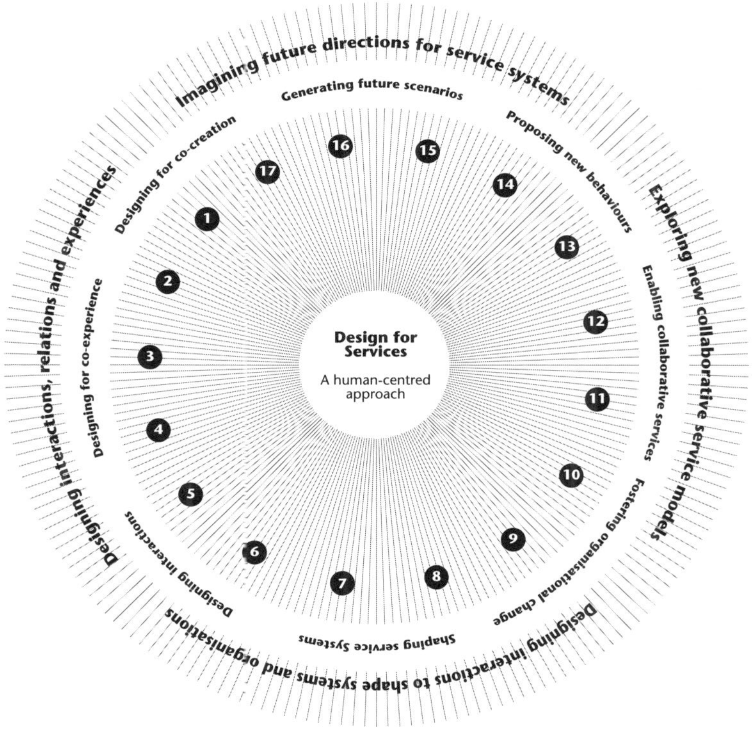

Figure 2.6.2 Map of design for services with case studies

CASE STUDIES

Designing interactions, relations and experiences

1 *Co-designing services in the public sector*
2 *Developing collaborative tools in international projects: PoliDaido project*
3 *Designing empathic conversations about future user experiences*
4 *Driving service design by directed storytelling*
5 *Exploring mobile needs and behaviours in emerging markets*

Designing interactions to shape systems and organisations

6 *There is more to service than interactions*
7 *How Service Design can support innovation in the public sector*
8 *From novelty to routine: services in science and technology-based enterprises*
9 *Enabling excellence in service with expressive service blueprinting*

Exploring new collaborative service models

10 *Service Design, new media and community development*
11 *Designing the next generation of public service*
12 *A Service Design inquiry into learning and personalisation*
13 *Mobile and collaborative. Mobile-phones, digital services and socio-cultural activation*

Imagining future directions for service systems

14 *Using scenarios to explore system change: VEIL, Local Food Depot*
15 *Designing a collaborative projection of the "Cité du Design"*
16 *Enabling sustainable behaviours in mobility through service design*
17 *Supporting social innovation in food networks*

DESIGNING INTERACTIONS, RELATIONS AND EXPERIENCES

Design for services can focus on evaluating and designing service interactions, relations and experiences as its main area of intervention. In this area designers aim to design better services by improving and enabling better experiences and supporting more empathic and effective interactions among people and the service system.

The main design contributions in this area are based on the capacity and methods to:

- Deeply understand, visualise and interpret people's behaviours, experiences and practices as a starting point to improve services; designers here aim at generating 'empathic conversations' among project participants, gaining insights into people's experiences and interactions with the services and imagining new (or improved) service experiences and interaction modes.

- Evaluate and design the conditions for more empathic interactions among users and staff (or users and users), in such a way as to stimulate people's social intelligence; by 'social intelligence' we mean the combination of social awareness and emotional intelligence (Goleman 2006) that lies behind constructive and meaningful interactions. Designers here aim to create situations where service participants can realise and express their emotional status, being recognised for their attitude, capacities or needs.

- Facilitate co-design processes among people directly or indirectly affected by the service in order to generate meaningful design solutions as well as to augment people's participation and engagement into service improvement processes.

When designers focus on service experiences, relations and interactions they qualify themselves as experts in improving services by making them more desirable, useful and usable. In so doing they apply existing design theory and practice coming from empathic design (Leonard and Rayport 1997), experience design and interaction design and related applied disciplines such as participatory design, ethnography, and social and cognitive psychology. These disciplines support designers in their understanding of people's behaviours and practices, of usability issues related to service interactions and of participation and engagement within co-design processes.

Most of the tools used in this area support designers in their observation of people and in the collection and visualisation of stories: examples are design documentary, storytelling, video-blog, or user diaries. Some methods, used to visualise and evaluate service interactions, are instead the interpretation of existing tools and concepts coming from service marketing and service operations management; see for example the 'emotional map' or the 'customer journey map' as simplifications and elaborations of a blueprint.

DESIGNING INTERACTIONS TO SHAPE SYSTEMS AND ORGANISATIONS

This area considers the redesign of service interactions as main driver for innovation, organisational change and business development. Service interactions are interpreted in a wide way, including user–staff interactions, staff–service system interactions and service systems interactions. The designers' intent here is to improve the service by suggesting new or improved interaction modes based on a more human-centred service culture.

The main design contributions in this area are based on the capacity and methods to:

- Evaluate and improve service interactions and interfaces at different levels, within and among service systems. Designers aim to reduce service interaction breakdowns, improving service usability, generating clearer processes, seamless experiences and effective communications.

- Promote new service system configurations by exploring new service ideas that better answer people's needs and by looking at new potential or improved collaborations and interactions within and among stakeholders.

- Foster organisational change by promoting a human-centred service culture. Designers introduce a demand-driven innovation approach that brings people's needs and experiences to the centre of service provision and service development.

When designers work in this area they look at services as complex social systems that are resistant to change and whose behaviours cannot be controlled or predicted. Their approach is a transformational one and they qualify themselves as agents for change. They apply knowledge and tools from interaction and system design to look at issues of usability and system complexity. They also apply knowledge from studies of service marketing and behavioural science on service encounters, co-production and user behaviour, and from organisational studies and innovation management, when they deal with issues of organisational change.

EXPLORING NEW COLLABORATIVE SERVICE MODELS

Designing for services can work on imagining and experimenting with new service models. Designers here develop new service ideas and explore their social, economic and technological feasibility working with people and within interdisciplinary design teams. The aim here is to transform existing service delivery models into the new 'open source' and distributed paradigm that relies on social networks and collaborative solutions.

The main design contributions in this area are based on the capacity and methods to:

- Engage people to experiment with new service models and more collaborative solutions. Designers here develop platforms, often based on social and mobile technologies, that enable people to connect and collaborate in new ways, using existing and more distributed resources, while transcending more traditional service delivery models.

- Apply transformational and experimental approaches to generate the space for change to happen. Designers use pilot projects and service prototypes as a way to allow people to inhabit and co-create new collaborative solutions, exploring resistances and motivations for change.

- Explore and propose new behavioural patterns that challenge existing unsustainable lifestyles. Designers here observe and interpret current social trends, in order to get inspiration for conceiving new behavioural models and for identifying promising examples to be replicated and supported by adequate solutions and policies.

In this area of application services are seen as platforms that enable people to participate and collaborate within their communities to achieve their goals and transform their lifestyles. Within these projects designers qualify themselves as interpreters of society demands and as innovators, acting as facilitators of transformation processes. Experimenting with more collaborative solutions, designers here look at management studies on co-production and network organisations to better understand and develop collaborative and value-oriented service models. They apply and adapt methodologies and tools that come from participatory and experience design traditions, such as experience prototype and hands-on collaborative design processes. In addition studies of psychology (see for example Positive Psychology) and behavioural sciences provide useful concepts to identify motivations and conditions necessary for certain behaviours to emerge.

IMAGINING FUTURE DIRECTIONS FOR SERVICE SYSTEMS

Within this area designers generate scenarios for the future development of regions, places and service systems. Designers here imagine alternative directions for more sustainable futures on a regional scale, and use these visions to engage stakeholders and citizens, through 'strategic conversations' (Nardone and Salvini 2004), to participate in longer transformation processes.

The main design contributions in this area are based on the capacity and methods to:

- Generate and share visions for the future. Designers use scenario building and storytelling methods as a way to imagine in a collective way the future of a place; sharing those visions helps different stakeholders to converge toward a united development strategy.

- Visualise and manifest future scenarios through stories and service ideas. Designers use service ideas to represent in practical terms how future scenarios will impact daily life and what changes people will experience in their territory.

- Work with and within communities to create the conditions for long-term transformation processes. In these projects, designers move from a user-centred approach to a community-centred one, as communities become the right interlocutor when acting for change on a regional scale.

In this area of application services are seen as manifestations of scenarios, showing tangible ways to implement more desirable futures. Within this kind of project designers qualify themselves as visionary and facilitators of strategic conversations among different stakeholders. They apply methodologies from strategic design and scenario building using idea generation and visualisation tools to facilitate creative collaborations and discussions around possible futures. They also derive knowledge from social psychology and sociology to understand the drivers and motivations to engage stakeholders in regional development plans and adapt tools from project management to help guide the design process. Finally, working on regional or urban scale, designers have explored tools and methods and collaborated with professionals from urban planning and future studies backgrounds.

References

Buchanan, R. 2001. Human dignity and human rights: thoughts on the principles of human-centered design. *Design Studies*, 17(3), 35–9.

Goleman, D. 2006. *Social Intelligence: The New Science of Human Relationships*. New York: Bantam Books.

Leonard, D. and Rayport, J. 1997. Spark innovation through empathic design. *Harvard Business Review*, November–December, 102–13.

Nardone, G. and Salvini, A. 2004. *Il dialogo strategico*. Milan: Ponte alle Grazie.

2.7 What Job Profiles for a Service Designer?

As a final reflection extracted from the collection of case studies, we have imagined how these areas of applications and contributions could be translated into job profiles. The main difficulty for design for services, as often for design professions in general, is to communicate the role and impact designers can have in organisations, society or the economy. This is particularly true when designers enter new fields of practice or when their roles overlap or integrate with existing ones. Think for example of the role of design management or strategic design where designers need to build an identity and role, negotiating their position with existing managerial ones; or consider the current confusion and overlapping of service design with service marketing, in particular when marketing is increasingly moving toward similar topics such as relationships, co-production and experiences.

At the risk of distancing ourselves from the case studies and emphasising roles that are still ambiguous, we will now suggest four job profiles that seem to emerge from the map. As described in the previous chapter, designers can work on four main areas related to service experiences, service systems, service models and service scenarios. These areas represent possible roles for designers working within or for service organisations and/or regional authorities. They can co-exist, of course, creating a complete profile of a designer for services, or be emphasised individually as specific job descriptions within organisations, institutions or design studios.

- *Designer for service experiences*: designers can work for and within service organisations to observe and evaluate service experiences and interactions as a way to improve existing services or suggest new functionalities and ideas. They work to engage users and staff within service improvement processes, designing the conditions that will stimulate more empathic interactions among service participants. Their role necessarily overlaps with service marketing, with which they can collaborate to generate more effective customer relationship strategies.

- *Designer for service policies*: when designers enter in a more strategic position, they can contribute to the development of a more human-centred design approach to service development and innovation. Their work is to verify that organisational policies and configurations are in line with people's experiences and demands. They can work to improve service interactions (at different levels), suggesting minor or radical changes to existing business models and service configurations. This role is close to what Buchanan describes as 'Interaction Design within organisations', that is 'to rethink the pathways of organisational life' (2004: 58). Their work necessarily overlaps with that of service management or service innovation management, with the aim of introducing more demand-driven strategies to service development.

- *Designer for service transformation*: designers can work with institutions, communities and/or service organisations to foster and experiment with new service models that rely on more collaborative and democratic patterns. Collaboration is, in fact, the interaction model that characterises the contemporary phenomena of social networking and open source innovation. Designers here facilitate the shift toward this new paradigm by creating platforms and tools for collaboration to engage people in cooperative actions and to prototype new ways of doing and living. New social media play a crucial role in this practice and become a specific area of design competence. This design profile overlaps partially and collaborates with community and regional development agents as well as with commissioning and innovation roles within public and private organisations.

- *Designer for service systems development*: designers can support urban and territorial development agencies and institutions as well as single organisations in imagining future directions for their sector and/or region. Designers work with local communities to generate visions of the future, introducing design thinking methods and imagining new services as a way to translate wide scenarios into everyday life experiences. Their role overlaps and collaborates with urban and territorial planning units as well as with commissioning and innovation roles within public and private organisations. The difference between this role and the service transformation one is the regional/urban divide and the timescale of the initiatives: the first one suggests and experiments with solutions that can be implemented immediately, while the second one imagines service scenarios for long-term development processes.

In conclusion, we observe that design for services seems to apply and partially transform existing design skills and roles such as those of design for experiences, strategic design, transformation design and scenario building. However, the application of these skills in the service sector requires integration with new competences and roles related to service marketing, service management, service operation and organisational studies, when designers relate to organisations, and with community and place development, spatial planning and participatory design when they act on territory and with local communities.

Each of these job profiles would need further work and research to develop their competences and skills effectively, as well as to explore their role and impact within service innovation and sustainability. As the four roles we propose are already hybrid ones, we think that research into comparison and integration with close disciplines would benefit the discipline. Links with these subjects need to be strengthened, making it possible to identify new interdisciplinary profiles that better answer contemporary needs for service innovation.

The design for services map (Figure 2.6.1) provides a first tool to interpret and navigate this emerging discipline. It completes the journey into its practical application while opening up new questions on its relevance, links and position within existing organisations and professions.

It also provides an initial response to the question of what design brings to the theory and practice of the emergent 'service science', defined as 'the study of service systems, aiming to create a basis for systematic service innovation' (Maglio and Spohrer 2008: 18).

Services are defined, by the service science community, as the application of resources for the benefit of another; while systems are defined as configurations of resources, such as people, organisations, technology and shared information, that interact with other service systems to create mutual value (Spohrer et al. 2008). A service system could be for example a family, a city, a company, a non-governmental organisation or even a nation. What shapes the history and identity of a service system are the interaction episodes with other systems to co-create value. Design for services applies a human-centred design approach at different levels in the exploration, design and innovation of service systems and their reciprocal interactions. It works to improve and redesign interactions within and among service systems, to reconfigure their networks and organisation, imagining new value propositions or new interaction modes for the near or distant future.

Design for services, however, needs increasingly to work and collaborate in an interdisciplinary way to make these contributions visible and more effective. In a recent collaborative effort the Arizona State University's Centre for Services Leadership (CSL) has managed to summarise a set of interdisciplinary research priorities for the science of service (see Table 2.7.1), integrating the perspectives of 300 academic and business representatives (Ostrom et al. 2010). Among these design for services, as an interdisciplinary effort, is gaining more visibility and recognition. Mary Jo Bitner suggests that 'effective service design is not something that can be isolated to operations researchers, designers, engineers, technologists, or marketers alone' (Ostrom et al. 2010: 14). While better defining the core identity of design for services, this book suggests its evolution in the expansion and strengthening of its interdisciplinary nature (see Figure 2.7.1).

Table 2.7.1 A synthesis of the main future research priorities as reported by the Arizona State University's Centre for Services Leadership

Business areas	Research priorities	Research topics
Strategy priorities	**Fostering service infusion and growth**	1. Identifying business models for growth and expansion based on service 2. Evolving goods-based organisations into service-oriented enterprises 3. Integrating and aligning goods, services and solutions strategies 4. Developing and managing a services–goods portfolio
	Improving well-being through transformative service	1. Improving consumer and societal welfare through service 2. Enhancing access, quality, and productivity in healthcare and education 3. Delivering service in a sustainable manner 4. Motivating the development and adoption of green technologies and related services 5. Planning, building and managing service infrastructure for metropolitan areas, regions and nations 6. Democratising public services for the benefit of consumers and society 7. Driving service innovation at the base of the pyramid
	Creating and maintaining a service culture	1. Recruiting, training and rewarding associates for a sustained service culture 2. Developing a service mindset in product-focused organisations 3. Creating a learning service organisation by harnessing employee and customer knowledge 4. Keeping a service focus as an organisation grows, matures and changes 5. Globalising a service organisation's culture across different countries

Table 2.7.1 *Concluded*

Development priorities	Stimulating service innovation	1. Identifying drivers of sustained new service success 2. Designing emergent and planned processes for incremental and radical service innovation 3. Identifying and managing customers' roles throughout the service innovation process 4. Infusing creativity and arts into service innovation processes 5. Aligning organisation structure, customer and supplier relationships with service innovation 6. Generating, prioritising and managing service innovation ideas 7. Using modelling and service simulation to enhance service innovation
	Enhancing service design	1. Integrating 'design thinking' into service practices, processes and systems 2. Integrating the performing and visual arts into service design 3. Designing dynamic, flexible services across economic cycles, maturity stages and market segments 4. Aligning service design approaches with existing organisational structures 5. Learning about how to best engage customers and employees in collaborative service design 6. Using service design to influence the behaviour of people within service systems
	Optimising service networks and value chains	1. Optimising interorganisational service network collaboration around customer experiences 2. Creating and improving distributed service networks globally 3. Developing effective pricing to share gains and losses across a service system 4. Managing upstream and downstream migration in the service value chain 5. Using outsourcing for enhanced service productivity and success
Execution priorities	Effectively branding and selling services	1. Effectively branding service and solutions and identifying ways to assess brand value 2. Developing consistent brand experiences across touch points 3. Harnessing social media's impact on service brands 4. Achieving effective solution selling and defining the new role of the sales force 5. Forging closer relationships between employees and the brand
	Enhancing the service experience through co-creation	1. Managing the customer experience across complex and diverse offerings, touch-points and customers 2. Defining the customer's role and developing methods for motivating customer contributions to enhance service success and loyalty 3. Driving customer/service collaboration through technology (for example, Web 3.0) 4. Creating, managing, and measuring the impact and returns of customer communities 5. Determining intellectual property rights to and the pricing of co-created services
	Measuring and optimising the value of service	1. Measuring the value and return on investment from service 2. Creating and enhancing tools for capturing the value in use for services and communicating value to customers and throughout the firm 3. Integrating service value and the costs of service delivery into joint optimisation models 4. Creating and enhancing service standards and metrics that link to financial outcomes of the firm 5. Managing the sales and service channel portfolio to maximise value 6. Integrating the role of customers, employees and technology for value optimisation (for example, the use of self-service technologies)

Source: Ostrom et al. (2010).

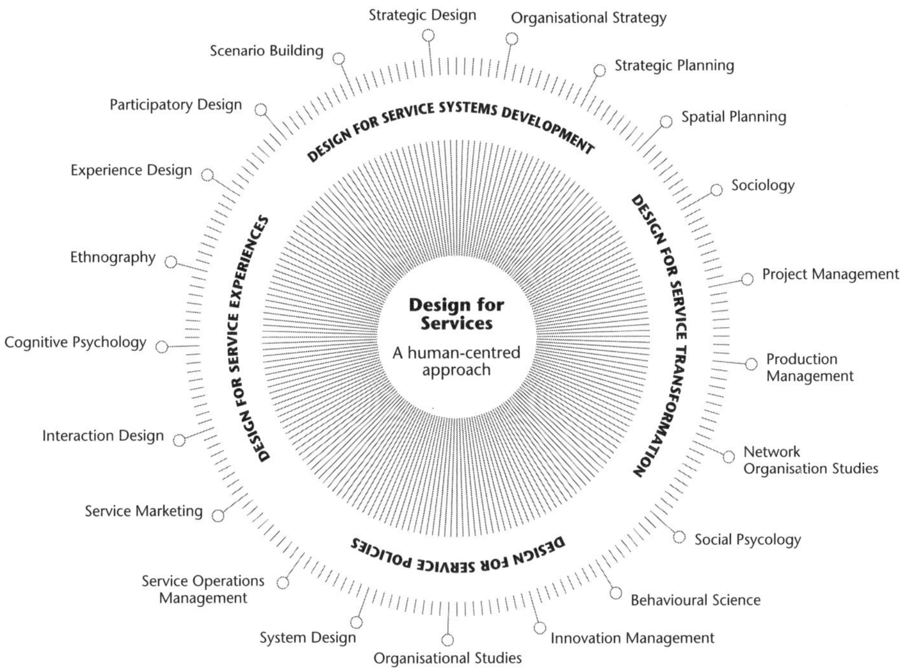

Figure 2.7.1 Map of design for services with related disciplines and job profiles

Most of the future research areas suggested by the CSL document touch current interests and practices within the design community and suggest a common ground for future research collaborations. In a smaller effort, but with a similar intent, we have dedicated the last section of this publication to the exploration of future directions for research and practice for this discipline. In particular, we have used existing theories about the emergence of a new economy to question the role of design for services and its necessary future development. In addition, we have also asked 17 key researchers and practitioners to report on their perspectives on the need for future research in the field. This collection is reported in Appendix 1. These final considerations conclude this publication and hopefully represent the incipit for a growing conversation and collaboration for the development and possible diversification of design for services as a discipline.

References

Buchanan, R. 2004. Management and design. Interaction pathways in organizational life. In *Managing as Designing*, edited by R. J. Boland and F. Collopy. Stanford, CA: Stanford University Press.

Maglio, P. and Spohrer, J. 2008. Fundamentals of service science. *Journal of the Academy of Marketing Science*, 36, 18–20.

Ostrom, A.L., Bitner, M.J., Brown, S.W., Burkhard, K.A., Goul, M., Smith-Daniels, V., Demirkan, H. and Rabinovich, E. 2010. Moving forward and making a difference: research priorities for the science of service. *Journal of Service Research*, 13(1), 4–36.

Spohrer, J., Vargo, S.L., Caswell, N. and Maglio, P.P. 2008. *The Service System is the Basic Abstraction of Service Science: Proceedings of the 41st Hawaii International Conference on System Sciences.*

Section 3

Future Developments

3.1 An Emerging Economy

In the previous section we introduced and discussed 17 case studies as the basis for generating a description of what we believe design for services is today. We have created a map that depicts four main areas of design application related to service experiences, service organisations, service models and service systems. Abstracting from the map we then suggested four possible job profiles, indicating ways designers can contribute to services in the current economy.

In this last section we will take a further (and last), step imagining how designers working for services could contribute to the future of the economy. To do this, we have reflected on future scenarios as illustrated by a selection of visionary contemporary authors, such as Ezio Manzini, a renowned expert in design and sustainability, Charles Leadbeater, a leading thinker in innovation and creativity, Robin Murray, Geoff Mulgan and July Caulier-Grice, economists focusing on social innovation and third sector companies, Eric Von Hippel, an expert in distributed and open innovation, Shoshana Zuboff and James Maxmin, theorists in innovative models of management, and Stephen Vargo and Robert Lush, renowned marketing theorists. Although they are from different disciplinary perspectives, their visions all converge into key concepts; we then used these concepts to imagine which directions design for services should take to actively participate in the shaping of a more sustainable future. As a further support to these considerations we have also invited different designers and researchers from around the world, who are working on design for services, to provide their vision for the future of the discipline. We asked them to suggest which kind of research they think would be relevant for the future of the field and of the economy. Their answers (reported in Appendix 1) together with this chapter bring the book to a closure and at the same time open up themes and questions for further research and practice.

Three Pillars

A different economy is emerging, as manifest in current phenomena and discussed by several contemporary authors. It is not the expression of mainstream practices and behaviours, but it is apparent in spread yet pervasive initiatives that can be observed all over the world and are sustained by specific sociotechnical circumstances. Different definitions and scenarios have been proposed to describe where this economy is (and should be) going. The authors we selected talk about the emergence of a 'social economy' (Murray et al. 2008, Murray 2009), a 'support economy' (Zuboff and Maxmin 2002), a 'co-production economy' (Leadbeater 2008, Von Hippel 2005, Ramirez 1999, Vargo and Lush 2004), or a 'next economy' (see Manzini's introduction to this book).

The ongoing change in the current economy is affecting the private and the public sector, as well as the profit and not for profit economy, suggesting a shift from a concentrated and hierarchical capitalism to a 'distributed' one. A new enterprise logic is rising, knitting technologies and people together, and allowing people to voice their need of self-determination, expression and interconnection (Zuboff and Maxmin 2002, Von Hippel 2005, Inghilleri 2003).

This emerging economy appears to be founded on three pillars:

1. Its social character, strongly linked with the phenomena of social innovation;

2. Its environmental reorientation, leading to a green revolution and to a renewed territorial linkage;

3. Its technological innovation, supported by an unprecedented technological breakthrough.

The combination of these three factors has contributed to the redefinition of its key characteristics.

A first impact of this emerging economy is in the definition of 'value' and of 'value production'. Together with economic value, social and environmental concerns are gaining recognition as determinants for value generation. At the same time, the growing collaborative and interactive nature of the current economy is reshaping the traditional sequential 'value production', as added to goods, into the synchronic one of 'value co-production', as co-created by people (Ramirez 1999). The relevance of active participation of people in shaping the value, instead of being a passive recipient of value-added products and services, qualifies this economy as a 'co-production economy' (Von Hippel 2005).

A second consideration regards the definition of markets. Business opportunities lay in the unmet needs of contemporary individuals and communities that ask for flexible and open solutions. Conventional organisational models are not in the position to answer these needs. Parker and Heapy (2006) describe the emergence of a new enterprise model which is no longer focused on providing products or services, but aims to provide 'the support' people need to lead their own lives as they wish and to navigate a complex world. Manzini, describing what he calls a 'next economy', talks about 'platforms for actions' that enable people to express and use their capabilities to co-create the solutions they need. In this way, people become part of the answer rather than being part of the problem. This change in the purpose of markets qualifies the economy as a 'support economy' (Zuboff and Maxmin 2002).

With similar bases, Manzini speaks about a 'social' character of the economy: contemporary challenges are often social in nature and can be solved only engaging different actors, and fostering significant changes in people's behaviour and lifestyles. This character connects economy with the dynamics of social innovation. Murray affirms that radical social innovation is needed to change the ways systems of production and service provision are conceived and implemented. Deeper social changes are necessary to actually reduce the need for consumptions and to lead toward a more sustainable development.

All these visions have services as central component: according to Vargo and Lush (2004) service provision, rather than goods provision, is becoming fundamental to economic exchange. Today for key stakeholders and users in production systems, a service-oriented approach (that is inherently user-oriented and relational) is needed and emerging in every sector. This implies that value is co-created with and defined by the user, rather than embedded in products, and that it lies in use when the offering is actually employed (Vargo et al. 2008). Considering services as the paradigm for the co-production of value, the attention of organisations is therefore moving towards processes and relationships.

The hybrid and heterogenic nature of services and the growing role of people in the shape of solutions and value represent the challenges for design in this emerging economy. The acceptance of this complexity and the consequent impossibility of predicting the future (see Manzini's introduction to this book) led design to work closely with scenario building as one of the best ways to collectively shape visions of the future, in a continuous dialogic relation with other stakeholders and the society.

Looking closer at the visions of a new emerging economy, some common characteristics which represent challenges can be discerned, but there are also opportunities for design for services to foster its development.

Characteristics

In the descriptions of this new economy, common characteristics become apparent. Together with the three pillars already mentioned – social character, environmental reorientation and technological innovation – the emerging economy is characterised by new kinds of artefacts. These characteristics altogether are increasingly affecting the work of designers.

NEW ARTEFACTS

Design artefacts are substantially different from those of the past economy. Traditional consumption goods are substituted by systems aiming at providing solutions, where the role of users as co-producer is crucial (see Manzini's introduction to this volume). The 'prosumer', conceptualised by Toffler (1980), is a person who wants to have an active role in the production of what they consider to be of value; being a passive recipient of generalised services and commodities is no longer desirable.

For this reason, the role and contribution of active users are increasingly part of the design process and part of the design 'outcome'. Leadbeater (2008) suggests how good ideas often come from ordinary people with skills that could be labelled as professional. The possibility of their developing ideas depends on the opportunities to collaborate without relying too much on formal organisations, instead finding the way to self-organising. In this sense innovation is being democratised (Von Hippel 2005): users of products and services are increasingly able to innovate by themselves. It is becoming easier for many users to get exactly what they want by designing it for themselves. In the words of Von Hippel, this leads to an increase of the social welfare as a sense of diffused satisfaction and self-realisation. 'Lead users', who are at the cutting edge of important market trends, engage in the modification of their interactions with products/services. Their design capacity and influence on other users is increasing thanks to the power of web technologies. In a similar way Leadbeater (2008) talks about 'pro–ams' ('professional amateurs') as dedicated, educated and well-equipped amateurs who are leading some of the most powerful movements to transform the contemporary world: they are people who engage in activities for the sake of it and perform to very high standards. These people seem to increasingly engage in modifying and creating solutions by themselves as traditional markets lack what they search for. Moreover they enjoy innovating and problem solving (Zuboff and Maxmin 2002, Von Hippel 2005). Thus innovation is becoming a mass creative activity, often involving large groups of professionals and amateurs, designers and users.

Companies and institutions need to be able to capture and convey such diffused creativity in order to gain advantage from this wave of potential innovation: several authors suggest a way to do it by creating 'innovation communities' supporting this attitude to flourish.

In the lexicon of marketing, Vargo and Lush (2004) make an analogous distinction between *operand resources*, resources (materials and goods) on which an operation or act is performed to produce an effect, and *operant resources* (knowledge and skills), which are employed to act on operand resources. In the emerging economy, the very nature of the new artefacts is very much related to operant resources. Skills and knowledge are the fundamental units of exchange, while goods are the distribution mechanism for service provision. Marketing is then conceived as a continuous learning process aiming at improving operant resources.

This shift from goods and commodities to enabling systems and people's competences and skills is changing the way designers have to work. Blurred boundaries now separate production and consumption, market and social economy.

SOCIAL CHARACTER

This emerging economy lies in the community dimension: value springs from relationships of trust among different stakeholders, users included (Zuboff and Maxmin 2002) and is no longer 'created' inside factories or offices. It is a social economy, because it is a system oriented to social needs and aspirations, where social innovation, the innovation in the creation of social outputs regardless of where they come from (Murray et al. 2008), is the crux of all paradigmatic changes.

This implies that the assets for value realisation need to be as distributed as the sources of value themselves. The co-production paradigm is making firms and institutions more permeable, overlapping and changeable (Ramirez 1999); it is pushing them to mobilise and manage stakeholders according to a logic of decentralisation.

Emphasis is on collaboration and interactions: peer-to-peer, disintermediation, wikis, open source are the new lexicon of the distributed systems (Murray 2009). Collaboration, cooperation, trust-based networks and user involvement in design for services are concepts now on the cutting edge of business (Murray et al. 2008). Production *for* the masses has been replaced by production *by* the masses. In addition multifunctional and multidisciplinary teams become the necessary and ordinary way of working; this is a consequence of the complexity of the new artefacts and of the hybrid and interdisciplinary nature of design work (see Manzini's introduction to this book, Ramirez 1999).

TECHNOLOGICAL INNOVATION

New technologies have a critical role in decentralisation, collaboration and interaction. The open source movement is often seen as a form of rebellion against the established corporate order and as a way of transforming traditional corporations.

Thanks to the breakthrough digital revolution, the already mentioned 'innovation communities' can actually exist and operate: very much locally rooted, these communities create in the household a new epicentre of entrepreneurship (Murray 2009) and become the key point and the beating hearts of several distributed systems. The way householders are directly collaborating, reconfiguring institutions and inventing new ones, is completely unprecedented; initiatives and innovation are widely dispersed and connected by networks, as small units in a large system. The very idea of small and large is actually changing, because the impact of an activity is not necessarily linked to its physical dimension, but to the quantity and quality of its links (Jégou and Manzini 2008).

Technology is bridging past and future: according to Leadbeater (2008), at least one part of the future could be a peculiar mixture of the 'peasant and the geek' and of pre-industrial and post-industrial combined, where ancient ideas will be partially rediscovered and reinterpreted.

ENVIRONMENTAL RE-ORIENTATION

It is no more an option but a 'must'. This emerging economy is committed to an environmental reorientation: ecology, ethics and reciprocity are key value points (Murray 2009) that can actually lead to benefits and profits for organisations. 'Green' is perceived as a complex concept, where several issues converge. Economies of scope become as important as economies of scale, because they can achieve substantial gains in effectiveness by providing more integrated and sustainable solutions. Moreover, ecological short product life cycles become possible and advantageous at the local and global scale.

This environmental reorientation is finally complemented by a relational one: in fact, large groups of people voluntarily commit their labour, not seeking financial reward or being told what to do, to create complex products and services of a recognised social value (Leadbeater 2008). Their aim is quality of relationships and personalisation (Murray et al. 2008) and the development of innovative products and services that better answer contemporary needs, matching the interest of the individual with the one of the community and the environment.

Objectives

The above-mentioned characteristics are driven by specific objectives. It is possible to identify some key ones to get a deeper understanding of these visions:

- *To introduce a preventative approach to policies and design*: adopting a preventative approach in the design of any public and private policy, related to issues such as heath, pollution, or waste reduction, is a necessary change of perspective. Instead of acting afterwards to deal with effects, preventative solutions can help in reducing production, dematerialising and detoxifying, while helping to reduce use and maintain products for longer (Murray 2009). As a consequence, a preventative attitude calls for a new generation of products, conceived in the light of the service provision. This empowers designers to think in terms of services instead of goods, and represents an opportunity to expand the market by supporting the user in knowledge and value creation activities, instead of merely consumption ones.

- *To provide individualised support and advocacy for people*: in a framework of trustworthy relationships, this new economy aims to support people in their life choices and activities. This 'support' is the new purpose of production and commerce; it is becoming the 'meta-product' that people ask for, to gain an adequate social participation and self-realisation.

- *To shift economy to a network paradigm*: a network paradigm has the potential to transform the relationships between the organisational centre and the peripheries. It takes advantage of the knowledge that lies at the borders and reduces the asymmetry of information that traditionally exists between the producer and the user. It means distributing complexity to the margins (i.e. to the household and the innovation communities) as a strategy to activate the peripheral knowledge, rather than standardise and simplify. It also creates the conditions for a continuum dialogue with stakeholders and the society as whole about the future, opening up possibilities that are more related to people's lives and needs.

- *To create a more open and democratic approach to innovation and competition*: society as a whole can benefit by the reduction of entry barriers and professional control on knowledge and information that have characterised organisations and markets thus far.

These characteristics and objectives describe an ongoing transformation, but also a vision for the future that needs to be adequately supported and cultivated, if we want to achieve the hoped-for reorientation of the economy toward more sustainable patterns. A deep understanding of these phenomena as they manifest themselves today and the ability to evaluate how designers can work for and within these dynamics is strategic and necessary. Starting from our map of what we believe design for services is, we have suggested some possible actions that designers can take as part of their contribution and participation to this ongoing transformation.

Designers' Actions

The depiction of this emerging economy is enriched by the authors with the discussion of possible actions and measures to support it to flourish and strengthen: some of them can be regarded as particularly relevant for the field of design for services and its future developments. We consider these actions as areas where the discipline needs to grow stronger, gaining more visibility in the field and providing a notable contribution at different levels. Some of these actions are, for example:

- *The re-conceptualisation of products as part of services*: the central role of design for services is evident here. In this perspective services can be seen as the starting point for innovation and the 'reason why' for designing goods. This implies understanding the value of services in the creation of new meanings and new behaviours (Verganti 2009). This point is crucial for progressively shifting the models of production and consumption towards more sustainable ones, based on accessing and using instead of owning and consuming. Taking a step further, this means considering design for services as a key contribution to any design education. The emergence of a 'service logic' (Vargo and Lush 2004) implies the need to learn in terms of processes, relationships and networks, this independently of which design discipline one belongs to. How is design for services positioned and recognised today within design education? How can this wider transformational role be enhanced in the development of the discipline?

- *The generation of accessible and distributed technology-based interfaces*: as already widely recognised, information and communication technologies (ICT) are the production system and one of the main innovation drivers for services. In this new emerging economy technology is acquiring a special role in supporting its social, open and collaborative, development. Proper access systems and dedicated interfaces are required. Design for services needs to develop a greater understanding and familiarity with ICT potentials and their relation with social innovation and service model change. Designers should make technologies affordable, accessible and operable for a variety of potential users, while creating networks of collaboration and mutual support. Understanding the deep interconnection of people and technologies in all dimensions of life is a vital skill for designers working in the service field (and not only there). Technology and digital economy, finally, can help to distribute and organise assets around the people, so to bring competences and design tools to the periphery of the productive system and thus to reshape business processes from the point of view of the final user.

- *Managing distributed networks*: distributed networks are another key component of this emerging economy, as they represent the backbone that supports and connects the operative 'cells' of the social economy. They request platforms that create the right conditions for stakeholders and users (organised in 'innovation communities') to engage in co-production. To do so, and to make this diffused creativity become effective, the reduction and simplification of the number and the role of players acting as intermediates with the market and the institutions is crucial. Participating in the shape of these platforms and developing proper tools to support creative collaborations and co-production is the way design for services can contribute to this action, enabling stakeholders and users to interact with competence and creativity. This capacity to connect and facilitate collaborative and distributed processes is becoming strategic for any innovation project. It implies a deeper understanding of 'innovation communities' and networks, design thinking methods and tools as well as of facilitation techniques and platforms.

- *Open innovation for complex projects*: contemporary issues such as chronic disease, ageing, environmental degradation and economic breakdown require complex set of interventions that cannot be solved by individuals and single organisations alone and that need creative solutions. The 'open innovation' paradigm tackles complex problems by modularising them in tasks, and activating core teams which invite other actors to contribute to the problem-solving process by conducting experiments in parallel. As a consequence, these distributed 'self-governing communities' need overall rules and tools to contribute to the project (Leadbeater 2008). Design for services (and design in general) needs to familiarise itself with open innovation models to support and contribute to wider programmes for change. Designers can help develop briefs for collective challenges while conceiving the 'social structure' (Leadbeater 2008) that allows people to contribute with different degrees of engagement and capabilities. This requires the development of tools for participation that need to be cheap and easy enough to be widely employed.

- *The development of a creative and collaborative society*: the growth of this emerging economy requires people's participation and collaboration if it is to increase. To achieve this it is fundamental that the expansion and diffusion of this kind of 'amateur work' is supported. As Leadbeater suggests (2008), thanks to the rising of educational attainments and to cheaper and diffused communication technology, innovation and creativity are actually already more distributed and can come from a different range of sources. Learning to co-design can happen while interacting with coaches, peers, clubs, networks or events: strong emphasis has been given to the role of the figures such as 'tutors' or 'coaches' working as personal advisers to support design initiatives and community empowerment (Zuboff and Maxmin 2002, Leadbeater 2008, Manzini, introduction to this book). Designers can act as visionary facilitators and catalysers of ideas, while allowing people through participation to become active designers of their own solutions. Design for services is already engaging in community-based initiatives, adopting a transformational approach to design projects, but little research has been done on its effectiveness and its methods.

This list of actions confirms that the already relational, co-produced and interactive nature of services is growing in a considerable way. It is actually expanding, characterising the economy and innovation processes as a whole. These actions suggest the need to multiply the possibilities of interaction and creativity, providing platforms and tools for creative and open collaborations and enhancing skills and capacities for people to engage in change initiatives. Services are becoming a paradigm for a more relational economy and society; design for services is in a good position to provide a relevant contribution to this transformation.

To visualise this contribution we should imagine two parallel transformations and integrate them: society and design both moving toward more open and collaborative patterns and identities. Design for services is developing in between these two bigger changes (see Figure 3.1).

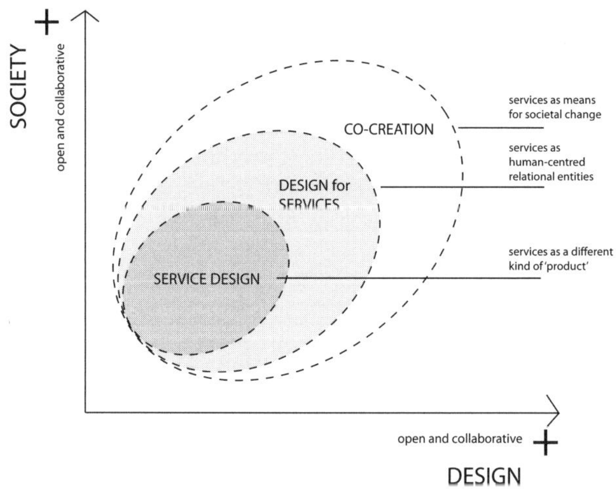

Figure 3.1 Ongoing transformations in design and society

In this process, services themselves are changing in their nature and conception. At the beginning of this book we talked about how design has been working for services that were conceived as a different kind of 'product', referring to the IHIP qualities – intangibility, heterogeneity, inseparability and perishability. We then made another step forward interpreting services as complex and relational entities that include products in processes where the human component is determinant, so that they cannot be fully designed, meaning predetermined. This step has led us to the use of the term 'design for services' (instead of design of services) with its interdisciplinary and emergent qualities, as well as potential areas of intervention. Finally in this last chapter we are moving this conversation forward, looking at services as a potential engine for wider societal transformations. As these conversations about the future of economy are suggesting, services are no longer considered as a design 'object', but as a 'mean' for supporting the emergence of a more collaborative and creative society and economy. Within this progression, co-creation is taking a significant role. We believe that this progression needs to be made more explicit to better understand and experiment with, through further research and discussions, how design for services can evolve in this scenario and contribute to a more sustainable future.

References

Inghilleri, P. 2003. *La ' buona vita'. Per l'uso creativo degli oggetti nella società dell'abbondanza.* Milan: Guerini e Associati.

Jégou, F. and Manzini, E. 2008. *Collaborative Services. Social Innovation and Design for Sustainability.* Milan: Edizioni Polidesign.

Leadbeater, C. 2008. *We Think: The Power of Mass Creativity.* London: Profile Books Ltd.

Murray, R. 2009. *Danger and Opportunity. Crisis and the New Social Economy. Provocation 09.* London: NESTA.

Murray, R., Mulgan, G. and Caulier-Grice, J. 2008. *How to Innovate: The Tools for Social Innovation.* Working paper. London: SIX Social Innovation Exchange.

Parker, S. and Heapy, J. 2006. *The Journey to the Interface. How Public Service Design can Connect Users to Reform.* London: Demos.

Ramirez, R. 1999. Value co-production: intellectual origins and implications for practice and research. *Strategic Management Journal*, 20, 49–65.

Toffler, A. 1980. *The Third Wave.* London: Collins.

Vargo, S. L. and Lush, R. F. 2004. Evolving to a new dominant logic for marketing. *Journal of Marketing*, 68, 1–17.

Vargo, S. L., Maglio, P. and Archpru Akaka, M. 2008. On value and value co-creation: a service systems and service logic perspective. *European Management Journal, 26,* 145–52.

Verganti, R. 2009. *Design-driven Innovation: Changing the Rules of Competition by Radically Innovating What Things Mean.* Boston, MA: Harvard Business School Publishing.

Von Hippel, E. 2005. *Democratizing Innovation.* Cambridge, MA: The MIT Press.

Zuboff, S. and Maxmin, J. 2002. *The Support Economy: Why Corporations Are Failing Individuals and the Next Episode of Capitalism.* New York: Penguin Books.

Appendix 1: An Open Conversation

This first appendix reports a conversation we had with a selection of key researchers and professionals working in the area of design for services. We thought it would be a good idea to integrate and conclude our reflection on current areas of research and practice of design for services with an open conversation on possible new ones for the near future. As the discipline is gaining a wider transformational role for society and the economy, we wanted to hear from professionals what future they were thinking of for design for services. In particular we asked what were the key areas they would like to work in or see research on in the coming years.

Their answers recall in some ways the key issues and characteristics of the 'emerging economy', as we discussed earlier. They all suggest a shift in the economy, where the role of products, people and organisations are subject to profound change. Their main drivers are people's activation and creativity, together with a strong call to include sustainability as a priority in service projects. Interventions in the public sector and skills and tools for organisational change are considered particularly relevant here. As a discipline they suggest the need to consolidate its history, identity, credibility and methodology and, at the same time, to reflect on its influence on other design fields such as product or communication design. Josephine Green suggests there is more here than just designing for services, and brings in the role of technology. She talks about a 'context economy' where:

> *Technology is embedded into our everyday environments, our walls, floors, clothes, so that we no longer consume but rather relate to an evolving ecosystem of information ... what is a service, a solution, an experience in this new integrated contextual space?*

In this appendix we summarise briefly the key emerging points of this open conversation, and then report the individual answers. Readers can use these quotes as inspiration for research directions as well as a mapping tool to realise where and on which topic design for services is currently developing in the world. Thus we can elicit the following as potential key areas for future research:

PEOPLE'S ACTIVATION AND CREATIVITY

- Developing the contribution of design for services to facilitate people's engagement and contribution to public and private initiatives (Morelli, Staszowski, Franqueira, Green, Down);

- Understanding the role of design for services in enhancing and supporting social creativity, entrepreneurship and co-creation (Franqueira, Young, Staszowski);

- Understanding the opportunities that exist in the 'unorganised' service sectors in fast developing countries, creating useful design solutions to support this kind of 'un-formalised economy' (Mehta).

SUSTAINABILITY

- Understanding the contribution of design for services in enhancing sustainability and social innovation (Brass, Staszowski, Malaguti);
- Developing tools and methods to tackle social and environmental problems (Brass);
- Supporting the shift from ownership to access (Down, Malaguti).

ORGANISATIONAL CHANGE AND INNOVATION

- Investigating the role of design for services in changing production and delivery systems and networks (Miettinen, Tonkinwise);
- Developing methods and tools to catalyse organisational change (Heapy);
- Investigating the role of design for services to enable deep customisation and open solutions (Green);
- Measuring the impact of design for services in innovation of service systems (Mager);
- Identifying and investigating the impact of design for services on products and communication artefacts (Malaguti, Green);
- Exploring methods and issues related to diffusion, replication and industrialisation of services (Morelli, Yongqi).

PUBLIC SECTOR AND URBAN DEVELOPMENT

- Understanding and developing the contribution and value of design for services in the public sector (Morelli, Young, Staszowski, Miettinen, Franqueira, Green);
- Investigating the role of design for services in retrofitting urban infrastructures and buildings (Staszowski);
- Developing the potential of design for services to safeguard or regenerate the commons (Franqueira);
- Helping to resolve how policy impacts on people in real-world contexts through design for services (Young).

DESIGN FOR SERVICES AS A DISCIPLINE

- Demonstrating the value and meaning of design for services in terms of its identity, impact, credibility and legitimacy (Mager, Young, Johansson);

- Understanding and developing the relation (and cross-fertilisation) with other disciplines (Mager, Johansson, Yongqi);
- Investigating design for services in the history of design and within product service systems historical innovation (Collina, Tonkinwise);
- Investigating the meaning of aesthetics in design for services (Collina);
- Investigating the emotional dimensions of service encounters considering all actors involved (Penin).

Short Interviews

CLARE BRASS, MANAGING DIRECTOR, SEED FOUNDATION, UK

With a service sometimes offering an alternative to a product, there has always been an incidental social and environmental benefit in service design. However, the relationship between service design and sustainability needs to become explicit. More research and case studies that explain this principle would be useful, and I would like to see a set of tools evolve from service design thinking and methodology that enable designers to tackle social and environmental problems. Mapping, service blueprinting, user-centred design and co-creation are all essential ingredients that should be embedded in the skills every designer has and become part of the everyday toolkit.

LUISA COLLINA, FULL PROFESSOR OF DESIGN, CHAIR OF THE PRODUCT SERVICE SYSTEM DESIGN MASTER, SCHOOL OF DESIGN, POLITECNICO DI MILAN, ITALY

Services are quite a new field of research for designers and for this reason there are several areas where it would be interesting to have a better understanding in the future. One of these is historical research: what are the origins of service design? Are there any examples of service design in the history of design? Achille Castiglioni designing the Splügen Bräu (1960), Domus Academy developing the Agronica project (1995) or more recently Michele De Lucchi designing the new Italian post offices and Deutsche Bank. Aren't these examples of service design?

This kind of research is important in order to understand the deep relationship between design and services as something that is not new but embedded in the history of design. What is new is the growing importance of services in our everyday life in comparison to products and awareness of the necessity to develop a service design approach.

The second area of research I would suggest is related to the aesthetic of service design: how can we give shape to services? How can we design a final service that is attractive, enjoyable, user-friendly and not only appropriate from a functional point of view? The enrichment of pure functionalism that has already happened in products, communication and interior design is still weak in service design.

CHRIS DOWNS, NON-EXECUTIVE DIRECTOR AND SHAREHOLDER, LIVE|WORK, UK

Service design offers up an enormous number of valuable research opportunities. It is a young discipline with an incredible potential to make profound change. From the very beginning it has always been live|work's ambition to use design to develop services that were more socially, environmentally and financially sustainable than owning products. But there's a very real problem. People love owning products. And that is where I would like to see some research focus. What attributes of a shared service are needed to convince people to give up the alternative of owning a product? What do we really have to do as designers to inspire the shift from ownership to access and from consumers to participants?

TERESA FRANQUEIRA, ASSISTANT PROFESSOR AND UNDERGRADUATE DESIGN COURSE COORDINATOR, COMMUNICATION AND ART DEPARTMENT, UNIVERSITY OF AVEIRO, CAMPUS UNIVERSITÁRIO DE SANTIAGO, PORTUGAL

I would like to develop design tools and platforms for a creativity-based collaboration and mass participation in the fields of urban and social renewal. These would aim at bridging top-down initiatives with bottom-up ones, designing an interface capable of nurturing and sustaining social and economic innovation and stimulating an active citizenship, providing tools for citizens to collaborate, create and contribute in the process.

In this respect, I would like to see real projects where those strategies and tools could be trialled and tested to further advance us towards a more active and collaborative society, for a more sustainable world.

It would be interesting to study ways of shifting the focus on the market and industry to a focus on people and their interactions with their governments and institutions, engaging design in the process of promoting active citizenship and open governance dynamics – ultimately translated in more participation, collaboration, inclusion and well-being.

JOE HEAPY, CO-FOUNDER AND DIRECTOR, ENGINE, UK

Almost as quickly as it appeared, the term 'transformation design' dissolved into the ongoing debate about the value of design. Too hard to formulate into a practical discipline (for now at least), the idea that design – all design – is in some way transformational is motivational for designers, but too self-conscious and presumptive to expose beyond design. Engine works with many large organisations all seeking to deliver better services. These organisations share similar problems and seek to transform in similar ways. We've found four recurring approaches that seem to stimulate demand for design-led approaches: culture change through influencing organisational behaviours, optimising existing business processes, developing or acquiring new capabilities and getting better at listening and responding to customers. The nature of 'design-led' has something to offer each approach. How effective is the service design method – design thinking – in catalysing change in organisations? Can the practice of design be formulated into a legitimate and codified process for organisational improvement?

JOSEPHINE GREEN, STRATEGIC DESIGN CONSULTANT, FORMER SENIOR DIRECTOR, SOCIAL INNOVATION, PHILIPS DESIGN

We hear a lot about services but unfortunately the talk is too often about combining services to products and about designing services for people rather than by people themselves. But service design is much more than this, and precisely because it is so much more then maybe it can no longer be isolated as a 'service' under the heading of service design

We are shifting from a consumer economy to a 'context economy', one in which technology is embedded into our everyday environments, our walls, floors, clothes, so that we no longer consume but rather relate to an evolving ecosystem of information, services, solutions and experiences within those environments. This is a major shift in behaviour and so in design and gives rise to a design strategy based on deep customisation and open solutions. A strategy in which passive consumers become active producers of their own services, solutions and environments. For me the big design questions are: in a relational environment what is the role of design? How can we make tangible deep customisation? What are the open tools towards open solutions? How do we interface and interact with this new world? What is a service, a solution, an experience in this new integrated contextual space? Perhaps most importantly, is the context economy a way to rethink some of the big social challenges such as the delivery of meaningful health, education, care of the elderly, mobility etc. For me these are fundamental research questions that cover the 'what' as much as the 'how' and the 'who'.

ULLA JOHANSSON, TORSTEN AND WANJA SÖDERBERG PROFESSORSHIP IN DESIGN MANAGEMENT, DIRECTOR, BUSINESS AND DESIGN LAB, UNIVERSITY OF GOTHENBURG, HDK-SCHOOL OF DESIGN AND CRAFTS AND SCHOOL OF BUSINESS, ECONOMICS AND LAW, SWEDEN

There is a need of good ethnographic research that can conceptualise and verbalise (or illustrate in pictures) what service design is about in order to make it possible to grasp the potential and possibilities for those who are going to use service designers. Those working with service design do have an identity and tacit knowledge about what it is, but those employing service design need to have a better understanding of what is meant – or what could be meant – by service design.

Also, I want research that, from an artistic point of view, compares service design with service management as an academic area. Since the two areas are in one way overlapping each other and looking at the same phenomena – the user and their requirements/needs and how they can be taken care of. But on the other hand the two areas are like alien worlds. How to conceptualise and compare them in a way that is fair and respectful to both of them? And is there a possibility for a merger or at least a connection between the two? What would that connection look like and what are the epistemological prerequisites for a good interdisciplinary meeting?

BIRGIT MAGER, PROFESSOR OF SERVICE DESIGN, KÖLN INTERNATIONAL SCHOOL OF DESIGN, GERMANY

The value of design in goods and manufacturing industries is proven and well understood, and companies using design in a systematic way are significantly more successful in the market. There is a deep body of knowledge related to the effective design of information, orientation, tangible products and user interfaces. Fifteen years ago service design began to emerge and since then many projects have shown that design has enormous power to improve and innovate service systems.

Still the discipline is young, and one research challenge will be to evaluate and measure in a systematic way the impacts of service design. This will support the integration of service design into business models.

It will also be important to learn more about culture- and market-specific needs for the design of services. What are the specific challenges? How do methods and processes have to be adapted in order to get the best result? How can service design be applied to B2B (business-to-business) systems?

Cross-fertilisation among disciplines and the integration of different approaches is another challenge. Learning from structures, processes, roles and interactions of performing arts, for example, is one of the research fields that is inspiring and promising.

Design has always been about influencing the behaviour of the customer or receiver. In the future we will need to broaden this knowledge in order to influence behaviour of other people within service systems. Services are co-created and co-produced, so the design of settings that enable all actors to perform easily and successfully is crucial.

CYNTIA MALAGUTI, PROFESSOR OF DESIGN, DESIGN COURSE, TECHNOLOGY DEPARTMENT, FACULTY OF ARCHITECTURE AND URBANISM, UNIVERSITY OF SÃO PAULO, BRAZIL

In what concerns service design and its relations to traditional design fields, it would be interesting to know, for example, what kinds of new products as well as changes and innovations are created in connection to the service peculiarities. Another relevant topic could be to investigate, in a particular case, how the partnerships and cooperation links created amidst the supply chain – production, distribution, commerce – influence visual identity and other design aspects.

Nowadays we face many situations where people from different countries, places and cultures meet each other for different reasons; therefore it would be important to study how service design deals with and helps multicultural dialogue and interchange.

And finally, it is crucial to research the ways in which service design initiatives contribute to sustainability, either by giving strength to habits such as hiring, sharing or repairing products instead of buying them or creating a better support for conviviality.

SHASHANK MEHTA, PROFESSOR OF INDUSTRIAL DESIGN, FACULTY OF INDUSTRIAL DESIGN, NATIONAL INSTITUTE OF DESIGN, AHMEDABAD, INDIA

In the context of India and other developing and densely populated countries, services offer great opportunity for employment at the individual level, utilising the person's existing skills, resources and the availability of time. It thus helps individuals to gain economic independence and confidence. Services are generally low on investment and help connect people at the individual and societal level.

A valuable area to investigate would be understanding the opportunities that exist in the 'unorganised' service sectors in India, developing useful design solutions for these kinds of organisations; I think that there is still a need to develop a systematic approach for this kind of design intervention.

Services that are generally pursued by industries aim to improve their customer relationship and the service interface, while the ones that I am talking about here are largely part of an unformalised economy that utilises limited skills and resources to offer employment opportunities at the individual level. A research project to document various examples of such typology of services has been planned.

SATU MIETTINEN, CO-ORDINATOR, DA, COMPETENCE CENTRE FOR INDUSTRIAL DESIGN, SAVONIA UNIVERSITY OF APPLIED SCIENCES, FINLAND

One of the areas of service design is and will be the transformation of public services. The means and funding of the public sector in Western economies is decreasing while at the same time the pressure in this area is increasing. We need new solutions that cross over the organisational and administrational boundaries. A service design and user-centred design approach can provide new service solutions for this area.

New public services will include the end user, the community member, the citizen in the service design process. The service chain will include the private and the public service providers as well as the third sector. These new service chains can be designed with service design methods.

Tourism and the leisure industry also offer more and more opportunities for service design. Services contribute to a major part of the turnover in this business area. Experience design will play an increasingly important part in the production process.

Service design and experience design are close partners when user experiences are produced in the leisure industry.

NICOLA MORELLI, ASSOCIATE PROFESSOR, SCHOOL OF ARCHITECTURE AND DESIGN, AALBORG UNIVERSITY, DENMARK

I would like to see research in two main areas: service design as a discipline and service design methodology.

The research on service design as a discipline should focus on the areas in which service design can make a difference in social and life quality. I think public services should be primarily considered as the main source of social and economic innovation. A new design approach based on citizens' participation and activation can introduce a paradigm shift in the way public services are organised.

The methodological research area could focus on the industrialisation of services. At the moment the most innovative services are developed as isolated cases. The methodological effort should concern how to design highly innovative services, taking into consideration the heritage of the industrial age, based on reproducibility, division of labour and codification of knowledge.

LARA PENIN, ASSISTANT PROFESSOR, SCHOOL OF DESIGN STRATEGIES, PARSONS THE NEW SCHOOL FOR DESIGN, NEW YORK, USA

The area I would like to see research on is about the emotional quality of the service encounter from the perspective of service jobs. This is now being studied in regard to non-commercial services (for example collaborative services, peer-to-peer) when the service exchange is freed from the burden of a commercial transaction. When it comes to commercial services (and this can mean an extremely diverse range of service provisions), this aspect is mostly focused on the user side. The provider side is normally approached at the organisation level but less often at the level of the agents of the provider, that is, people at the front desk of the service encounter. During the design process, we normally fail to acknowledge the point of view of these service agents who are themselves being (emotionally) affected by all touch-points from uniforms to space, not to mention protocols and scripts; and their emotional input is critical to determine the quality of the service encounter. I am particularly interested in exploring this aspect within healthcare services, where the management of the emotional tension between service users and providers is critical.

EDUARDO STASZOWSKI, ASSISTANT PROFESSOR OF DESIGN STRATEGIES, SCHOOL OF DESIGN STRATEGIES, CITIES/SERVICES/ECOSYSTEMS, PARSONS THE NEW SCHOOL FOR DESIGN, NEW YORK, USA

There is a growing interest in how (service) design thinking can be introduced in the public sector and at policy level to create more sustainable forms of urban living. I would like to see more research on how (service) designers could help cities and their governments to cope with the ever-growing urban challenges, in particular in the design of innovative urban services that would inspire and enable people to adopt more sustainable lifestyles. More specifically, I am interested in two directions:

1. The potential of services to retrofit the already built infrastructure of our cities in opposition to definitive solutions that come within the notion of 'urban renewal'. These include how services could deliver solutions to the lack of affordable housing, reduce traffic congestion and promote sustainable food systems, particularly through the re-functionalisation of

existing structures, networks and systems like bringing the farm to the city instead of bringing the food from the farm.

2. New community-engagement models to increase the adoption and diffusion of original service ideas and stimulate entrepreneurial creativity based on cultural specificities, cultural heritage and tacit knowledge of individuals and groups.

CAMERON TONKINWISE, CHAIR DESIGN THINKING AND SUSTAINABILITY, PARSONS THE NEW SCHOOL FOR DESIGN, NEW YORK, USA

As Dolores Hayden documents in *The Grand Domestic Revolution* (1996), late nineteenth-century USA saw a proliferation of product–service system innovations. These centred on outsourcing private domestic production – food production, clothing care, child care, etc. – to collectives. One of the most iconic examples comes from King C. Gillette, who may have bequeathed to the twentieth century the unsustainable economy of disposability, but who actually wanted to bequeath to the future aggregated and therefore more efficient domestic service industries. Hayden describes the convergence that led to these initiatives: the arrival of technological innovations that worked best at scale (steam power), and the socio-political changes that discouraged domestic servants whilst wanting to liberate bourgeois women from isolated domestic labour, as well as a bit of utopian socialism. I would love to research more closely this 'road not taken' of product–service systems that nearly prevented high eco-impacting household activities from disappearing into private and therefore resistant-to-change kitchens and laundries. It is crucial that service design not think of itself as brand new and unprecedented. Historical maturity is essential if the kinds of more sustainable service systems now being proposed are not to suffer the same fate as these late nineteenth-century innovations.

Households become their own designers, processors and assemblers, and their houses mini-offices.

The key intermediaries are those that have the knowledge and trust to bring together the relevant packages of support. They are the assemblers of the knowledge economy.

LOU YONGQI, PROFESSOR OF DESIGN, COLLEGE OF DESIGN AND INNOVATION, TONGJI UNIVERSITY, SHANGHAI, CHINA

The awareness of a paradigm shift from design doing to design thinking is already well recognised. As a new field, service design provides an approach that can manipulate and adjust society without destroying or severing its structure. It has already become one of the ideal design tools to encourage social innovation and sustainability. To improve prospects for impact and implementation, service design should enter more fields including economics, policy, environment and society. Prototyping, networking and popularising promising cases indicate new fields and new roles, by making them more and more visible. The methodology of service design and related skills, methods and tools still needs to be well developed through conversation and interaction with other disciplines. The management of service design and the related new economy should also become one of the main topics for this new discipline.

ROBERT YOUNG, ASSOCIATE DEAN, RESEARCH AND INNOVATION, SCHOOL OF DESIGN, NORTHUMBRIA UNIVERSITY, NEWCASTLE, UK

We have come to recognise that the quality of services depends on the responsibility and accountability of both those who deliver and those who receive and this requires different mentalities and behaviours to that which societies have become accustomed through product consumerism. Service experiences are transformed by human encounters and their 'narrativity', and therefore an important function of service design teams is to orchestrate these through co-designing processes. What we can infer from our study of service design as an evolving field of practice is that whilst it is not a subset of product design but its own meta- or interdiscipline, it is nevertheless a further evolution of good design thinking and practice to realise a better world; in the face of three horizons that define our contemporary existence – artifice, the market and social and environmental sustainability – design plays a key role using creativity to promote human dignity.

Service design will continue to evolve organically through practice, helping to resolve how policy impacts on people in real-world contexts. A key task for research is to bring clarity to the interpretive methodologies that connect people and policy, theory and practice to enable existing policy makers from disciplines with influence to see design as a credible and reliable process. There is a corresponding critical action for academia to revise how creative education is developed to address service issues.

References

Hayden, D. 1996. *Grand Domestic Revolution: History of Feminist Designs for American Homes, Neighbourhoods and Cities*. Cambridge, MA; Massachusetts Institute of Technology Press.

Appendix 2:
Tools of Design for Services

The design tools presented in this second appendix to the book have been derived and selected from the 18 cases studies. They don't cover all the existing set of tools of designing for services, but they provide a good overview of the kind of methods that are currently applied in the field.

Tools have been clustered in four main activities: analysing, generating, developing and prototyping. These activities can easily represent the four common stages of a design process. The tools, listed in the following pages, are briefly described in terms of *what* they are, *when* they are generally used and *how* they are generally applied. It is not a detailed description, but it works as scaffolding instructions and examples that professionals and researchers can pick up and reinterpret in their own processes. Moreover, given the iterative nature of any design process, the same tools can actually be used more than one time and at different stages by different people.

The four design activities of analysing, generating, developing and prototyping can be described as follows:

1. *Analysing*: these tools help in collecting, recording and sharing contextual information, using different media such as videos, sound, images or text. They can be supplied to users or used in interaction with project participants to explore their perceptions and experiences – *Myspace; customer journey map; directed storytelling; emotional map; design documentary; video-blog; film diary; user diary; story collection.*

2. *Generating*: these tools help in constructing a shared meaning out of collected experiences through direct or mediated conversations with project participants. They use different kinds of visualisations to suggest service ideas, aesthetics or stories – *idea sketches; glimpses; service moodboard.*

3. *Developing*: these tools provide different kinds of formats with which to elaborate and develop service ideas into more detailed and rich stories and systems. They support designers to explore parts in relation to the entirety of the service while evaluating its feasibility – *micropanoramic; storyboard; service blueprint; expressive service blueprint; visual service scripts; service breakdown; system map; service interaction design guidelines; desirability, viability, feasibility.*

4. *Prototyping*: these tools provide modes to quickly test out new service ideas during workshops or in real settings with people. They allow people to experiment with new service models, reducing the risk of failure and enhancing the possibility of generating more meaningful and desirable

futures – *Video sketch; living labs; FASPE (fast service prototyping and simulation for evaluation); experience prototype.*

The tools presented in this collection have been outlined by the different authors of this book, and edited by Meroni and Sangiorgi.

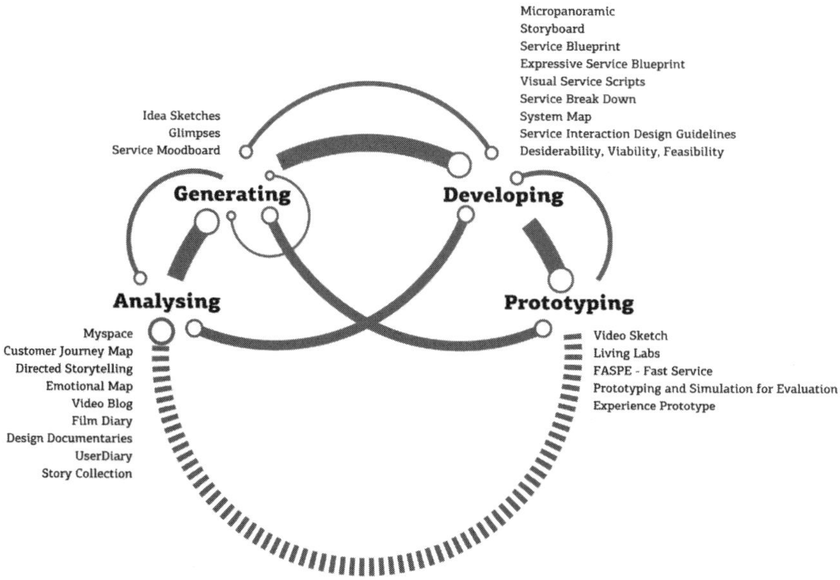

Figure A2.1 A diagram that represents the iterative nature of a design process and the tools presented in this book that populate the different stages

Analysing

MYSPACE

DANIELA SANGIORGI AND SABINE JUNGINGER

What – *Myspace* is a tool that encourages and facilitates participants to identify, express, record and share aspects of their lives. The booklet's structure, targeted to a specific inquiry, enables designers to draw in people's experiences without violating or invading participant's privacy.

When – *Myspace* can be used as an exploratory tool at the early stages of a design project. It works best as part of an inquiry when it is coupled and complemented with other research methods, such as observation, shadowing or interviews.

How – *Myspace* has been thought as an offline version of the well-known community website. It works like a scrapbook that project participants can use to communicate their lives, answering overall questions such as: 'what matters to us in our lives?'. It can be semi-structured with sections and prompting questions (for example talk about your life, share who you like and why, etc.); participants may be given cameras and be encouraged to download images from the Internet or cut-outs from magazines, make hand drawings, use personal photos, stickers, text or whatever else they saw fit. The booklets can then be used in workshops where participants present their scrapbook, get to know each other better and identify common themes, interests, issues, etc. A facilitator can then map out what emerges from the conversations, clustering emergent topics in thematic groups.

Figure A2.2 An application of Myspace in a project for a secondary school in east Lancashire, UK

Source: ImaginationLancaster, Lancaster University.

CUSTOMER JOURNEY MAP

ANNA MERONI AND DANIELA SANGIORGI

What – The *customer journey map* is a simplification of a blueprint and an evolution of the storyboard. It maps out the customer journey through the service, identifying the main encounters, evidences and key actions of the supplier. A strong emphasis is given to touch-points and their role in the interaction to make the process more tangible, clear and accessible. It also provides dedicated space to synthetically visualise identified issues and possible improvements to be undertaken.

When – The *customer journey map* can be used at an exploratory stage as well as later on when the detail of a new service is being specified. It can help stakeholders inside and external to organisations identify problems in an existing service and generate recommendations for making improvements.

How – Designing services typically involves several parts of an organisation such as marketing, operations, and finance. Cross-functional teams and end users working together to visualise the service journey generates a more accurate representation of when and how value is co-produced. Ethnographically inspired methods during which researchers observe or shadow stakeholders, capturing key moments with photos, for example, provide some of the data with which to populate this template. But it is through co-creation workshops when different stakeholders work together to map out the journey that valuable opportunities to improve the service emerge.

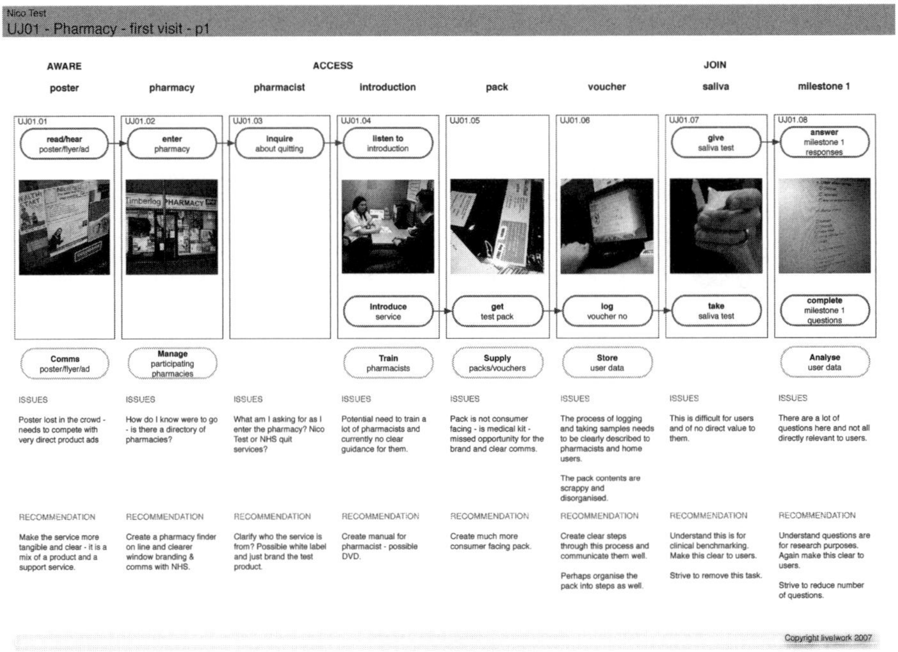

Figure A2.3 An example of a customer journey map
Source: live|work.

DIRECTED STORYTELLING

SHELLEY EVENSON

What – Stories have been shared among people as a way of entertaining, teaching, and preserving culture. Drawn from the technique of narrative inquiry from anthropology *directed storytelling* is a method that designers use to facilitate participants in expressing and sharing the details of their service experience.

The process quickly reveals consistent patterns in people's experiences and for reinforcing or validating what the designer may already know.

When – *Directed storytelling* can be used as an exploratory tool at the early stages of a design project. It should be used as a way to inform what should be done in other research methods, such as observation, shadowing, participatory design, etc.

How – The session leader asks the storyteller to begin the story by asking the subject to recall a specific instance – 'Tell me about the last time you had a communication at a distance' – and encouraging the subject to use props if they are related to the experience and are at hand. As the story unfolds, the documenter writes one idea per page (ideally on Post-its). Ideas are elements of the story that seem to be important either through the emphasis that the storyteller has given or through the documenter's own interpretation of the information given by the storyteller. The telling and recording continues as long as it takes to recount the experience.

Figure A2.4 An example of the results of a directed storytelling session organised into a map
Source: Politecnico di Milano.

EMOTIONAL MAP

DEBORA SZEBEKO

What – The *emotional map* is a tool to map and then describe emotional touchpoints as people journey through the service. It helps all the subjects involved in a design process to understand the experiences of the users, their challenges and where priorities for improving the experience lie, giving everyone an opportunity to evaluate and decide on those priorities.

When – *Emotional maps* are used in the first stages of an experience-based design process, helping to find the key points of the service experience, to define priorities by voting and to start discussing their possible improvement, redesign or rethink.

How – The *emotional map* is built directly by each subject involved in the service with the support of the designer. Everybody is requested to map and describe the experience within the given context of the service and/or extend the reflection beyond this, maintaining a manageable scale. This allows subjects to consider all environments users come in contact with during the service journey. The result is a paper map evidencing the different touchpoints and the related emotions.

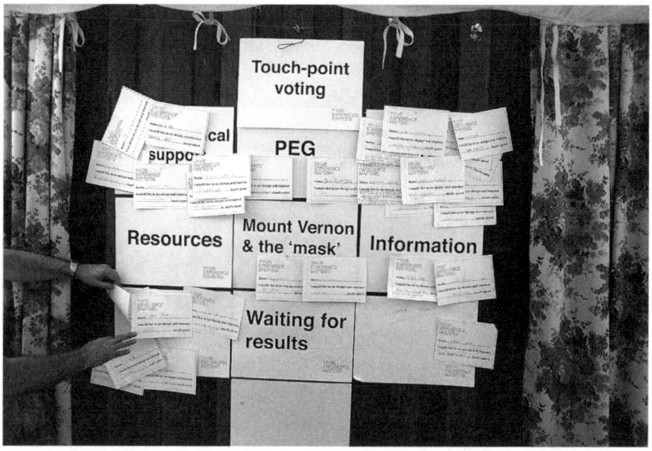

Figure A2.5 An example of emotional maps built in a co-design process for the NHS Institute for Innovation and Improvement at Luton and Dunstable Hospital, UK
Source: *thinkpublic*.

DESIGN DOCUMENTARIES

BAS RAIJMAKERS

What – The *design documentaries* bring the techniques and ideas documentary film-makers use to video ethnography for design. The aim of the tool is to tell stories about relevant practices and motives of people through a short film. This allows the team to empathise with the future users of their designs. The team can step into the shoes of the future users and think from their perspective about the services they are designing.

When – *Design documentaries* are particularly useful at the very early stages of a design process when it is still necessary to create insights about the people you are designing for, and develop opportunities for service design. They are mostly used to get a good understanding of the future users before concept development starts.

How – Four types of film techniques are used in *design documentaries*: *observation*, *compilation*, *intervention* and *performance*. All of them can be applied in many variations, as documentary film-makers have done for over 100 years. The best way to learn is to watch documentary films and appropriate the techniques you see. Design documentaries are empathic conversations between the researchers making the film and the people in the film. This can be literally a conversation, but also a constructed conversation, for instance when the film observes people and has a voice-over from the film-maker. The films are mostly used to inform and inspire design teams in conceiving workshops as well as during later stages of the design process.

Figure A2.6 Still from Debra, a design documentary to understand and empathise with heart patients, for Philips Medical Systems USA

Source: STBY.

CREDITS
www.designdocumentaries.com

VIDEO-BLOG

BAS RAIJMAKERS

What – The *video-blog* is a tool used to share videos collected during research with the design team. By putting individual video clips online and tagging them, designers can organise the clips any way they prefer. At the same time a video-blog has pages that bring a selection of the clips together in stories. Both stories and tagged clips help designers to explore issues around a certain question or topic they encounter while designing.

When – *Video-blogs* can be used at any design stage but they are most useful at the start when a design team needs to learn about the people they are going to design for.

How – The *video-blog* uses any blogging tool. It is easiest to upload the video clips to sites such as Vimeo or YouTube and embed their reference code in the posts and the pages of the blog. Each post contains one video clip and is tagged with relevant keywords for the project. The pages function of the blog is used to present stories about relevant topics for the design. These stories are mainly a series of video clips with brief texts in between where needed for telling the story. Such stories can take several formats, for instance it can be a persona, a guided tour, or a day in the life of someone or something.

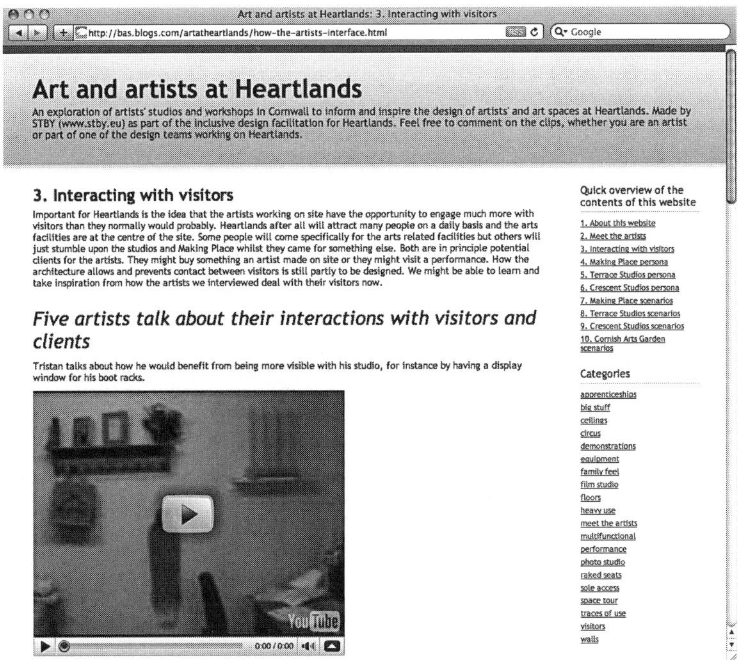

Figure A2.7 *Heartlands*, an example of a video-blog
Source: STBY.

CREDITS

http://bas.blogs.com/artatheartlands/

FILM DIARY

DÉBORA SZEBEKO

What – A *film diary* is a movie collection of interviews with service users and providers in different contexts. People are invited to tell their stories following the chronological unfolding of the experience. The aim is to expand the service experience to experiences before, after and around the service pathway, to gain a more holistic view of all the subjects involved in critical service experiences, such as hospitalisation.

When – *Film diaries* are valuable tools which help the design team to empathise with the people involved in the service, understanding the critical moments of the service interaction (memorable touchpoints) and thus identifying the areas of design intervention. They are also an effective way to kick off the idea generation. In the case of a project of experience-based design for the NHS in the UK, while the initial intent was to facilitate a conversation around users' and providers' experiences, films have also become staff-training and promotional tools.

How – A *film diary* is the result of unstructured and open interviews conducted using a 'clean language' approach to storytelling, one that seeks to elicit honest responses that ensure little to no steering from the interviewer. In the case of the NHS project, over 30 hours of storytelling footage by the patients and staff have been edited to create a succinct 30-minute film to capture the most common spoken themes in head and neck cancer experiences.

Fiqure A2.8 An example of a film diary for the NHS Institute for Innovation and Improvement, UK

Source: *thinkpublic.*

CREDITS

http://vimeo.com/thinkpublic/videos/page:3/sort:newest

http://www.institute.nhs.uk/quality_and_value/experienced_based_design/ebd_approach_videos.html

USER DIARY

ANNA MERONI AND DANIELA SANGIORGI

What – The *user diary* is a self-reporting tool, aiming to capture the subjective experience of people in a specific situation or in their everyday life, by using traditional diaries, notebooks and a camera. It is a design tool used to gain insight into patterns of behaviours.

When – *User diaries* help in understanding the structure and meaning people give to their behaviours, gaining intimacy and probing matters of emotions that might be overlooked in the presence of a researcher. In service design, *user diaries* can help understanding areas of unmet needs that can be covered by new services, or capture the emotional impact of a service interaction on a person's life. Hence they help to frame the areas of opportunity for innovation and feed the idea generation phase.

How – Very close to the cultural probes, which use creative kits of tools for user self-reporting, a user diary is normally obtained by supplying individuals with a diary and asking them to keep a written record of their impressions, circumstances and activities, related to the relevant aspects of their lives. A simple guide is often supplied to help the person focus on specific activities. A pre-printed notebook can facilitate the work. The period of self-observation can be a week or longer. Results are both discussed vis-à-vis with the researcher or just returned without additional talks. This tool is best used in conjunction with interviews, using the photos or entries to trigger discussions about behaviours that may normally be out of your user's awareness.

Figure A2.9 An example of a user diary made by an elderly woman to document her food habits

Source: Politecnico di Milano.

STORY COLLECTION

FRANÇOIS JÉGOU

What – The *story collection* is a tool that enables different stakeholders to project and share their views on possible usages of a developing service. A simple narration format allows to engage different participants on the same basis and to accumulate a mosaic collective projection of expected usages.

When – The *story collection* should be used at early stages of definition of a potential service, to explore users' expectations in a creative and open way. It is a particularly efficient approach for prompting the convergence of a large group of players with multiple backgrounds, complex and conflicting visions and limited previous experience in mutual interaction.

How – The *story collection* is a storytelling activity developed in various ways (on- or offline; collective workshops; individual meetings) involving a range of different profiles and as many participants as possible. The light but systematic narration format (character, age, profession, 10 lines written in the first person and situated at a medium-term horizon) allows everyone to engage at the same level with relatively little effort for very different populations. A typical story collection process requires the collection of a significant corpus of stories (50 to 150 according to the service), the exchange and cross-fertilisation between contributors (using an interactive Web repository and offline group sessions) and the consolidation of a consistent short list. It takes therefore between one to three months. Further development of the tool consists on the one hand in disseminating the collective projection obtained (see also the *video sketch* tool) and on the other hand in deriving from the corpus of stories a draft of the service technical specifications.

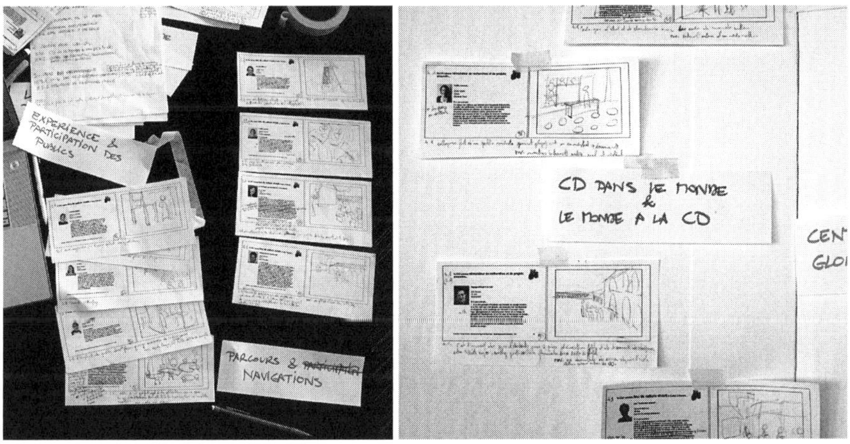

Figure A2.10 An example of story collection: different stories collected in paper form
Source: François Jégou.

Generating

IDEA SKETCHES

ANNA MERONI AND DANIELA SANGIORGI

What – Idea sketches is a simple tool or format to visualise initial ideas as a sketch or an image. These ideas can represent completely new service solutions, improvements in the interactions or in individual touch-points. They can suggest the appearance and functioning of the proposal and add simple notes to better understand the nature of the problem and of the solutions.

When – Idea sketches can be used both when analysing customer journeys in an existing service, when sketching improvements to existing encounters or when proposing entirely new ones.

How – In the study in which live|work designers were observed using a version of this tool, three designers spent around 30 minutes generating several sketches each, following an extensive critique of an existing service which they had mapped out on the wall into a representation of the customer or stakeholder journey (see the *customer journey map* tool). These sketches can then be used in meetings with clients or users to discuss and brainstorm on feasibility and desirability of the proposals or to generate new ones.

Figure A2.11 An example of idea sketches
Source: live|work.

GLIMPSES

DIANNE MOY

What – Glimpses is a collaborative tool that helps people to explore and envision sustainable futures. The tool is a schematic and open scenario which investigates system changes at a local level. Designers and non-designers use it to explore a portfolio of solutions against specific local conditions and opportunities, identifying which ones are best suited to the area.

When – Glimpses are part of the scenario-building process. They can be used in exploratory workshops to probe, excite and move participants from the constraints of the present to the opportunities of the future. The tool helps people to create stories around how their local area has changed. From this process, specific localised service solutions and opportunities, along with specific actors, motivations and pathways are identified. The tool can be used as the basis of design briefs or as a tool to enable more collaborative conversations.

How – Glimpses are idea prototypes of new relationships: they are deliberately indefinite so that they have to be adopted and adapted for different localities. They are presented to workshop participants as a kit of possible solutions either as a simple solution seed (a text-based narrative) or as a more designed visualisation. Current elements from a local area are often incorporated into the glimpses as this assists people in understanding the very real possibilities of change. With a direct investigation of how an initiative might operate within their local area people can understand the 'who, how and why' of system change. A variety of complementary tools help participants rewrite the glimpses for their local context. At the end of the workshop participants tell their newly created stories to each other, and a facilitator identifies commonalities, innovations and the possible steps to implementing the glimpse, that can be developed further by designers.

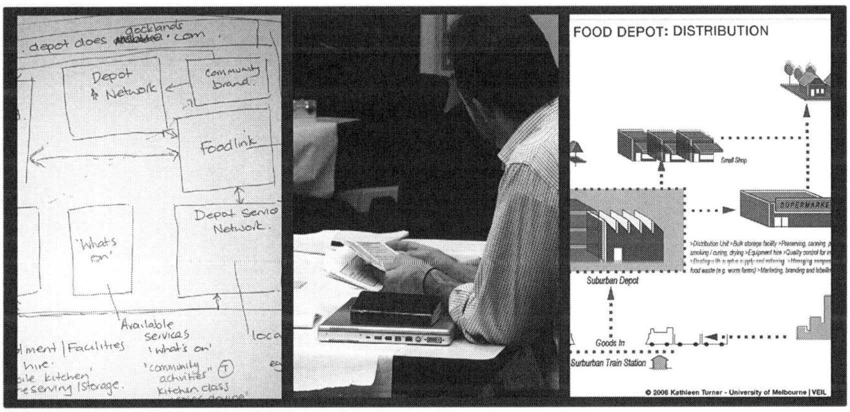

Figure A2.12 An example of glimpses used for a food system scenario
Source: VEIL, Melbourne.

SERVICE MOODBOARD

ANNA MERONI AND DANIELA SANGIORGI

What – The *service moodboard* is a visualisation that represents the mood, atmosphere and style of a service. It derives from the adaptation, to the service context, of a tool usually applied in areas such as fashion, interior, communication or product design. Its purpose is to make the character of the service interaction emerge.

Where – The *service moodboard* can be used either for the analysis of an existent service, by depicting it, or for the design of a new one, by envisioning it. Made of pictures, images, textures, key words and colours, it aims to transmit the 'feel' and the 'style' of a service interaction and of its context. A moodboard, in a design activity, works as a visual tool designers can use to quickly communicate their idea of the service 'mood'. Thus it is used to develop and vsualise the phenomenology of a service idea.

How – A *service moodboard* is usually a composition of images and visual stimuli, like photos, taken from a specific context (if referred to an existing case) or taken from magazines or image repertoires. A moodboard works as an analogy, not as a metaphor: therefore, the meaning and the significance of the different images must converge and be consistent with the purpose of the communication and the phenomenology of the service. A moodboard for services focuses mainly on the style of the interactions and of their contexts.

Figure A2.13 An example of a moodboard for a service of do-it-yourself urban agriculture
Source: Politecnico di Milano.

Developing

MICROPANORAMIC

ANNA MERONI AND PAOLA TRAPANI

What – The *micropanoramic* is a white maquette reproducing the three-dimensional spatial layout of a service and its principal performances, graphically labelled according to a colour-coding legend. The *micropanoramic* places the service into a context, even though the white blurs the scene to an abstract dimension, that is proper for a model to be adapted and adopted in different situations.

When – The *micropanoramic* can be applied as a visualising tool to represent concepts generated at an early stage of a design project. It works best as part of a visualising toolkit, when it is coupled and complemented with other visualising methods, such as moodboard, system map, storyboard, or action board.

How – The *micropanoramic* makes the layout of a service tangible and helps with visualising it in a given context. All the main evidences of the service are represented: human resources, logistics and infrastructures, communication and other goods. The reconstructed scene can then be used during brainstorming sessions, where participants are free to move, add or delete the elements from the scene according to their personal point of view. The final version can be filmed to obtain still pictures and/or movies for discussing ideas in a larger session or for communication purposes. The colour white helps to abstract the concept of the service, so that project participants are free to project and imagine their own idea of it.

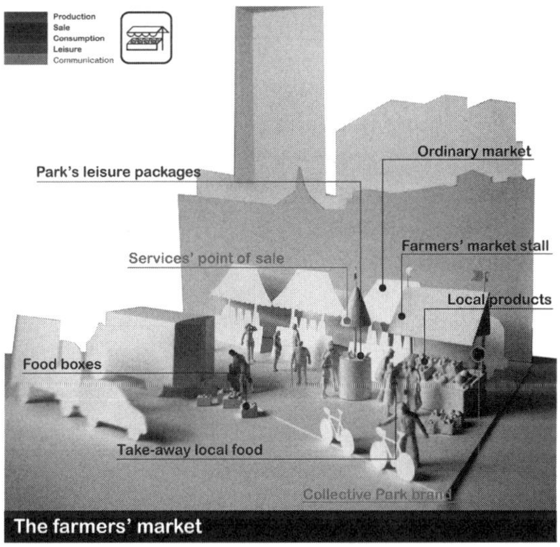

Figure A2.14 An example of a micropanoramic of a farmers' market designed for the city of Milan, Italy
Source: Politecnico di Milano.

STORYBOARD

ANNA MERONI AND DANIELA SANGIORGI

What – The *storyboard* is a well-known tool used in several design fields to describe the occurrence of an action or of an interaction. Adopted and adapted from the film industry, it is a narrative technique that describes, by images and captions, the script of a service, creating a sequence of actions in an established time frame. Linking time, space, physical evidences and people interactions, it is a fundamental tool in service design, which makes the possible experience of the user emerge.

Where – The *storyboard* has been an essential tool of service design since the very early stages of concept development. It precedes the creation of the *service blueprint*. From simple sketches representing the basic elements of the interaction, to complex and detailed realistic visualisations, the storyboard can intervene in different stages of the design process, and help to imagine interactions; stimulate a discussion around the service; design the prototyping phase; provide the details that will enable the design of the setting where the service will take place (touchpoints, environment, or communication); design the style of the service interaction.

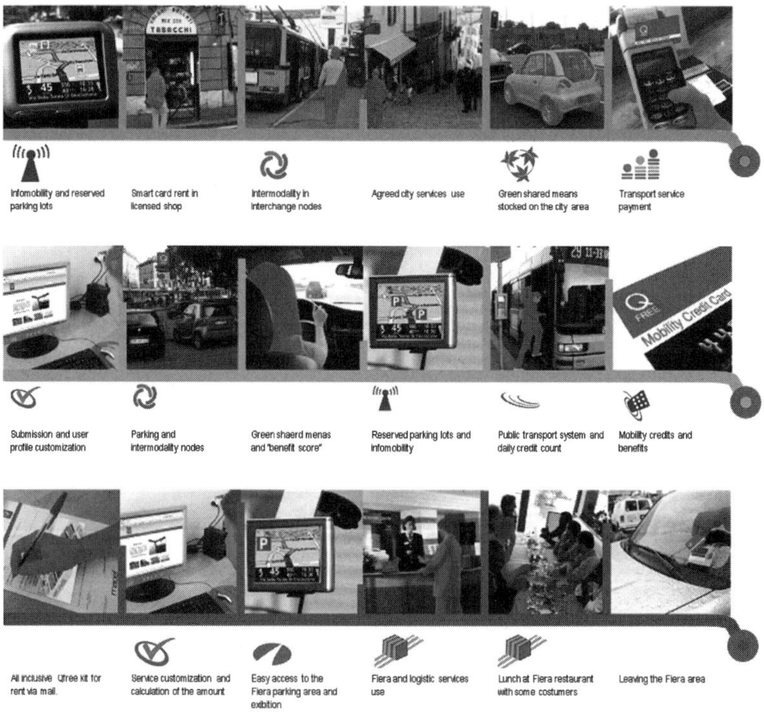

Figure A2.15 Examples of story boards of mobility services
Source: Politecnico di Milano.

How – Key points of a good storyboard are: the proper organisation of the sequence of frames for the comprehension of the narrative; the presence of an adequate amount of details in the images according to the purpose of the design phase; the accuracy of the elements that influence the user experience. A storyboard can be made by drawings, pictures, images and photo compositions or 3D graphics whose sequence can be organised in different forms of visual strips.

SERVICE BLUEPRINT

ANNA MERONI AND DANIELA SANGIORGI

What – The *blueprint* is a holistic representation of a service used to help manage the complexity of a service system. It maps a service starting from the user's perspective to then add the actions and processes the organisation needs to perform in order to support it, together with service evidences and incidental failure points.

Where – The *blueprint* can be used both to analyse an existing service and to design a new one. It helps designers to evaluate the processes, actions, tools and resources that are needed to implement service ideas and offerings as well as to understand their mutual dependence.

How – The *blueprint* can be used to design the overall service performance or single encounters and processes. Once chosen the time focus the blueprint is built by visualising the visible actions of users and service staff as divided by the so-called 'line of interaction'; then visualising the related, but invisible (to the user) actions and processes conducted in the backstage by service employees divided by the so-called 'line of visibility'. Any action or processes not conducted in parallel to the user's actions are mapped as support processes. Service evidences and incidental points of failures are then signed on the map as further design and management information.

Figure A2.16 An example of a blueprint
Source: ImaginationLancaster.

EXPRESSIVE SERVICE BLUEPRINT

SUSAN SPRARAGEN

What – The *expressive service blueprint* is a tool used to represent visually the meaningful moments of a service engagement from the customer's perspective. The blueprint gives service providers a clear way to express their intentions and goals while linking them to customer's needs as the service activity progresses. The expressive components of the blueprint include notations that capture the customer's emotional responses to the service. These may be realised through observations, comments, or anticipatory behaviours and are mapped onto the blueprint in the form of text, icons, or graphics that mark these human attributes effectively.

When – *Expressive service blueprint* is most applicable in scenarios where there is a significant number of user–provider interactions. Also, if there is a need to distinguish between elements of the service that the users see and service actions that they do not see, the blueprinting framework can be very constructive. Most importantly, it is used to facilitate understanding of the customer's perspective of the service.

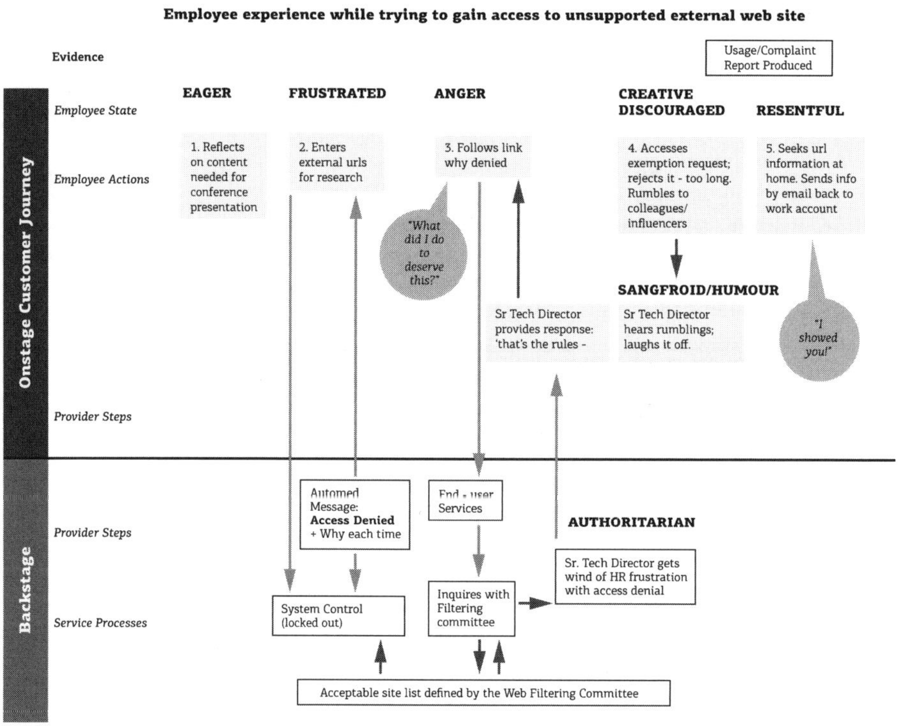

Figure A2.17 An example of an expressive blueprint

How – *Expressive service blueprint* should be constructed collaboratively among key service stakeholders. First the customer service journey steps are mapped out as it would proceed from the customer's perspective. Then the provider's actions, interactions and required backstage processes are linked to that journey. As an addition to a normal 'blueprint' the service actions can then be commented with text boxes, icons or graphics to mark people's emotions and opinions about a service performance.

VISUAL SERVICE SCRIPTS

ELENA PACENTI

What – *Visual service scripts* are an evolution of the role scripts used for guiding the front line operators in performing the service interaction with users. Visual scripts are task flows described with different kinds of visualisation techniques.

When – *Visual service scripts* are used during the implementation of the service to support the personnel in understanding the service procedures and adopting a behaviour that is consistent with the brand philosophy and the service performance targets. They are generally designed for personnel training sessions, but the scripts can also be used as support for personnel's operations in action.

How – The visual service scripts offer the service operator a description of the service procedures and provides indications on how to perform each stage of the process. For each process the script indicates objectives and tasks, the available tools and evidences to be used, and provides qualitative comments and advises on how to behave. The visual elements can be added both to better describe and emphasise the phases of the process as well as to visualise the required behaviour. In both cases symbolic and realistic images can be used to assist in envisaging the situation. As filming techniques are more effective

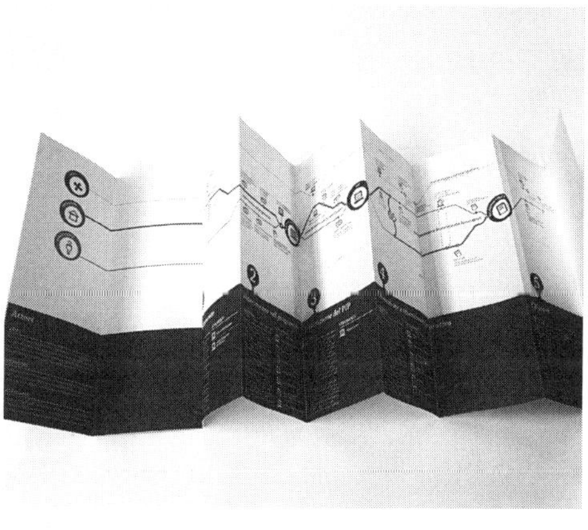

Figure A2.18 An example of visual service script
Source: Domus Academy Research Centre.

in communicating behaviours, the visual service script can take the form of a short movie.

SERVICE BREAK DOWN

ANNA MERONI AND DANIELA SANGIORGI

What – The *service break down* is a tool used to deconstruct a service in its constituent elements, the set of assessable and self-contained material or immaterial bits needed to produce and deliver it. Elements are then gathered in different categories that are consistent with each kind of solution. It generally consists of icons to represent each element of the system and their interrelationships.

Where – The *service break down* is used in the late stages of the design of a service, as it requires a clear definition of its structure and development. It allows design of the service in detail to match the required elements with the assets of the stakeholders delivering the solution, or to search for additional suppliers. It also helps to understand possible synergies within and outside the system.

How – The *service break down* is the result of a detailed work of analysis of the system the service is part of. It requires first the identification of the main self-contained categories of service elements to then identify all the various service elements that belong to each category. In its development it can help various

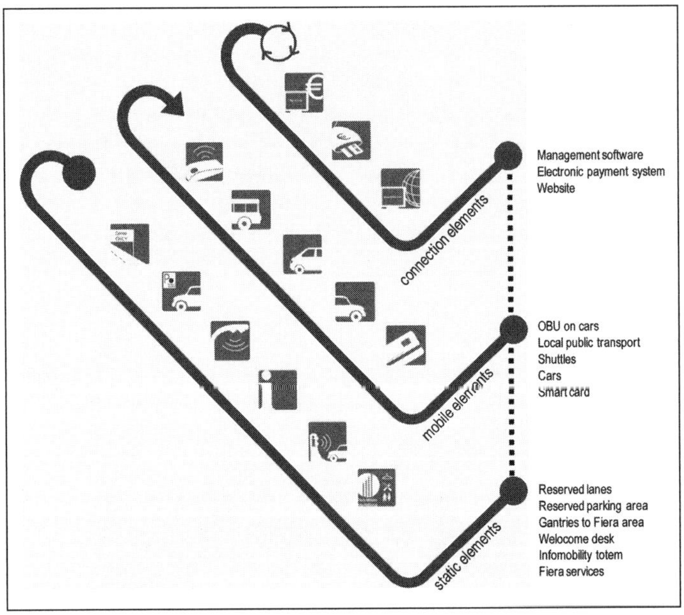

Figure A2.19 An example of service break down of a solution of integrated mobility
Source: Politecnico di Milano.

stakeholders to define reciprocal roles and synergies in the service supply; for this reason its application could be linked with theories and practice of operations management and strategies of modularisation of service architectures.

CREDITS

This tool is a development of the Solution Elements Brief presented in Jégou, F., Manzini, E. and Meroni, A. 2004. Design plan, a toolbox to facilitate solution-oriented partnerships, in *Solution-oriented partnership. How to design industrialised sustainable solutions*, edited by E. Manzini, L. Collina and S. Evans, S. Cranfield: Cranfield University, 108–19.

SYSTEM MAP

ANNA MERONI AND DANIELA SANGIORGI

What – The *system map* is a visual tool used to design and represent the working model of a service system. It represents the different stakeholders involved in the production, delivery and use of a product–service system as well as the flows of material, information and money linking the different partners.

When – The *system map* helps to understand the composition and organisation of a service system, visualising the main interactions and flows among key partner organisations and final users. It is therefore a useful tool for the initial stages of a service design process as it helps in evaluating the feasibility of a service idea and at the same time it supports various stakeholders to understand the implications of a service delivery partnership.

How – The *system map* represents a conceptual model of the service partnership and illustrates the service from the point of view of the providers. It represents, 259

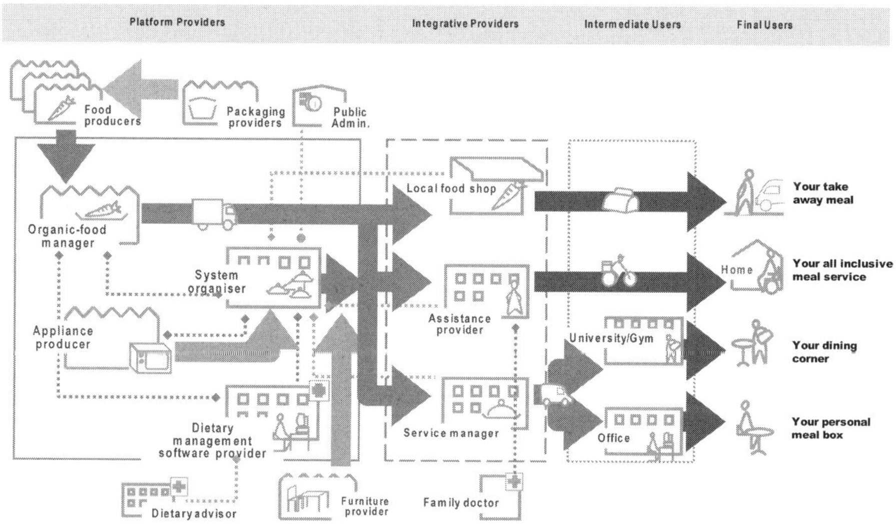

Figure A2.20 An example of system map of a series of interrelated services of food delivery
Source: Politecnico di Milano.

through icons, the different stakeholders and, through arrows and lines, the exchanges among them. A frame is used to depict the boundaries of the core service delivery partnership in the map, while other suppliers are drawn in a smaller size outside the frame to symbolise their secondary role in the system. Only the main exchanges of material goods, information and money need to be visualised at this stage. Short texts can be used to explain the different flows. As the tool is supposed to be easily used also by non-designers, a set of predefined icons is suggested and provided.

CREDITS

Jégou, F., Manzini, E. and Meroni, A. 2004. Design plan, a toolbox to facilitate solution-oriented partnerships. In *Solution-oriented partnership. How to design industrialised sustainable solutions*, edited by E. Manzini, L. Collina and S. Evans, S. Cranfield: Cranfield University,108–19.

SERVICE INTERACTION DESIGN GUIDELINES

ELENA PACENTI

What – The *service interaction design guidelines* are a tool for the analysis and design of service interactions. The guidelines are basic principles, mainly inspired by human–computer interaction design criteria, which can be used for the design of effective interactions with complex service interfaces.

When – *Service interaction design guidelines* can be used as a tool to evaluate the quality of existing services, working as a checklist to guide the redesign of service touch-points and interactions, as well as a general reference for the design of new service interfaces.

How – The *service interaction design guidelines* are a set of principles to design effective and pleasurable service interactions. They are divided in four main groups: guidelines related to the creation of the interaction platform – shared language, consistency, accessibility; guidelines related to the interaction modes and styles – visibility, transparency, atmosphere; guidelines related to interaction tasks – feedback, undo, error-friendliness; and guidelines related to an adaptive service interface – listening, personalization, flexibility. The tool describes each principle to be used as a checklist during the analysis or the design process. Some of these principles – such as those used to create the interaction platform – represent essential requirements for any new service concept, so they are very useful in any concept generation phase; others – such as those guiding interaction tasks execution – are very useful during the evaluation phases of an existing service interaction, and can be used by designers together with customer journeys and touch-points maps.

CREDITS

The tool has been conceived by Ezio Manzini and Elena Pacenti in 1998.

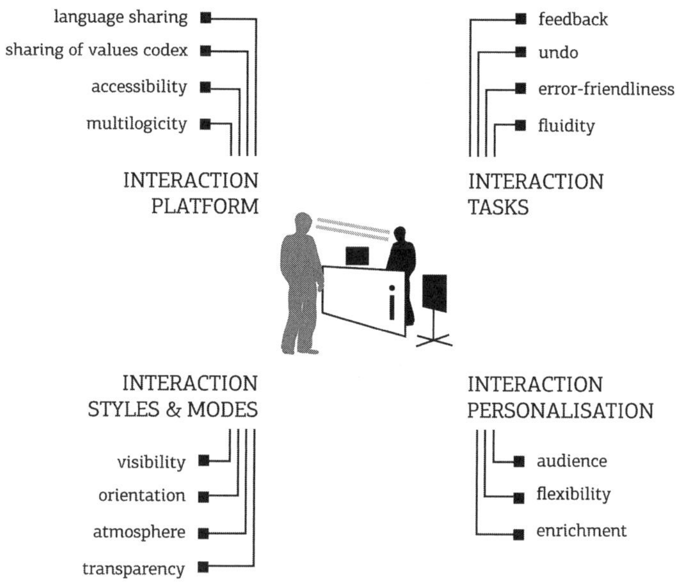

Figure A2.21 An example of service interaction guidelines
Source: Domus Academy Research Centre.

DESIRABILITY, VIABILITY AND FEASIBILITY

ANNA MERONI AND DANIELA SANGIORGI

What – Successful service innovations hit the 'sweet spot' between desirability (what people want), feasibility (what is possible) and viability (the business model behind it). Together, these three characters generate a self-consistent tool for service development.

When – The lenses of *desirability, viability and feasibility* are applied throughout the whole service design process; from the inspiration and insight that is the foundation of great design through idea generation and in guiding experimentation in building and delivering the service.

How – The *desirability, viability and feasibility* tool drives the search for inspiration, suggesting criteria for looking for peoples' unmet needs, behaviours and motivations, other business models or other technologies and infrastructure. In idea generation this tool can help in building a more successful service – 'how might we use existing infrastructure to meet people's needs?' or 'how might we leverage alternative business models to motivate people?'. The lenses may be translated into a set of principles or evaluation criteria and be used to guide iterative service development – the service must meet people's needs; align with strategy; and be implementable in this time frame. The key to applying the lenses for the most successful result is applying them simultaneously and iteratively, keeping all three perspectives in balance throughout the whole service design process.

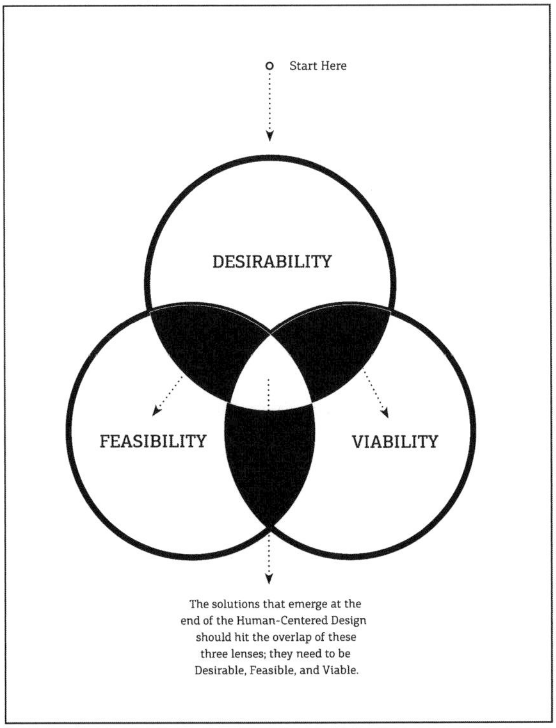

Figure A2.22 A scheme visualising the design tool desirability, viability, feasibility
Source: elaborated from IDEO.

CREDITS

IDEO. 2009. HCD Human Centered Design, Toolkit [Online]. Available at: http://www.ideo.com/work/featured/human-centered-design-toolkit [accessed: 31 January 2010]

Prototyping

VIDEO SKETCH

FRANÇOIS JÉGOU

What – Video sketch is a tool for co-designing a service. Literally, it is an instant sketch of the service, made up by using a video camera as a pencil to draft interaction processes with users themselves.

When – Video sketch may be used at the very first stages of a creative design process to focus the project team on the generation of ideas starting from the user point of view. It also allows the designer to generate highly communicative material quickly in order to engage wider circles of players in strategic conversation and early decision-making processes.

How – *Video sketching* is a hands-on creative thinking activity using a video camera to capture spontaneous mimicking of interaction processes in users' informal discussions: cameras instead of papers and pens are available on the table and participants in the brainstorming session are asked to 'act-in' their ideas and to film one another. They are then encouraged to review the video scenes, assess the credibility of the service from their point of view and eventually perform the interaction scene again, adapting the service design until they get a convincing representation. The scenes are performed and captured 'on the fly' in the order they should occur in the real service with no video editing. The resulting visual writing is a 'hybrid reality' mixing spontaneous user performance with a balance of realistic and simulated elements in order to serve the in-progress status of the design process.

Figure A2.23 The making of a video sketch
Source: François Jégou.

LIVING LABS

KEITH MITCHELL

What – *Living labs* are tools aiming to turn users, traditionally considered as a problem, into value creation within an experimental situation. As such, living labs are defined as environments for innovation and development where users are exposed to new ICT solutions in realistic contexts, as part of medium- or long-term studies targeting evaluation of new ICT solutions and the discovery of innovation opportunities. Fundamentally living labs offer a new research paradigm, integrating user-centred multidisciplinary research approaches and a user community-driven innovation based on real-life experiments in the wild.

When – *Living labs* act as an overarching approach which may encompass numerous tools and methodology for engagement at all stages of the design process. The purpose of this tool is to explore and evaluate new ideas and concepts and enable reusable experiments (that is data sets, research protocols and methods).

How – Within the *living lab*-based research approach, several disciplines such as computer science, ergonomics, economics, cognitive psychology, social sciences, environmental sciences, humanities and life sciences are necessary for designing and building user experience prototype environments, exploring new concepts and related artefacts, making proper observations and evaluation on different aspects according to the context of the specific research projects. End-users are not necessarily immersed individually but may be immersed as groups or whole communities. This leads to richer observations and greater quantities of data that, in turn, helps increase the reliability of the resulting analysis.

Figure A2.24 An example of living labs
Source: Infolab 21.

FASPE (FAST SERVICE PROTOTYPING AND SIMULATION FOR EVALUATION)

MARGHERITA PILLAN

What – *FASPE* is an approach to service test and evaluation based on paper prototypes and dramatisation activities. Service simulation is carried out through the *mise en scène* of the main service processes, so creating living storyboards. Critical aspects, related to human interaction and service procedures, can be explored effectively and borderline cases can be spotted.

When – *FASPE* activities should be performed as a physical design stage of the project, that is when the service concept is mature and its main features are set, in order to evaluate them. Simulations can also support the choice between different design options. FASPE can be also adopted as a didactic approach, to emphasise the difference between conceptual and physical service design.

How – Simulation activities can be performed in real contexts taken as a reference during design, or anywhere else. Dramatisations can focus on aspects of single processes, or on main procedures. In order to create realistic conditions most enabling physical solutions should be available or should be emulated using paper prototyping techniques (such as static interfaces for digital devices). Participants should be divided into three groups: a first team representing service staff, also emulating automatic processes if required by the system; a second team impersonating users (it is better if they are representatives of the real service target); and a third group acting as external observers, also in charge of the documentation production.

Figure A2.25 A paper prototype of a mobile phone service interface
Source: Politecnico di Milano.

EXPERIENCE PROTOTYPE

JENNIE WINHALL

What – *Experience prototyping* is a tool for shaping and testing out the kinds of interactions that might take place in a new service, helping to decide how it should happen. Compared to running a pilot, experience prototyping is more rapid, iterative and exploratory. It consists of 'sketching out' a new service in real time, by adapting the conditions that affect relationships and behaviours as you go along, in response to feedback from participants. Experience prototyping can lead to a greater understanding of how the goal can best be achieved;

what role the service plays in people's lives; how it could be implemented; what reduces cost; what affects how people experience it.

When – *Experience prototype* can be used at different stages of the development of a service: during idea generation (e.g. by the project team role-playing interactions to test out ideas); when identifying potential applications for a new service (e.g. by making a new technology available to people and seeing how they use it); when a service concept exists but is still very open ended (by allowing potential service users to further shape a rough idea through their interactions) or when the service content is defined but you want to compare different methods of delivery.

How – To stage an *experience prototype*, the questions to be answered are decided, and conditions for a proposed experience are set up with as few materials as possible and in a way that is as close to 'reality' as necessary to get useful feedback. Often members of the design team or client team play the roles imagined in the proposed service. Touch-points are mocked up so that the service feels real enough. The prototype might run for a number of hours, days or weeks. Regular reviews are held to get feedback, reject or iterate the concept and try different ways of doing things. It is easy for the design team to get attached to making the idea successful so it is especially important to find objective ways of capturing what is and is not working.

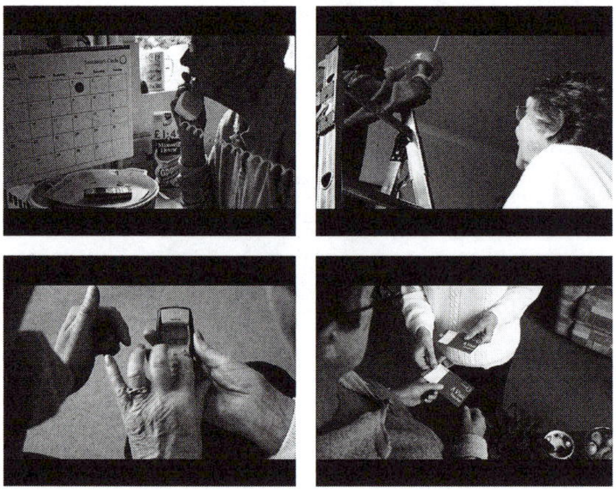

Figure A2.26 An example of an experience prototype of a service to provide practical help and social connections to older people in a London borough
Source: Participle.

CREDITS

Buchenau, M. and Fulton Suri, J. (eds) 2000. *Experience Prototyping*, paper to the third conference on designing interactive systems. New York City, 17–19 August.

Book Accreditation

We as authors, have worked hard to gather and make sense of the growing research and materials that belong to Design for Services and close areas of practice and research. We worked together to develop its structure and contents, looking at its past, present and potential future developments. For the purpose of this publication we would like to acknowledge our respective individual contributions to the writing of the following chapters:

1. Introduction to Design for Services (Sangiorgi)

2.1 Designing Interactions, Relations and Experiences (Meroni)

2.2 Designing Interactions to Shape Systems and Organisations (Sangiorgi)

2.3 Exploring New Collaborative Service Models (Sangiorgi)

2.4 Imagining Future Directions for Service Systems (Meroni)

2.5 A Map of Design for Services (Meroni and Sangiorgi)

2.6 What is Design for Services (Meroni and Sangiorgi)

2.7 What Job Profiles for a Service Designer? (Meroni and Sangiorgi)

3. Future Developments (Meroni)

Appendix 1: An Open Conversation (Meroni)

Appendix 2: Tools of Design for Services (Sangiorgi)

INDEX